About the author

Cynthia Cockburn is Research Professor in the Department of Sociology, City University London. She is the author of a number of highly acclaimed books, including *In the Way of Women: Men's Resistance to Sex Equality in Organizations* (Macmillan, UK and ILR Press, Ithaca, USA); *Machinery of Dominance: Women, Men and Technical Know-how*; *Brothers: Male Dominance and Technical Change* and *The Local Stage: Management of Cities and People* (London and Boston: Pluto Press)

The Space Between Us
Negotiating Gender and National Identities in Conflict

CYNTHIA COCKBURN

Zed Books
LONDON AND NEW YORK

The Space Between Us: Negotiating Gender and National Identities in Conflict was first published by Zed Books Ltd, 7 Cynthia Street, London N1 9JF, UK and Room 400, 175 Fifth Avenue, New York, NY 10010, USA in 1998.

Distributed in the USA exclusively by St Martin's Press, Inc., 175 Fifth Avenue, New York, NY 10010, USA.

Copyright © Cynthia Cockburn, 1998

Cover designed by Andrew Corbett
Set in Monotype Ehrhardt by Ewan Smith
Printed and bound in the United Kingdom
by Redwood Books, Trowbridge, Wilts

The right of Cynthia Cockburn to be identified as the author of this work has been asserted by her in accordance with the Copyright, Designs and Patents Act, 1988.

A catalogue record for this book is available from the British Library

Library of Congress Cataloging-in-Publication Data
Cockburn, Cynthia.
    The space between us: negotiating gender and national identities in conflict / Cynthia Cockburn.
       p.   cm.
    Includes bibliographical references and index.
    ISBN 1-85649-617-1. – ISBN 1-85649-618-x
    1. Women and war. 2. Women pacifists. 3. Nationalism.
4. Ethnic relations. I. Title.
HQ1236.C55 1998
303.6'6'082–dc21   98-19798
                              CIP

ISBN 1 85649 617 1 cased
ISBN 1 85649 618 x limp

Contents

Acknowledgements

So many people have contributed so much time, labour, encouragement and so many ideas to this complicated research undertaking and to the writing of the book that I despair of naming them all and thanking them enough. But to have a chance to put my thanks in writing gives me great enjoyment.

I want to thank first and foremost the women of the Women's Support Network in Northern Ireland, Bat Shalom of Megiddo and The Valleys in Israel and Medica Women's Therapy Centre in Bosnia-Hercegovina for being so open and welcoming, for entering into a real partnership and teaching me so much. I have never felt so privileged and satisfied by a research relationship as by these. But I want to thank them mainly for bringing their projects into existence, for doing what they do, and doing it so boldly and lovingly.

Dženana Husremović and Tagreed Yahia-Younis were my interpreters in Bosnia and Israel respectively – but they interpreted much more than interviews. They befriended me and enriched my understanding of the worlds I was trying to learn about. Thank you both.

If Jo Coppage and her women's holiday villa-hotel The Spanish Experience in Mijas, southern Spain had not existed, twenty-one of us would have been greatly the poorer. Thank you Jo, and other women who hosted us there, for the Mijas Workshop, a week that several of us have said was the most moving in our lives.

I have benefited greatly from being able to share ideas with researchers of the Women in Conflict Zones Network, based at York University, Toronto, and from the generosity of those who advised me on aspects of the project as I carried out the fieldwork. They include Nabila Espanioly, Monika Hauser and Hannah Knaz. I especially want to thank the following for their penetrating comment and constructive advice on the draft: Nadje Al-Ali, Cynthia Enloe, Gillian Gibson, Vera Jordan, Maja Korac, Andjelka Milić, Gabi Mischkowski, Hilary Prentice, Nora Räthzel, Carmel Roulston, Rada Stakić-Domuz, Joanne Vance and Nira Yuval-Davis. Nadje, Nora and Hilary were specially close to the project and helped facilitate the Mijas Workshop. Gabi besides was a very important companion, guiding me through the politics of Bosnia, as were Marie Mulholland in Belfast and Lily Traubmann in whose kibbutz I lived in Israel. Thank you all more than I can say. The book owes a lot to you – and the errors and misjudgements it certainly still contains are only there in so far as I failed to make good use of your help.

It is not usual to thank the other authors one refers to in writing a book. But knowledge is like a cloth, a kind of embroidery, woven and worked by successive hands. The small motif you add has no sense at all except in relation to the meanings others have made before you. So I want to thank the many writers I acknowledge in the text for what they have taught me.

In connection with the photographic exhibit, *Women Building Bridges*, that resulted from the research I want to thank John and Neil Webster of Jay's Displays for lending me their enviable skills to assemble and mount it. The exhibit would not have existed, though, without the input of Doreen Massey and the other editors of *Soundings: a Journal of Politics and Culture* who first took the risk of publishing the material as a series of rather experimental photo-narratives. I owe them, and Tim Davison, their graphic designer, a special debt of gratitude. A particular thank-you too to Louise Murray, Anne Rodford and others at Zed who guided this book to publication and to Ewan Smith who responded so skilfully to my hopes for the appearance of text and illustrations.

Finally, the project would not have been possible if I had not had a supportive academic home in City University London, who, besides, rummaged in some budgetary cupboard to find me a year's salary. I am greatly indebted to the following funding organizations who enabled the research and associated activities, in grants ranging in size from £50 to £5,000: the E. and H. N. Boyd and J. E. Morland Charitable Trust; the William A. Cadbury Charitable Trust; the Community Relations Council of Northern Ireland; the Global Fund for Women; the Lipman-Miliband Trust; the Network for Social Change; the Niwano Peace Foundation; the Scurrah Wainwright Charity; and Womankind Worldwide.

Introduction

When you stand in a silent vigil for an hour you have time to think. And one day in the autumn of 1993 as I stood with other 'Women in Black' on the steps of St Martin's Church in central London in our weekly demonstration against aggression in the former Yugoslavia I found myself thinking: we need to know more about *how peace is done*. I mean, really *done*. Not how politicians posture, demand and concede. Not how people tolerate each other by muffling their disagreements and turning a blind eye to their injustices. But how some ordinary people arrange to fill the space between their national differences with words in place of bullets. What do they say to each other then?

We ourselves had had difficulty in agreeing the words we would display on our placards and banners there in Trafalgar Square. And this was because of differences among us of both ethnic/national back-ground and political opinion. Not only were there Serb, Muslim and Croat women living in London who wanted to support a vigil, each bringing a political position that was (of course) impossible to read off from her ethnic identity. The women of English, Irish and other ethnic backgrounds too, although we all deplored aggression, had different interpretations as to who was to blame and what should be done. We had different points of political departure, some in the movement of principled pacifism, some in anti-racism or solidarity movements. We also came from different feminisms.

It was standing there on one of those Wednesday evenings, as the dark drew in, the street-lights came on, and the pigeons flew to roost, as the tourists and the buses moved in and out of my field of vision, that I decided to do the research on which this book is based.

The first step was to contact women in other countries with whom we already had links as feminist anti-war activists. Women in Black in its London manifestation of 1993 was anyway the offspring of a move-ment given its name years earlier by Israeli Jewish and Palestinian women demonstrating against the occupation of the West Bank and Gaza. It had been conveyed by Italian women to Belgrade, where women were currently demonstrating weekly with a Women in Black banner in Republic Square against the wars in the former Yugoslavia.

Through these and other contacts I identified three projects that seemed likely to be productive subjects for study and asked for their cooperation. Each project was in a country where there was war, current or latent. Each involved women of different ethnic backgrounds or national belonging, where those ethno-national collectivities were implicated, in different ways and for different reasons, in the fighting. (I leave till later the interesting issues of what ethnicity and nationality may be thought to be, their relation to politics and war, and the relation of women to all of those things.)

The *Women's Support Network* represents women's community centres in both Catholic and Protestant working-class districts of Belfast. In Northern Ireland there is a British military presence and policing that are experienced by many as violent or threatening. The Irish Republican Army wages war on the British state, and the IRA and Unionist paramilitary groups fight each other and violently punish disloyalty in the communities they consider theirs. The Network women's political origins differ widely. But, focusing on poverty and marginalization in both communities, they cooperate with the aim of getting working-class women's voices better heard and their interests expressed in peace processes, state policy and international funding programmes.

Bat Shalom (*Megiddo, Nazareth and The Valleys*) is an alliance of Israeli Jewish and Israeli Palestinian Arab women. The words Bat Shalom mean 'offspring of peace'. Their membership is drawn from Jewish kibbutzim and local Arab towns and villages in northern Israel. These are highly contrasted communities that normally have little contact, and are pulled apart by the violent realities of a militarized Israel and Palestinian resistance. The women campaign together for peace, an end to the occupation and the creation of a Palestinian state, and for the rights of Palestinian Arabs in Israel.

The *Medica Women's Therapy Centre* in Zenica, central Bosnia-Hercegovina, is a medical and psycho-social project established by German and Bosnian women in 1993 to respond to the needs of women and their children traumatized by rape, bereavement and uprooting in the nationalist aggression involved in the break-up of the Yugoslav federal state. The Medica project team, mainly Bosnian Muslim, also includes Bosnian Serb and Bosnian Croat women and others of mixed parentage and in mixed marriages, working together in a way that extremists' strategies have aimed to make unthinkable.

The projects welcomed my involvement but we were careful in establishing the terms of the research relationship. It is always difficult to ensure that the researched have a reasonable degree of control over the research process and its products. It is especially important to do so where they are experiencing privation, fear and physical danger, so that the disparities between researcher and researched are even more exaggerated than usual. The agreement needs to take account of the fact that the researched take greater risks and lack the mobility, resources and choices available to the researcher. I made it very clear that I would give the well-being of the projects priority over research interests.

We agreed that this would be action research and would involve participant observation. I would involve myself as closely as I could with the projects, living within them for some weeks, observing and taking part in as many activities as possible. Gathering documentation and meticulously recording observations and casual conversations would clearly be one aspect of the work. I would also interview in depth between twenty and twenty-five women in each project, using an unstructured but thematic approach appropriate to such qualitative research. And this is indeed how it worked out. The interviews were tape-recorded and fully transcribed. In both Bosnia and Israel I had the help of a thoughtful, careful woman interpreter. Neither was a member of the project we were studying, but each was familiar with it and well attuned to its concerns and those of my research.

It was agreed that in the writing and publishing process I would refer back to the projects, showing them drafts in plenty of time for them to react with criticism, comment and suggestions. This was not an agreement for them to censor what I wrote. But we all wanted to be sure that I had understood them well and interpreted what I learned in a way that seemed reasonable to them. It was not, either, that I intended to censor my own political views, that I would ignore the existence of right and wrong, oppressors and oppressed, aggressors and aggressed, in these countries. There are ethics involved in these wars and it is impossible for a researcher, even if she wants to, to position herself above and outside them. Even in the projects there were inevitably women to whose views on what we came to call 'big-P Politics' I felt closer than in the case of others. That is not the point. What the research relationship was based on was my unshakeable respect for the commitment of the women in these projects to listen to each other, negotiate across differences and allow for change and movement.

The result was a great deal of interaction over the writing. The draft, in whole and in parts, I made available to anyone interested to see it, through my agreed 'referees' in the projects. Everyone individually cited had a chance to see her own words quoted in this book and elsewhere, and a choice as to whether her real name or a pseudonym would be used. A few women preferred me to use their personal name only. In these cases I substitute 'X' for their surname. A few women wanted to be anonymous. I use their chosen pseudonym as first name, followed by 'Y'. Mostly, though, individuals were content to appear in the narrative in their own names and the small changes asked for by the projects were not difficult to agree. Only in one case did I eventually omit material at the project's request. This related to a response to violence in the local community over which there was bitter disagreement within the project concerned. To press any further for a version of the events agreeable to all its members threatened to damage relationships in the group. It was a loss to my analysis, but to persist would have meant a more serious loss to their alliance.

By action research we meant that I would not only participate in and observe the day-to-day life of the projects but also try to contribute in some proactive way to their goals. Of course, to someone concerned for 'scientific objectivity', this intervention would be muddying the water through which I was trying to look. But although rigour and honesty are indispensable, I believe that in all kinds of research it is more productive to acknowledge the active presence of the researcher than to wish it away. A second reason for an action component in this research was that I felt, given their tough circumstances, that I could hardly ask the projects to afford me their time were I not to devote some of mine to them.

But what could I usefully do? Photography has always been a form of expression for me in parallel with writing. It was agreed that I would photograph the people, activities and contexts of the projects. There were several intentions in this. First, I would make these images directly available to the projects, furthering a kind of reflexivity, a seeing of themselves through my eyes, and a seeing of me through the way I was seeing them. I believe, because of the high value they knew I ascribed to them and to the intelligence and generosity of their struggles with each other and with the outside world, that this re-presenting and re-perceiving was a positive process. The photographs were, I think, recognized by the women as affirmation of them and their work.

Second, I could, and did, use the photos in helping them develop publicity and fund-raising material, and in the case of Medica on my return to the UK I embarked on a funding appeal here. Third, the photographs would be used in my research publications as a kind of alternative narrative accompanying the written text. So in this book my intention with the photographs has been to afford a visual take, alongside the verbal take, on 'the space between us' – by which I mean both the social space between these women, and between them and me, and the physical and political spaces in which we were together living and working. The photographs are not put on the page with the suggestion that they depict some objective reality to 'verify' my written observations. On the contrary, as Susan Sontag says, 'despite the presumption of veracity that gives all photographs authority, interest, seductiveness, the work that photographers do is no generic exception to the usually shady commerce between art and truth ... photographs are as much an interpretation of the world as paintings and drawings are' (Sontag 1979: 6). This easily grasped fact should usefully jog the awareness that my written research 'findings' too are subjective and interpretive.

The material from the research has been published prior to this book mainly in one particular medium – a series of three photo-narratives in *Soundings: A Journal of Politics and Culture* (Cockburn 1996a and b, 1997). I used these as a basis for a mobile exhibit on a sequence of thirteen A1-size boards. Within the limits of a few words and pictures, I hoped this display, which was called *Women Building Bridges*, would increase awareness of the creative work some women can and do perform around the world in spanning divisive differences without denying them, counteracting violence while addressing the reasons for it. In 18 months with little prompting by me the display passed between 17 venues, travelled to six countries and was translated into several languages. I think and hope that this interest in it was due to the fact that, in our despair over intractable wars, people felt they gained by reading what is positive in the project's stories and achievements.

I began the research on 'the space between us' in September 1995. By September 1996 the next step of our planned action research partnership became a reality, with an international workshop we were able to arrange, linking the three projects. Sixteen women, drawn representatively from the three projects and the ethnic/national groups within them, flew to Malaga in southern Spain. They were joined by me and three other facilitators – variously of Iraqi, English and German background. There, in a sunny and supportive villa-hotel near the village of Mijas, run by women for women, we lived and worked together for an intense and memorable five days.

The Mijas workshop had several dimensions. The first was an exchange of experience between the three projects, a learning from each other's situations, struggles and analyses. So the groups were asked to bring and present short histories of their countries and conflicts, and descriptions of their projects, ways of working, successes and difficulties. From the start it was recognized that each project group would be a unity, with shared interests, but also bring with it internal differentiations and disagreements, some of which would have been in the open, some till then submerged. The discussions would give rise to hurt and conflict. Some of it would be old and practised pain. But because of the unaccustomed mixity[1] of the Mijas event, with each group bringing up material foreign to the others' customary agenda, some of it was bound to be raw and new. Most of the women spoke English. But communication was fostered by two women interpreters, and by the facilitators who put a great deal of thought into the creation of a safe, containing environment and a carefully paced process in which the participants could move trustingly, in a relatively short time, from being strangers to knowing quite a lot about each other.

Of course each woman was also coming as an individual, with unique kinds of experience, and would not necessarily be known intimately even by the others from her project. So we asked each participant to bring with her, in addition to project material, personal photos and other things that would illustrate what she might want us to know of her life. Gradually, as the days of the workshop went by, the walls filled with snapshots and women gathered round them asking each other questions, amplifying, comparing. This process, just as much as the working sessions, was about identities, difference, translation and recognition.

In the second half of the workshop we moved on to small-group discussion of themes that had emerged as relevant to all three projects. The questions women most wanted to explore were: 'Why are we women's groups? What are human commonalities?'; 'What is nationalism? And what is the relation of women to nationalism?'; 'What do we mean by tradition, culture and ethnicity?'; and 'How can we build democracy out of differences – in our projects and outside?' The record of these sessions, which I have reread many times, is a reminder of just how clear, focused and powerful the discussion was. From the start in this research it quickly became clear to me that women make theory through practice, and the Mijas workshop exemplified this wonderfully. This book not only cites dialogue that I heard at Mijas and uses the concepts women tried out on each other there. It is informed throughout by the theories, ideas of 'how it is', 'how it works', floated in that soft Mediterranean air, around the terraces of the Villa Maria Annunziata.

I have asked myself many times what is the disciplinary terrain of this research. I am based in a university department of sociology, but the reading it has led me into has spanned a wider range of 'social

---

1. I use the word mixity often in this book. It does not appear in English dictionaries, but in the form *mixité* is used in French in discussions of sex equality to refer to the presence of both men and women. I adopt the term into English because it can express a possibility of great political importance: a mixing that neither the word heterogeneity nor the word homogeneity captures, the interrelation and intermingling of elements that retain their distinctiveness.

science' concerns. I am in debt to feminist writers in two disciplines, though the concepts used and developed here are drawn mainly from a third.

The first is International Relations (IR), in which our theme often seemed to lie. Of course, these women were not negotiating sovereignty, drafting treaties or doing diplomacy. They were not among the important people, mainly men, who were simultaneously, elsewhere, sitting around negotiating tables making peace (or more accurately failing to make peace) for their various nations. But these were undeniably cross-national projects, well connected to an international feminist anti-war movement, developing detailed experience of handling ethno-political conflict and defying war machines.

Until recently it would have been unthinkable to posit women and women's concerns as having a place in IR. It is a discipline from which they have been absent and to which they have been invisible. Spike Peterson, who works in this field, says IR discourse is 'derived from what some men have done, what questions they asked, and what answers they generated, having consulted exclusively each other' (Peterson 1996: 16). With a handful of other feminists she has begun to draw back the curtain and show both that gender is utterly constitutive of IR and that women are in fact there too on the international stage. Women become more visible as you emphasize non-traditional aspects of the international: tourism, global production, the international division of labour, environmental and health issues (Enloe 1989). Then women step into the footlights, not so much as state leaders, more as 'transstate, non-state and antistate actors' (Peterson and Runyan 1993: 113).

So yes, what Medica, Bat Shalom and the Women's Support Network were doing certainly added up to international relations. But my reading of IR theory left me thinking: these concepts will not readily get voiced in these women's everyday vocabulary. So I turned to the newer literature of peace and conflict studies. There are two schools of thought here. There are those who stand above the conflict and look for rational, value-free solutions. They theorize that conflict arises through unmet human needs, insist that such needs can realistically be met and believe that the only value that should be permitted in processes of conflict resolution is the value attached purely to resolving the conflict (Burton 1987, 1990). And there are those who take issue with them over such 'neutrality', believing that it can sometimes compromise human rights. To succeed, they say, conflict resolution must not be afraid to recognize greater and lesser wrongs (Galtung 1975–80).

The women of the three projects would recognize themselves in these latter ideas. They are deeply aware of the structural violence of entrenched inequalities. They are not, on the whole, pacifists. What they are looking for is an opening to justice so that words can replace weapons sooner than might otherwise be the case. The notion of translation, 'transforming violence into creative, militant, positive non-violence' makes sense to them (Rupesinghe 1995a: 90). They would also recognize with Adam Curle that development and resource-building, the expansion of peace constituencies at the grassroots, is necessary if peace is to mean more than ceasefire (Curle 1971). Indeed it is one way of seeing what they are doing.

As with other disciplines, a feminist perspective on conflict has tended to disturb the academic paradigm. Seeing with eyes that are gender-aware, women tend to make connections between the oppression that is the ostensible cause of a conflict (ethnic or national oppression) in the light of another cross-cutting one: that of the gender regime. Feminist work tends to represent war as a continuum of violence from the bedroom to the battlefield, traversing our bodies and our sense of self. We see that the 'homeland' is not, never was, an essentially peaceful unitary space. We glimpse this more readily (I shall suggest) because as women we have seen that 'the home' itself is not the haven it is cracked up to be. Why, if it is a refuge, do so many women have to escape from it to 'refuges'? And we recognize, with Virginia Woolf, that 'the public and private worlds are inseparably connected: that the tyrannies and servilities of one are the tyrannies and servilities of the other' (Woolf 1966: 142).

So this research benefits from insights in both international relations and peace/conflict studies, but it has located itself more readily in a corner of a third discipline, political sociology. It draws on, and I hope may contribute to, debates concerning *democracy* and *identity*, especially *gender and national identities*. These words are continually in the air between the women in the three projects. They have many ideas about what they may mean, and are hungry for more.

It is also theoretically informed by the women's anti-war movement as practice. Italian activists developed a strategy they called 'transversal politics'. It was a conceptual move to get around and above the immobilizing contradiction in which we often find ourselves: between a dangerous belief in universal sisterhood and a relativist stress on difference that dooms us to division and fragmentation. The notion of transversal politics has been taken up and developed by Nira Yuval-Davis, who highlights its component practices of 'rooting' and 'shifting': 'The idea is that each participant in the dialogue brings with her the rooting in her own membership and identity, but at the same time tries to shift in order to put herself in a situation of exchange with women who have different membership and identity.' The process of shifting should not involve self-decentring, abandoning one's political and other sources of belonging. But neither should rooting render us incapable of movement, of looking for connection with those, among 'the others', with whom we might find compatible values and goals:

> In 'transversal politics', perceived unity and homogeneity are replaced by dialogues which give recognition to the specific positionings of those who participate in them as well as to the 'unfinished knowledge' that each such situated positioning can offer … The boundaries of a transversal dialogue are determined by the message rather than the messenger (Yuval-Davis 1997: 130–1).

The aim of this research is precisely to fill the container 'transversal politics' with content. I wanted to see what exactly is involved in the doing of it. Thinking of the starting points, moves and connections implied in 'transversalism' I have come to use the image of 'a space'. The metaphor operates at a number of levels. Sometimes the space is territorial, the land we share. Looking through the lens of a camera, now and then the space between people became something you could show in a two-dimensional image. The photos on pp. 148–9 are an example. You can almost see the words flying across the space. Mostly it is social. We can be thought of as on its periphery, looking for meanings that will bring us into relationship across it. The social space is sometimes too wide, sometimes too narrow. Sometimes it is empty and problematic, sometimes it is filled with useful, flexible structures.

My hunch was that the two key components involved in structuring the space between us (doing transversal politics) would be seen to be *democratic process* and what I came to think of as '*identity work*'.

On *democracy*, for instance, the discussion at Mijas showed that the women saw democracy and difference as being in play at various levels: in family, home and household; in the local collectivities of a neighbourhood, district or city; in their own projects; and in the domain of the state. My own analysis is of the projects, but I cannot altogether detach them from those other dimensions to which they are tied. I do not see the projects as communities, because to say 'community' is to skate over difference and division, to assume harmony and cohesion. The research is precisely about delaying that closure. So rather, the projects are represented as little polities – social and political entities – whose qualities we are bound to interrogate. When do they succeed and how? When do they fail and why?

As to *identity*, my hunch was quickly confirmed. The women were suffering a lot of what I came to think of as 'identity hurt'. The pain occurred where there was friction and disjuncture between a woman's sense of self and the identities with which she was labelled, that she was held to account for, or felt seduced by. The women were assailed by identities that contradicted their politics, that seemed to position them uncomfortably, and they were bereft of identities they would have liked to have. A good deal of the knitting, unravelling, texturing and tearing of the space between them therefore I interpret as identity work.

I do not want however to suggest, in choosing this focus for the research, that identity processes are the source of all evil. It is important to stress that inequalities are felt first and foremost materially, through the appropriation and squandering of wealth by a few, the exploitation by some of others' labour power and the abuse of others' bodies. Identity processes matter precisely because they are second only to force as the means by which power is effected in oppressive and exploitative systems.

It is through the creation of collective identities that ethnic and national movements, and the land-right claims they make, gain their force. The discourses emanating from influential social sources, such as intellectuals and the media, compellingly hail individuals as nationals – 'you who are one of us' – at the same time making it clear who is 'other'. They mobilize culture, tradition, religion, and notions of history and place to evoke a sense of unity, an ethnic or national identity. But it is not only in the matter of ethnic and national hegemony that identity processes have such importance. When control by any group is capable of being maintained without direct force it is always because compliance has been won through processes of identification. Those who benefit from class domination and male power make sure the working class and women 'know their place'.

The book is organized as follows. Chapter 1 introduces the three projects as *women's* projects, with a critical take on conventional, essentialist, representations of 'women' and 'nation'. I trace the historical emergence in their three countries, in always political and often violent processes, of today's ethno-national identities, the particular divisive differences that define the space across which the women have to reach each other. I draw on current theories that seem to reflect and further the understandings of people, nation and land that arise in the research. I explore the relation of women and gender to nation, and of feminism to nationalism, both in general terms and in the projects.

The central portion of the book has three sections, the first concerned with the Women's Support Network in Northern Ireland, the second with Bat Shalom in Megiddo, Nazareth and The Valleys, Israel, and the third with Medica Women's Therapy Centre in Bosnia-

Hercegovina. In each case an introductory chapter describes the social and political context out of which the project has emerged, while a second chapter describes the project itself, its relations and its contradictions. In these accounts abstractions like 'ethnicity', 'nation', 'place' and 'gender' take shape as vital issues – in fact as issues of life and death – for real women. The themes of alliance, democracy and identity wind through the women's accounts.

In the final chapter I take up the issue of identity and identity processes where the situated accounts break off. I look at ways of theorizing identity, putting forward an understanding of identity as social and relational, complex, always in process, taking shape in discourse: what people say, write, paint, make films about, legislate for, institutionalize. As the women in the projects do, I wonder about the nature of the link between our sense of self and those coercive identities in our own past and 'out there' right now, hailing us, flattering us, holding us hostage. How much choice do we have in producing our selves? We see the kinds of identity work the three alliances engage in to create a sustainable space between difficult differences, exacerbated by the violence all around them. They (mostly, at best) take care to listen to what a woman says about her sense of herself; remember not to inflict hurt by making assumptions; hesitate in the face of given, rigid formulations of identity; give weight to 'what she does' rather than 'who she is'; anticipate shifting and change.

I close by speculating on what we might learn from these women's projects about creating democratic, sustainable polities. How dangerous daydreams, whether they are of promised 'homes of our own' or of an apocalyptic demolition of all walls, might be let go. And replaced with the idea of something we could perhaps really have: a careful and caring struggle in a well-lit space.

I
Women and Nationalism

Belfast's streets, the parched hills of Israel and the villages of central Bosnia have become familiar places to people who have never visited them and live far away. Because they are sites of violence, and because violence is news, they are continually with us on our television screens and on the front pages of our newspapers. But the picture we get from the media is mostly a very particular rendering of those places and the events that happen in them. People who do not have firsthand knowledge of Northern Ireland for instance, but depend for their information on news reports featuring 'Catholics' and 'Protestants', often think the war is about religious belief. So you hear people say, 'They're all Christians. Why can't they agree?' The wars in the former Yugoslavia are often portrayed by media commentators as 'tribal' fighting, inspired by 'ancient animosities'. So readers say, 'The Balkans were always like that.' Israel's conflict with the Palestine Liberation Organization (PLO) and the Arab states is popularly explained by recourse to history – an age-old irreconcilability of Arab and Jew. In each case the claim of rights over land and a belonging to land are represented as primordial ties. Seen this way the wars are inescapable and will never end, just vary in intensity.

A more careful analysis shows that, while something of the past is active in the present, these wars are nothing if not modern (some might call them post-modern, but that is another matter). They are fought with modern weapons – Semtex explosive, helicopters, rifles with telescopic sites. The goals are modern goals – sovereignty, statehood, citizenship. But even more to the point, the sides in the fighting are the armed expression of contemporary political projects. They are today's apotheosis of nationalism, whether liberatory, defensive or aggressive. And nationalism has been one of the defining features of modernity. Besides, to represent 1990s national movements as vestigial, as throwbacks to some outdated past, is to underestimate the part played in them by twentieth-century world powers, particularly the USA, Britain and Germany.

Another characteristic of news reporting from Bosnia-Hercegovina, Israel/Palestine and Northern Ireland is a curious 'present absence' of gender. The picture we get is certainly sex-differentiated. We see men in combat fatigues, bearing weapons. Women we see expelled from their homes, raped, bereaved. But a certain naturalness is assumed in this too. Here are men and women acting out their age-old trans-historic roles. Facts that do not fit are sidelined. We hear very little, for instance, of the tens of thousands of Yugoslav men who evaded the draft and went into exile rather than fight.

These wars, we need continually to remind ourselves, are happening *now*. A century and more of women's struggles for legal emancipation, economic equality, control over our own bodies, have not been without effect. It was often enough modern, educated, well-travelled, politicized Yugoslav women who became, in a devastating moment in 1992, those 'Muslims', 'victims', 'refugees'. The women who went on the streets in the civil rights movement in Northern Ireland in 1968, and whose just demands signalled changes that would be used by all sides as an excuse for violence, were after all modern working women, university students, consumers in new markets. They were the same women who would soon join in a feminist movement with other just demands – for abortion rights, political representation, autonomous sexuality. How did *that* woman get translated into the mother we saw in the news reports, standing patiently in line outside the prison gates to bring succour to her interned son?

We cannot let traditionalist images of women and men in these wars pass unquestioned, any more than we can accept primordial explanations of the violence itself. We have to ask: what happened that the reality could sustain such images, and that those images could gain currency? Asking such questions uncovers an important idea: these apparently ethnic wars are, in a sense, also gender wars. The communal power these political movements, armed with guns, seek to establish or defend is (among other things) gender power, the regimes they seek to install are (among other things) gender regimes. As well as defining a relation between peoples and land, they shape a certain relation between women and men. It is a relation of male dominance, in some cases frankly patriarchal. It is constituted at best in a refusal to challenge the existing balance of gender power enforced by male violence, at worst in an essentialist discourse that reasserts a supposedly natural order and legitimates that violence.

Essentialism is not merely an interesting theoretical concept. It is a dangerous political force, designed to shore up differences and inequalities, to sustain dominations. It operates through stereotypes that fix identity in eternal dualisms: woman victim, male warrior; trusty compatriot, degenerate foreigner.

It is the pervasiveness of essentialism in warring national projects and in media discourse about them that seemed to me to give particular potential and meaning to women's organizations if, like the three introduced here, they throw conventional gender definitions into question. In doing so they might be the more likely, I supposed, to challenge prevailing identity processes as such, including those of ethnicity and nationality.

The Belfast Women's Support Network, the Medica Women's Therapy Centre of Bosnia-Hercegovina, and the Bat Shalom peace group in northern Israel are in some ways quite different. Each has a different job to do, a different rationale for existing. But they are similar in a number of ways that are significant both for their own ability to sustain a critique in an environment deformed by essentialisms and to my enquiry as a researcher concerned with the practice of 'peace'.

First, these are not women's projects by hazard. They have all made a political decision to work on a women-only basis. They respond to the idea that gender is a central issue in their war, that its violence is gendered violence. Their members are acting on the hunch they have that there is something at stake for women *as women* in conflict and peace processes.

Second, there is a consciously chosen ethnic, national and religious mixity in the projects. Further, the projects share a preoccupation not only with holding together their small but fissile collectivities, but also with building and maintaining bridges to a wider circle of women in their immediate environments, even more diverse in many dimensions than themselves.

Third, there is an ethos in all three that holds that what you think, say and do is more important than what you 'are'. At the same time, while they share certain political values and goals, they also accept that there remain divergences of opinion among them on significant political issues. They are alliances holding together differences whose negotiation is never complete, and is not expected to be so.

Finally, as alliances, a central concern of all three projects is democratic process, finding ways of assuring an equal voice and equal effectiveness for every member and for the 'sides' of whichever divisions may be salient. An important feature of this, in turn, is how to negotiate working relationships in which each individual is safe to show the self she really feels herself to be, and welcome others doing likewise.

A crucial issue for all the projects, as we shall see, is the relation between individual selves and collective identities. It is so problematic that I early made a decision about terminology that runs right through this book. I do not use the word 'identity' to describe what a person feels about herself. For that I use sense of self, self-sense or selfhood, and related terms like subjectivity and subject position. I reserve the word identity for other, more 'external' meanings. I write for instance of the identity that may be ascribed to someone, the identity discourses an individual hears, contributes to, responds to – and the collective identities such discourses generate. I describe the individual as caught up in identity processes. I have found that dividing the terminology like this is useful, arbitrary though it may be and too suggestive perhaps of a fault line between self and society. It helps to leave unsettled, as the women do themselves, the question of subject agency. It is better to avoid speaking of a person's identity so as to remain open to uncertainty about how, from moment to moment, she may (be able to) produce herself. I return to questions of democracy and identity, and the relation between them, in the final chapter.

The women of the projects, like everyone else in these particular social formations, have been caught up in coercive and narrowing identity processes. They come to the projects strongly marked by highly mobilized ethnicities, 'knowing' each other to be members of mutually exclusive national groups and to have different political affiliations. In working together now the question was: how could they construct a fully social space between and among them all? It had to be a space allowing distance, in which such differences would be respected, not collapsed into a spurious unity. At the same time it had to be a space allowing closeness, even intimacy, in which differences are not so reified as to determine expectations and limit the range of responses. What kind of relations could give shape and form to such a space?

Within this problematic emerge many more concrete questions challenging each individual woman but affecting the functioning of the collective as a whole. How may I understand and deal with the gap between my own sense of myself and the particular forms of ethnic, national, religious, gender and political identity with which others associate me? What sense can I make of the dramatic contradictions and shifts I feel in my sense of myself (and that of other women) due to the violent changes in our context? How can I explain and accept ambivalence – that I both want to feel I 'belong', yet suspect the power of identity, through which belonging is effected, to constrain and impoverish me? Can I hope, demand, to have a choice, or has the choice already been made for me? In what sense am I responsible for things done in my name? How can I avoid the labelling and limiting of others?

The very survival of these three 'difficult' associations seemed to their members to depend on finding coherent answers to such questions. They needed answers to guide the choices we shall see them making over their working agendas (what matters they deal with and what they leave aside), their process (how they go about making decisions, taking action, sorting out problems) and their operational links with other, different, women on the edge of and beyond the immediate alliance, many of them closer to the sources of violence.

To understand the current modalities of ethnic, national and place-related identity with which the projects are struggling, the political fields of force in which they do their transversal politics, it is important to know something of the histories out of which they emerge. At the Mijas workshop the projects made presentations to each other about their countries, nations and conflicts. Drawing on these and on my own reading I have constructed the following short narratives that may serve to give substance to words like 'Protestant', 'Muslim', 'Jew', 'country' and 'tradition' when they are deployed by the women themselves in later chapters.

A word of caution is necessary, though. The versions of history the women brought to Mijas had been carefully negotiated within the groups before they came. Because of course (to cite but one example) Jew and Palestinian Arab have experienced and interpreted the events of this century differently and one voice alone cannot tell a story that will be accepted as true by everyone. In the telling at Mijas, they often chipped in amendments to each other's accounts. These alternatives were allowed to just hang there, resonating alongside the original, somewhere between harmony and discord. But the written word fixes meaning more un-ambiguously. My version picks a careful course through multiple readings. I asked the women in the projects to check through the draft carefully and tell me where they flinched. Although what follows has been approved by them for inclusion here, this means only that there is nothing remaining, after I adopted the various amendments they pro-posed, that is too hurtfully biased. They feel, perhaps, that it 'will do', since it is me, not them, taking final responsibility for this telling. And, as for me, I put it forward not as a definitive account but as indicating some of the highly charged materials on which current identities selectively draw.

Northern Ireland: post-colonial limbo

'The island lies like a leaf upon the sea, green island like a leaf new fallen from the tree ...' On the map of Europe, the leaf-green island of Ireland floats on the extremity of the continent. It is the place where early westward migrations had to end. The people we think of today as 'the Irish' were assorted Gaelic-speaking tribes of Celtic stock who probably arrived on the islands from mainland Europe, via Britain, in the first millennium BC. But the Celts were not the last, as they had not been the first, to cross the Irish Sea. During the following centuries there were continual incursions from the larger island by English kings and adventuring nobles. And as England from the sixteenth century onward began to establish a worldwide empire, Ireland was its nearest overseas dominion. 'Blood in the yellow corn' is the refrain of Ewan MacColl's song, *The Island*. Even today, stories from that early violent history influence Irish feelings towards 'the British'.

The present pattern of ethnic difference, inequality and enmity in Northern Ireland has a rather specific origin: the colonial 'Plantation of Ulster' during the seventeenth century.[1] To suppress once and for all the resistance of the Irish to the British crown and to secure this strategically important offshore island against European rivals, English and Scottish settlers were purposely implanted on the island. The plantations were sustained first by the military might of the Stuart monarchs, then of Cromwell's Protestant army and later of King William of Orange.

The Plantation was focused particularly on the north of Ireland, till then least subject to British influence. Here the settlers drove the native Irish off the best farmland, defended themselves against sporadic counter-attack and built towns. Along with their crops they succeeded in planting on Irish soil, far more than earlier incursions had done, a new and different culture. One of the dimensions of difference was religion. The Irish people were Roman Catholic, as the English population had been until in the sixteenth century King Henry VIII rejected the rule of Rome and established the Church of England. With Henry's Reformation, Catholics everywhere in the British Isles became political outcasts.

But the distinction between native and settler, Catholic and Protestant, so destructive in Northern Ireland today, was never absolute. In her presentation to the Mijas workshop Joanne Vance stressed that 'in spite of attempts to keep the settlers and native Irish apart, the two communities gradually came into more contact with each other. Occasionally they intermarried and, while divisions were still apparent, evidence of mixing was visible too.' And in so far as the distinction was real it was politically manipulated:

---

1. I draw in this brief history on O'Leary and McGarry (1993) whom I follow in applying the term ethnicity in the Irish context. For a full discussion of its implications please see pp. 35ff. I am also indebted, among other sources, to articles in the volume edited by Aughey and Morrow (1996), to Bell (1978), MacCurtain and O Corrain (1978), Keogh and Haltzel (1993) and Ryan (1994).

These beginnings have been used since to create a myth of two ethnically pure identities, one Irish and one British. This simple analysis has been used in political argument, throughout Ireland's history, to ensure that the people will live politically divided and physically apart.

There were, besides, internal divisions among the colonizers, which still find expression in Northern Ireland politics today. Though all inimical to 'papists', they were not united as Protestants. The wealthier landowners and ruling class, many of whom were descended from English families who had owned land in Ireland for centuries, were privileged adherents of the Church of England (in Ireland it was called the Church of Ireland). Some of the new incoming settlers, the small farmers and craftsmen of the Plantation, would have been so too, but many were Scots, mainly of Presbyterian and other 'low church' denominations. And these Protestant dissenters, like Catholics, were penalized for their religious beliefs and obliged to pay tithes to the established church.

The new settler class did not remain for long the pawns of the British crown. They might despise the Irish, but they also kept their distance from the old aristocrats and landlords of the Anglo-Irish ascendancy, who tended to look down on *them*. In the same way, later they would strive to keep their autonomy from the British state. This ambivalence towards Britain became a theme in Ulster Protestant identity.

Meanwhile Catholics were excluded, socially, economically and legally, from many of the sources of wealth and power on the island. Their culture and language were suppressed. For this reason it is often supposed that agitation for greater independence for Ireland was a purely Catholic insurgency. In fact, it was some of the local Anglo-Irish who first became restless under British dominion. And some Protestants, alongside Catholics, were active in both successive reform movements and more militant nationalist and republican organizations such as the Fenian Brotherhood.

But as the nineteenth century advanced, as one nationalist uprising followed another, and as the British parliament considered successive proposals for Irish 'Home Rule', the fears of the Protestants for their future in a Catholic Irish state grew more acute. In 1912 a quarter of a million signatures were gathered for a covenant pledging resistance to separation from Britain. And in 1913 the Ulster Unionist leadership raised and equipped a paramilitary army, the Ulster Volunteer Force, which exists to this day. The Republican 'Easter Rising' of 1916 and a subsequent guerrilla campaign finally brought home to the British the impossibility of continuing to govern the rebellious island. But when, in 1921, a majority in the British parliament was finally mobilized to accord an Irish Free State, they were compelled to negotiate an arrangement that took account of Ulster Protestant fears.

This is how Ireland came to be partitioned. The six north-eastern counties, where the proportion of Protestant to Catholic was high, remained within the 'United Kingdom of Great Britain and Northern Ireland'. But as the new country pursued its national trajectory towards today's Republic of Ireland its constitution retained clauses enshrining the age-old Irish aspiration to being an island state bounded only by its seashores. Irish nationalists, North and South, mainly Catholic, continued to fight (sometimes literally) for a united Ireland. And the Protestants of Ulster, mainly Unionists, began a beleaguered history of semi-autonomy in Northern Ireland. They profited from the relative industrial development of their corner of an otherwise poor and rural country. And they pointed to the Republic's relationship, enshrined in the constitution of 1937, with its particularly conservative Catholic Church: this was the fate threatening them should their union with Britain ever be annulled.

From 1921 to the late 1960s the Ulster Unionist Party ruled Northern Ireland by means of a devolved parliament, and the Protestant demographic majority enabled it to do so exclusively in its own sectarian interests. These it interpreted as the maintenance of an unbreached border between North and South and vigilance against any inclination by Britain to default on its guarantees of union.

But the Unionists met with continuous political defiance from Northern nationalists and Republicans. The Catholic one-third of Northern Ireland's population were discriminated against in every sphere, but most importantly in jobs, in housing and in representative democracy. The British parliament in Westminster for its part allowed the local Protestant rulers in Stormont to do as they pleased, devoting minimal attention to Irish affairs.

In the 1960s, however, things began to change. Civil rights activism among Black people in the United States inspired a similar movement in Northern Ireland. This was a different protest from those that had gone before. Its demands were not the removal of the border between North and South but fair treatment for Catholics within the British state. The demands of the marchers were for free speech, fair local government, jobs on merit, houses on need, and what was termed (despite the prominent presence of many women in the movement) 'one man, one vote'. This movement did not reprise the old Fenian repertoire but, in harmony with the 1968 generation everywhere, sang *We Shall Overcome*. Marches were ruthlessly repressed by the local police force, recruited almost exclusively from the Protestant community. But the Unionists were divided on how to handle the unrest. The governing Ulster Unionist Party (representing mainly the old Protestant ruling class) was increasingly challenged by ultra-loyalists in the settler tradition, inspired by the fundamentalist Free Presbyterian Reverend Ian Paisley. Paisley formed a new party, the Democratic Unionist Party (DUP), in 1971.

The Protestant working class felt their cherished sense of advantage over the local Catholic minority being eroded. In August 1969 Protestant mobs took things into their own hands and attacked Catholic homes and businesses. Intimidation and torching forced many Catholics to abandon their homes and relocate in the relative safety of Catholic areas. Estimates vary of the number affected by this wave of expulsions – a kind of aggression for which, a quarter-century on, extremists in another corner of Europe would coin the foul term 'ethnic cleansing'. An official report suggests that between 1969 and 1972 between thirty and sixty thousand people were driven out, 80 per cent of them Catholic, 20 per cent Protestant. At the time it was the largest enforced population movement in Western Europe since the Second World War (McKittrick 1994: 39).

Riots ensued in Londonderry/Derry and Belfast. The Irish Republican Army was given a new lease of life and paramilitary units became active in defence of Catholic neighbourhoods. The British government sent detachments of the army to Northern Ireland. The soldiers were at first welcomed by Catholics as protectors, but their brutal treatment of civilians quickly came to be felt as a profound injustice. The IRA split to give birth to the Provisional IRA (the Provos), who abandoned the organization's formerly leftist and internationalist politics and rapidly concentrated their focus on the issue of Irish unification, committed to a war that would continue until the border between North and South was wiped from the map. The security forces became their main target: they wanted the British removed once and for all from Irish soil. But sectarian attacks on Ulster Protestants and their organizations were frequent.

In 1971 the UK government suspended what remained of justice in Northern Ireland and introduced internment (imprisonment without right of early trial) for suspected 'terrorists'. In January 1972 the army fired on a peaceful civil rights demonstration in Londonderry/Derry, killing 13 civilians in what was soon known to an appalled world as Bloody Sunday. In March the Stormont administration was disbanded and direct rule from Westminster imposed. The Protestant paramilitary organizations, the historic Ulster Volunteer Force, the Ulster Defence Association (formed in 1972) and their offshoots, rapidly grew in membership to defend their own neighbourhoods, matching IRA intimidation with equal violence.

During the 1970s and 1980s a succession of initiatives was produced by the British government searching for a constitutional arrangement capable of bringing the violence to an end. Britain was now increasingly inclined to involve the government of the Republic of Ireland in a solution. This threat was met by an Ulster Workers' Council strike that paralysed Northern Ireland. A decade later a further Anglo-Irish agreement provoked a boycott of local council business by Unionist politicians. While many ordinary Protestants were simply confused and fearful, the more militant were still ready to defend themselves with weapons against British betrayal.

Meanwhile, the cost of Northern Ireland to the British taxpayer was escalating. Bomb attacks by the IRA on the mainland were unsettling British public opinion. The government was also paying a price in Britain's deteriorating reputation: hunger strikes and protests of IRA prisoners were deeply disturbing to world opinion. A ban on British media giving airtime to representatives of Sinn Féin, the Republican party popularly seen as the political wing of the IRA, was widely felt unjust. The strategic importance of Ireland to Britain was by now, in a supersonic thermonuclear age, greatly reduced. Britain was ready (even if it could not admit it) to see the Republic of Ireland shoulder the problem of governing these troublesome six counties. But by now the Republic was ambivalent about taking in this Trojan horse.

The situation in Northern Ireland had seldom been worse than it was in the early 1990s. Already, in two decades between 1969 and 1989, 3,000 people had died because of political violence, more than ten times that number had been wounded, and there seemed no end in sight to the killing (O'Leary and McGarry 1993: 37). So long as the Unionist parties refused to share power with the parties representing the Catholic minority, the British government could not abandon direct rule. While it stayed, it was resented by Republicans and obliged to enforce security. So the army remained a threatening presence, especially in Catholic areas.

Then, following an initiative by the Social Democratic and Labour Party leader John Hume to begin unpublicized talks with Sinn Féin, slowly the ice began to melt. Denying every move, the British government also pursued behind-the-scenes contacts with the Republicans. Almost as if by sleight of hand, an agreement emerged to halt hostilities. The IRA declared a ceasefire on 31 August 1994 and on 13 October the Combined Loyalist Military Command followed suit.

The hope now lay in all-party talks to seal a lasting peace. But the

IRA refused to give up its arms until its political goal was in sight, while the Unionist parties would not sit round a table with Sinn Féin before decommissioning. Despite pressure from the USA, the British government hedged and delayed. A vulnerable Conservative Party could ill afford to alienate the Unionist parties, on whose MPs it was crucially dependent for its diminishing majority at Westminster. Impatient, the IRA broke its ceasefire with a massive explosion on 9 February 1996 in London's Canary Wharf business centre. Loyalist paramilitaries breached their own ceasefires and violence broke out anew in Belfast, Drumcree, Ballymena and other areas of Northern Ireland. Army helicopters were soon circling overhead again. A front-page headline in the *Independent* on 17 July 1996 read 'Ethnic cleansing in the UK ... 600 Ulster homes emptied by the mobs in ten days'. At the end of 1996, where this account must close, an end to the suffering of Northern Ireland seemed as far away as ever.

Israel/Palestine: wrong and wrong again

Palestine is the name historically given to the land between the southern part of the Eastern Mediterranean shore and the River Jordan, which flows parallel to the coast forty or fifty miles inland. This strip of sun-baked littoral, no more than two hundred miles from end to end, contains sites sacred to all three of the world's great monotheistic religions: Judaism, Christianity and Islam. That is often given as the reason why Palestine has been the subject of a lethal ownership dispute for most of the present century. But a more immediate reason may be its geopolitical significance to the Western powers, who have never ceased to conspire for influence there. Close to the Suez Canal, Palestine is located at the meeting point of Europe, Africa and Asia, and Western European and US strategists value it as a potential foothold in the oil-rich, Arab-owned Middle East.[2]

Among the Semitic tribes that occupied Palestine in the pre-Christian era was a group with a distinctive religion, the forebears of today's Jews. For long periods they were self-governing, but military and political pressures led to the dispersal of many of these Judaeans (or Hebrews, or Israelites) out of the region into what eventually, over millennia, became a worldwide Jewish diaspora. Today they are designated in three

---

2. I am indebted to the following sources on which I have drawn selectively for this summary account of the history of Israel: Jiryis 1976, Lustick 1980, Flapan 1987, Halevi 1987, Davis 1987, Ashkenasi 1992, Orr 1994, Abdo and Yuval-Davis 1995 and Usher 1995. I give page references only where citing specific data.

important groups, with different cultures and variants of religion. The Sephardim are those who settled in Spain until driven out in the fifteenth century by a Catholic monarchy. The Ashkenazim flowered in Eastern and Central Europe and Russia. Both made a substantial contribution to the cultures of Western Europe and the Americas. A third remnant, later to be known as 'Oriental' or Misrahi Jews, continued to live in Palestine and neighbouring Arab lands, speaking Arabic but maintaining their religious, cultural and linguistic difference into the Christian period and beyond, as Islam became the dominant force in the region. The Jews met with different treatment in different societies. In Arab societies they were, in the main, tolerated as distinctive minorities. But within European Christendom they were often persecuted, discriminated against and confined to prescribed occupations and quarters (Halevi 1987).

From the late eighteenth century small numbers of diaspora Jews were travelling back to re-establish themselves in Palestine. The flow of migrants increased and changed in nature with the growth among some European Jews in the late nineteenth century of a political movement, Zionism, a project to create a 'national home' for the scattered Jewish people in what many continued to think of as 'their' Holy Land. Zionist enthusiasts tended to portray Palestine as sparsely populated, 'a land without people for a people without land'. In reality, at the beginning of the twentieth century it was one of the more prosperous areas of the Middle East, peopled by Arabs, mainly Sunni Muslims, under the hegemony of the Ottoman Turks. Most were agriculturalists and herdsmen, but there were several important cities with a thriving bourgeoisie, among whom were many Arab Christians, involved in commerce and seafaring.

With the collapse of the Ottoman Empire after the First World War, a League of Nations mandate placed Palestine under the control of the British government, who lent support to the Zionist plan for the eventual creation of a Jewish 'homeland'. In this the British showed their disregard for the Arabs, whom they had promised their own post-war sovereignty in the region in return for their military support against the Germans.

In the 1920s and early 1930s Jewish migration went on apace, encouraged at first by the British authorities. After years of ghettoization and stereotyping, the Jewish migrants longed more than anything else for normality and self-sufficiency. Their colonizing strategy was what they termed the 'three conquests'. The first was the conquest of land. The World Zionist Organization's agencies purchased large rural estates from Palestinian speculators and absentee land owners, who first dispossessed their tenants. They established Jewish settlements and farms, including many agricultural collectives (kibbutzim) and cooperative villages (moshavim), reflecting the predominantly socialist Zionist ideals of the time. The second 'conquest' was that of labour. The Zionists were determined to rely on their own capacity to do every kind of work from the most skilled to the most menial, rather than paying others to work for them. Third, the settlers aimed to conquer the market, depending on the local population neither as a source of goods nor as customers (Abdo and Yuval-Davis 1995).

At first, the arrival of Jewish settlers among them had not met with organized resistance by native Palestinians. But the post-war migration was on a threatening scale and clearly a political project with powerful backers. It was evident that there would be no place for Palestinians in this strange new society being installed among them. By the 1920s an angry Palestinian educated class was campaigning to stem further Jewish incursions. Sporadic violence spread, to become, in the late 1930s, a large-scale peasant revolt. The British forces were involved in suppressing both the Palestinian uprising and, increasingly, Jewish armed terrorism.

But these events in Palestine were overtaken by cataclysm in Europe. Anti-Semitism was at its most extreme in Germany under the National Socialist regime during the 1930s and 1940s, culminating in the systemic programme of genocide in which six million Jews are estimated to have been murdered. The Allied governments did not intervene to save the Jews; they had different motivations in fighting Germany. The war over, many in Britain and the USA welcomed the project to create a state for Jews in Palestine as a way of salving their bad consciences, while avoiding an influx of Jewish refugees into their own societies.

In 1947 the United Nations acted to resolve conflict in Palestine by ending the British mandate and partitioning the area. Under General Assembly Resolution 181 (II) just over half the territory was allocated to a Jewish state. The Arabs, two-thirds of the population, were designated somewhat less than half for a neighbouring Palestinian state (Davis 1987: 21). On 15 May 1948 the Jewish authorities issued a Declaration of the Establishment of the State of Israel.

Most Palestinian Arabs rejected the partition and, with aid from neighbouring Arab countries, began attacking Jewish shops and houses in the cities, and raiding kibbutzim and other rural settlements. Before long the new state of Israel was fighting for its life against a union of several Arab states. Quickly welding its pre-state militias into a national army, Israel not only survived but pushed its eventual armistice borders far beyond the area allocated under the United Nations resolution, acquiring not 57 per cent but 68 per cent of Palestine (ibid.: 18). The additional land included Galilee in the north and part of the much-prized city of Jerusalem. The independent Palestinian Arab state provided for by the United Nations was never created. Instead, what was left of Palestine came under the control of neighbouring Arab states.

Eighty per cent of the Palestinians within Israel's *de facto* borders lost their homes and land, many in armed expulsions, others in temporary flight made permanent by subsequent Israeli actions (Abdo and Yuval-Davis 1995: 295). Hundreds of thousands clustered, where their descendants still remain, in refugee camps just outside the borders of Israel. Between four and five hundred Arab villages were erased from the map at this time, to be replaced by Jewish settlements.

For the Israeli government the challenge was now to populate the newly acquired land and consolidate the state. In 1950 the Israeli parliament, the Knesset, enacted the Law of Return, which affirmed the right of Jews anywhere in the world to citizenship in Israel. Two-thirds of the territory accorded to Israel in the 1949 armistice had been in Palestinian ownership before the fighting broke out (Davis 1987: 18). It was on this land that many of the 300,000 Jewish refugees from the Holocaust started their lives anew in hardship and hope, soon to be joined by a further million Misrahi and Sephardic Jews fearing for their futures in the now hostile Arab countries. But the Jews were compensated for the wrongs that had been done to them only by means of a wrong inflicted on others: they built among the ruins of a dispossessed people. Jews had come 'home', Palestinians had become the new wanderers.

The Knesset passed legislation that, ignoring a United Nations resolution to the contrary, denied the departed Palestinians the right to return home, vesting their land titles in a new national body, the Custodian of Absentee Property. Pre-war Zionist movement organizations such as the Jewish Agency, the Jewish National Fund and the Histradut, the General Federation of Jewish labour, were forged into powerful para-state apparatuses, consolidating Israel as a Jewish state.

But in one important respect the reality differed from the Zionist vision: the Jews were not alone in their new state. A vestigial Palestinian Arab population of about 150,000 remained. They were now virtually landless and property-less, many of them 'internal' refugees, clustered mainly in towns and villages of the north. They were granted Israeli citizenship, but as non-Jews they lacked rights and resources. As Arabs they were considered potentially disloyal and for this reason until 1966 they were permitted only limited mobility and held subject to military law (Jiryis 1976; Lustick 1980).

So the state of Israel came into existence beset by enemies wishing to see it destroyed. After a period of disarray and despair, exiled

Palestinians in 1964 formed a Palestine Liberation Organization (PLO) pledged to regain Palestine for Palestinian Arabs. Fired by the distress in the refugee camps, PLO terrorism soon acquired an international reach. The Israeli Defence Forces were involved in frequent armed incidents, ranging from raids and reprisals to episodes of outright war.

The most far-reaching in its effects was the Six Day War of 1967, in which Israel repulsed an invasion by combined Arab states and retaliated by seizing control of the neighbouring West Bank (from Jordan) and the Gaza Strip and Sinai Peninsula (from Egypt). The occupation split Israeli opinion. To some Jews it fulfilled the Zionist dream of an Israeli state across the entire Promised Land. To others it cancelled the benefit they had gained by emptying Israel of most of its Palestinian inhabitants.

Holding down this territory containing a million resentful Palestinians destabilized Israeli society. The army had been trained for the battle-front. The new role of policing a subject people was distasteful. Liberal Israelis increasingly lost confidence in the justice of Israeli policies and the honour of their soldiers. The Israeli economy began to depend on Palestinian labourers entering Israel from the Occupied Territories on day-permits, undermining both Jewish self-sufficiency and border security. Renewed contact with other Palestinians politicized the Palestinian minority in Israel. Jewish settlers, belonging to intransigently Zionist groups, encroached into the West Bank, involving yet more land appropriations from Palestinians. Rifts developed between those willing and unwilling to trade these lands for peace with the Arab states.

In 1987 Palestinian resentment flared into rebellion against Israeli rule in the Occupied Territories. The Palestinians called it the *intifada*, a waking up and shaking off of Israeli authority. They boycotted Israeli goods, refused Israeli employment and created an alternative infrastructure. Young men and schoolchildren hurled defiance and stones at the Israeli troops. The army retaliated with arrests, detention, harassment and house demolitions.

Meanwhile a peace process, too, stumbled along. In 1988, PLO Chairman Yasir Arafat, from his headquarters in Tunisia (he had been hounded from Jordan and Lebanon), declared a Palestinian state. But time was also driving the PLO towards the recognition of Israel. Three years later representatives of the two sides met cautiously for the first time, in Madrid. Then once again the local conflict in Palestine was recast by shifts on the world stage. The Soviet bloc disintegrated, and with it the Arab states and PLO lost their counter-weight to the USA, which now became the uncontested world power. In early 1991 an unexpected challenge to American authority came from Iraq, whose provocative invasion of Kuwait was decisively punished. By expressing support for the Iraqi regime the PLO isolated itself, incurred the expulsion of 400,000 Palestinian workers from the Gulf States and forfeited $10 billion in assets and revenue.

The United States, looking for a general stabilization of the Middle East in the wake of the Gulf crisis, used its influence to push the peace process onward. The Israeli government, faced with the alternative of Hamas, the extremist Islamic resistance movement now challenging the PLO's hegemony in the Occupied Territories, had begun to see value as a negotiating partner in this weakened Yasir Arafat. While the public peace process crawled along, secret talks went on in parallel in Oslo, brokered by the Norwegians. In 1993 they resulted in a Declaration of Principles involving mutual recognition, the creation of a Palestine National Authority and the gradual transfer to its control of parts of the Occupied Territories – starting with the Gaza Strip and the town of Jericho.

In recognizing Israel without winning instant statehood, without securing a share of Jerusalem and without stemming the tide of Jewish settlers in the West Bank, many Palestinians considered that Yasir Arafat and the PLO had sold out: the Oslo accords were 'a Palestinian Versailles' (Said 1995: 34). In sharing the policing of the Occupied Territories with the Israelis the PLO became dangerously compromised. The organization was rapidly drawn into corruption and brutality. The fundamentalist Hamas and Islamic Jihad took up the rejectionist banner where the PLO had dropped it, striking fear into the heart of Israel in suicide-bomb assassinations of Israeli civilians in 1995 and 1996.

A matching breed of nationalist extremism had also been festering on the right wing of Israeli opinion, bolstered by some religious elements. Its exponents pursued aggressive settlement tactics in East Jerusalem, Hebron and other West Bank areas. Innocent Palestinians were murdered in notorious incidents. And, most shocking of all to liberal Israeli opinion, Prime Minister Yitshak Rabin was assassinated – by a Jew. In 1996 the Labour-led government that had initiated the peace process was ousted by the hawkish and conservative Likud party, led by Benyamin Netanyahu. As 1997 began, there was little prospect of credible leadership emerging on either side, and violence appeared set to continue.

Bosnia-Hercegovina: ethnicity as destiny

Like Palestine, the Balkan territory that is today the state of Bosnia-Hercegovina (BH) is a region across which ethnic and political boundaries have continually shifted and flowed. Successive empires have confronted each other across these mountains, so that war and population movements have been frequent. But the southward movement of the Slavs into the Balkans in the sixth and seventh centuries AD is usually taken as the starting point for any history of Bosnia. Today's Bosnians, whatever other designation they may give themselves or be given by others, are mainly, simply, the Slavs living in the Bosnian geographical region (Malcolm 1994: 2, 8).[3] But these Slavs were soon to be differentiated by religion. The Bosnian mountains were at different times on the west and on the east of the dividing line between the Holy Roman Empire and the Byzantine Empire, so that both Catholic and Orthodox communities existed there from early in the Christian era.

For periods in the late Middle Ages Bosnia was itself a state. The thirteenth and fourteenth centuries were a time of particular prosperity under a line of Bosnian Christian kings. But Christianity itself was now being challenged by the Ottoman Empire. In AD 1389 the Turkish army defeated the Serbs at the battle of Kosovo Polje. In 1463 they took control of Bosnia. By the early seventeenth century a majority of the people living in the territory of today's BH were Muslim by religion. Conversion of the Slavs had been gradual and unforced, because Christianity and other religious traditions were accommodated in the Ottoman system. But attractive careers in the Ottoman administration were open only to Muslims, and a privileged urban class of Muslim Slavs emerged.

Ottoman governance of the Balkans continued for 400 years. It began to falter in the mid-nineteenth century, with an upsurge of Christian and nationalist feeling among those Slavs who now (to the north and west) celebrated Croatian identity and those (to the south and east) who identified themselves as a Serb *narod*, or nation. Both nationalist movements had ambitions not only to end Ottoman rule but also to add the territory and population of BH to their domains. Croats claimed that Muslims were really just 'Turkicized' Croats, while Serbs asserted that they were merely lapsed Orthodox. Muslim attitudes hardened in response.

In the 1870s Serbia and Russia launched a war against Ottoman rule that led to Bosnia becoming part of the Austro-Hungarian Empire. The

---

3. This account of Bosnian history prior to the mid-twentieth century draws mainly on Noel Malcolm's *Bosnia: A Short History* (Malcolm 1994). I follow him in sometimes, for the sake of brevity, using the term 'Bosnia' (or alternatively BH) to refer to the whole territory of modern Bosnia-Hercegovina. In narrating the history of Bosnia from 1980, including the war of 1991–95, I draw mainly on Susan L. Woodward's *Balkan Tragedy* (Woodward 1995), on *The Death of Yugoslavia* by Laura Silber and Allan Little (Silber and Little 1995) and the journal *War Report*, published by the Institute for War and Peace Reporting.

economy now developed quickly, mineral resources were exploited, and factories and railways were built. But political life became increasingly ethnicized, with the main political parties of the region claiming to represent distinct Croat, Serb and Muslim interests. It was nationalist ferment in the Balkans that sparked the First World War in which Russia, France and Britain defeated Germany, finally eclipsed the Austro-Hungarian and Ottoman Empires and replaced their hegemony in Europe.

From early in the twentieth century a project of unity among the 'south Slavs' had been in the making, and soon after the end of the First World War BH found itself part of a 'Kingdom of Slovenes, Serbs and Croats', later renamed 'Yugoslavia'. Rivalry continued between expansionist Catholic/Croats and Orthodox/Serbs, but under the leadership of Mehmed Spaho the Bosnian Muslims maintained political leverage.

So Bosnia developed as a territory of extraordinary ethnic mixity. 'We saw it as a specifically Bosnian spirit,' the Bosnian women told us at Mijas. There were Jews, Germans, Hungarians and Roma (Gypsies). Among the majority Slav population were Bosnian Orthodox and Bosnian Catholics, who might or might not think of themselves as respectively 'Serb' or 'Croat'. But the largest single component of the Bosnian population was the Bosnian Muslims. They spanned all economic classes, from landowner to peasant. The educated, professional and owning-class Muslims had become gradually more secular and more 'European' during the late nineteenth and early twentieth centuries.

It is important to stress that these groups were indistinguishable in physique. There were small regional differences in spoken dialect and religious cultures differentiated them to some extent, but economic class differences were probably always more divisive (Malcolm 1994). Enmity between the ethnic groups did not normally arise unless provoked by outside forces. The Second World War is an instance of a wider conflagration in which Bosnian differences were inflamed into ethnic war. In 1941 Yugoslavia was invaded and defeated by Germany and its allies. The Germans installed a Nazi puppet regime in Croatia and Bosnia. Croatian Ustaša fascists participated in the extermination of Jews and Roma, and are remembered for extreme brutality to Serbs. Fierce bands of monarchist Serb resistance fighters, the Četniks, fought the Ustaša. But the force that won through to control Yugoslavia at the end of the Second World War was not the Četniks but their rivals, the revolutionary anti-fascist Partisan resistance movement. Led by Josip Broz 'Tito' (part-Slovene, part-Croat), the Partisans began as a mainly Serb guerrilla army. In the later phases of the war they were joined by anti-fascist Croats and Muslims, many from Bosnia, and received support from Britain and the Allies. Sarajevo was liberated by the Partisans on 6 April 1945.

Two million Yugoslavs died in the Second World War, the majority killed by other Yugoslavs. Bosnians had fought on all sides. No process of healing or reconciliation followed – indeed, Stalinist reprisals ensued, and Tito's control was imposed at a heavy price. Agriculture was collectivized, dress modernized and education standardized. But in 1948 Yugoslavia broke with the Soviet Union and developed its own kind of socialism, with a characteristic system of economic 'self-management'. It traded with the capitalist world and allowed more individual freedom of movement than other communist-bloc countries. Yugoslavia took advantage of its geopolitical significance to the Western powers during the Cold War period. They were obliged to court it as leader of a non-aligned movement of Third World countries.

Tito's policy for containing nationalism was to give the strongest 'nations' their own republic within a federal system. The six republics (Serbia, Montenegro, Slovenia, Croatia, Macedonia and Bosnia-Hercegovina) followed more or less the old Ottoman boundaries. Each had large minorities, for whom individual rights were guaranteed. As many as one-quarter of all Serbs and Croats lived outside 'their' borders. The structure of the state was federal, and a quota system assured equal representation in all important federal bodies.

Bosnia-Hercegovina, though, had no majority ethnic group. One-third of its population was of Orthodox and one-sixth of Catholic background. Mostly they were born and bred in BH. For all that, they were conceived in Yugoslav ideology as having their 'homeland' in Serbia and Croatia respectively. But the state could not identify the largest group, the Bosnian Muslims, just under half the population, as 'coming from' anywhere but Bosnia. In the post-war Yugoslav constitution Muslims were treated as an anomaly, so that given a choice in the census of identifying as Serb, Croat or 'Yugoslav', many opted for the latter. The 1961 census, however, furnished a new option: to identify as 'Muslim in an ethnic sense'. The 1971 census developed this official identity one step further to 'Muslim in the sense of nation'. Between 1953 and 1971 the number of Bosnians declaring themselves 'Yugoslav' consequently fell by two-thirds, as many shifted to 'Muslim' (Bringa 1995: 28).

The tendency of constitutional changes in 1963 and 1974 was to erode the federal Yugoslav ideal, decentralizing power, particularly over economic development, to republican leaders. Inter-republic trade throughout the 1970s was no more than 20–25 per cent, and 99 per cent of all investments came from within the republics (Djurić 1995: 125). Then in 1980 Tito died leaving a weak and inefficient successor, a collective eight-man presidency. During the 1980s the Yugoslav economy was failing. Experiments with a 'socialist market' and price liberalism had led to spiralling inflation and a mountainous national debt. As a condition of aid to the ailing country the Western powers, represented by the International Monetary Fund, called for the imposition of drastic austerity measures, including cuts in the country's extensive public sector. Economic reforms forced the federal government to constrain the republics, tightening control over banking, taxation, budgets, investment and foreign trade. The pressures led to quarrels between the ambitious leaders of the rival republics, and between them and the federal authorities. Unemployment and shortages sharpened class inequalities, civil disorder grew and governmental authority was eroded.

In these circumstances, communist ideology progressively lost its hold over Yugoslav minds. Serbian and Croatian nationalisms were surging back to life, feeding off each other. The leaderships, feeling power slipping from their hands, changed from communist to nationalist rhetoric. On 28 June 1989 at a rally in Kosovo, near the historic battlefield of Kosovo Polje, Slobodan Milošević, president of the Republic of Serbia, used the anniversary of the defeat of the Serbs by the Ottoman Turks to whip up Serb feeling, turning the discontent and fear of Serbs living alongside significant minorities (Hungarians in Vojvodina and Albanians in Kosovo) into a source of political power. The Orthodox Church lent its authority to his project, parading the relics of saints and heroes through the land. Irresponsible academics in Belgrade disseminated inflammatory nationalist tracts.

The media manipulated people's anxieties. Press and television in Yugoslavia were rapidly losing any federal identity and ideology they may once have had and were converted into tools of the nationalist movements (Article 19, 1994). Opinion in the country lurched to the right as anti-communist émigrés to the West now flooded back to Yugoslavia, while educated and mainly democratic young people left. The old enforced ethic of 'the class interest' yielded without apparent difficulty to one of 'the national interest' (Milić 1993: 110).

In the first Yugoslav multi-party elections in 1990 nationalist parties swept the board. The relatively developed northern republic of Slovenia now saw advantage in slipping the bonds that tied it to the poor Yugoslav south and looked to join the wealthy nations of 'Europe'. The nationalist regime of President Franjo Tudjman in Croatia looked for ways of increasing its distance from a belligerent Serbia. But Milošević refused to accept a looser confederal compromise. His vision was no longer a

Yugoslavia of any kind, but a Greater Serbia. Slovenia and Croatia proclaimed their independence in 1991, and were quickly given international recognition. Slovenia, with few Serb inhabitants, escaped with only token resistance from the Yugoslav Army (JNA). Not so Croatia. The JNA and Serbia supported a violent insurrection by the large Serb minority there.

In Bosnia-Hercegovina the elections of 1990 had been fought by three parties organized on ethnic lines. The subsequent government was dominated by the Muslim Party of Democratic Action (the SDA), led by Alija Izetbegović. Against the nationalist strategies of the neighbouring republics, the SDA played two contradictory cards: strengthening Muslim political representation, and simultaneously emphasizing the multi-national, multi-religious character of BH. Afraid of eclipse within a Yugoslavia looking more and more like Milošević's Greater Serbia they too declared independence, in April 1992.

Some Bosnian Serbs, under extremist leadership, swiftly declared certain areas of BH autonomous Serb regions. Milošević was now leader of a Yugoslavia comprising only Serbia and Montenegro, but he still deployed the greater part of the formidable weaponry of the JNA, much of which was now stationed in BH. Concealing his role behind a front of Bosnian Serb paramilitary forces and bands of irregulars from Serbia, he backed a military campaign with the aim of taking control of large areas of Bosnia. The territory targeted lay across the north and east of the country, a potential land bridge from Serbia proper to enclaves of Serbian population in Croatia. Given the close intermingling of the three ethnic groups throughout the republic, this was bound to be a bloody exercise. 'Ethnic cleansing' of the selected areas – by means of military action, murder and imprisonment, rape, intimidation and propaganda – was a central part of the political project.

Within weeks the JNA had control of 70 per cent of BH. The Bosnian government, despite its lack of weapons, ammunition and trained men, quickly mobilized a defence force. But the alliance of Bosnian Croats and Bosnian Muslims under SDA leadership felt apart in 1993, when some Bosnian Croat nationalists, with support from extremist elements in Croatia itself, opportunistically began 'a war within a war', seizing from Muslim control areas in west and central Bosnia, and in Hercegovina in the south, with the aim of creating a Croatian mini-state they termed 'Herceg-Bosna'. For 18 months the Croatian HVO (Croat Defence Council) party and associated para-militaries, the HOS (Croat Paramilitary Force), in the same manner as the Bosnian Serb Army and its supporters, engaged in campaigns against the (mainly) Muslim civilian population, involving massacres, rapes and expulsions.

Not all Bosnian Serbs and Bosnian Croats approved what was being done in their name. Many remained loyal to the ideal of the mixity and unity of BH and fought in its defence. Unlike the other two parties to the war the Bosnian government did not use 'ethnic cleansing' as deliberate strategy. Their war was a defensive one. But the Bosnian *Armija* too, as the wars progressed and Sarajevo and central Bosnia were besieged, was drawn into the logic of securing territory by killing, terrorizing and expelling civilians.

The European powers had a lot to answer for in the descent of Yugoslavia into war. Germany had irresponsibly endorsed the secession of its old ally Croatia. Russia uncritically supported the Serbs. Western governments looked strictly to their own interests. It was convenient to define this as a civil war, a flare-up of those 'age-old hatreds' among the Bosnian population. The United Nations sent a peace-keeping force but would not allow it to counter aggression. International mediators dreamed up ill-advised solutions that involved partition between ethnic groups, unachievable in BH without huge population movements. By playing with ethnic maps they precipitated the Croatian aggression. An arms embargo imposed in September 1991 cost Serbia little but prevented the self-defence of the Bosnian state. The BH Armija was obliged to rely on military aid from Islamic countries, including a draft of extremist *mujahedeen* troops.

In the autumn of 1995 the United States government, driven by public opinion in the USA, began to play a more active role, enabling air strikes against the Serbs and eventually bringing the parties to a peace conference at Dayton, Ohio. Meanwhile military action by the Croatian government had assisted the BH forces in turning the tide against the Bosnian Serb army. Milošević, cornered by economic sanctions and vilified worldwide, now tactically distanced himself from the Bosnian Serb leadership. But at Dayton, agreement was pressed upon the three parties to the satisfaction of none. Bosnia-Hercegovina would retain its independence and its borders, but it would be divided into two ethnic parts. Bosnian Serb aggression was rewarded with 49 per cent of the country and a semi-autonomous entity, the Republika Srpska. A Muslim–Croat Federation would govern the remaining 51 per cent of the territory. This was bound to be an uneasy alliance. Though the partners shared a common enemy in the Bosnian Serb aggressors, and Croatia had taken in hundreds of thousands of Muslim refugees, Croat separatists had by no means relinquished their plans to seize some of the Federation territory.

Very large numbers died in the three and a half years of war, probably more than two hundred thousand. Many more were wounded, and at least two million people were turned out of their homes and became refugees, either in the areas of central Bosnia held by the BH forces, or abroad. The Republika Srpska largely refused cooperation in the government of BH, failed to hand over indicted war criminals and made the return of refugees to their homes impossible. In many areas (and most notably in the town of Mostar) Bosnian Croats acted as though a state of Herceg-Bosna had become a reality, guarding checkpoints and refusing reintegration.

In 1996 the Bosnian economy lay in ruins and the country was still heavily dependent on humanitarian aid. Hundreds of thousands of refugees remained in limbo. Meanwhile the world's attention had turned to other catastrophes. There was little recognition that this had been, in a sense, not a 'Balkan war' but Europe's war, the world's war. The conflict had been sparked by stress in the domestic Yugoslav polity and economy. But that stress was the local effect of transformations in the European and international order, in which far greater powers were the key actors. And those external agents, no less than the local ones, had made the racist error of seeing an ethnic logic as incontestable (Woodward 1995: 13).

People, nation, land

These then are some of the events that, differently experienced, variously interpreted, with divergent motivations, have brought into being the collective identities in play in the contemporary conflicts. This is how some people have come to 'be' Catholic, Protestant, Palestinian Arab, Israeli Jew, Bosnian Muslim, Serb or Croat. We can see how any one of those names has different meanings and values when spoken from, or heard in, different positions. But while history has furnished the materials that shape and influence today's actors and that they in turn can reinterpret and deploy in their plots, history has not written the script. Today's Unionists are not yesterday's British settlers, even though they still celebrating the Battle of the Boyne and get called 'planter' by those who hate them. As Brendan O'Leary and John McGarry put it:

The present conflict is not an exotic rave from the grave of Europe's past, a 'replay' of twelfth-century feudal wars of conquest, or a 'repeat' for modern television audiences of seventeenth-century wars of religion. The key ideas of nationalism and unionism, the central political doctrines which polarize the communities in contemporary Northern Ireland, were not present, and made no sense, in the twelfth or seventeenth centuries (O'Leary and McGarry 1993: 55).

It is when present events make collective identity politically important that we reach for history, spanning the gap between present and past with stories that stress 'people', nation and land. They are slippery concepts, because they all refer simultaneously to 'real' material phenomena and to interpretations of them whose cogency lies in what people say and sing, paint and write, and how others take up and act out their meanings. To the women in Bat Shalom, Medica and the Women's Support Network, understanding these three concepts and positioning them in relation to their own politics is no mere theoretical pastime. It is a pressing practical need.

'*The people*', 'our people' are words we use to differentiate ourselves on the basis of culture and to denote a sense of belonging. With the same intent we might use tribe, community, religious tradition, or 'tongue'. The preferred word of academics, and latterly also administrators and the media, is 'ethnic group', deriving from the Greek *ethnos*, 'own' people, and *ethnikos*, 'other' people.

It is hotly debated how 'real' ethnicity is. Can people legitimately be differentiated and categorized in distinct collectivities on grounds of culture? After all, ethnic groups are never entirely homogenous. For example, many distinctive cultures (North American, Russian and Ethiopian to name but a few) go to make up 'Israeli Jews'. And Palestinian Arabs, as we have seen, are culturally subdivided into Christian and Muslim, and they in turn are internally differentiated. Besides, people of upper and lower social classes in a single ethnic group often have very different cultures. Sometimes, as in Ireland over the centuries, a dominant ethnic group operates as a ruling class, in such a way that class and ethnic boundaries are inscribed one over the other and it is unclear which is salient (O'Leary and McGarry 1993). At the cultural edges of an ethnic group the similarities with other ethnicities may be greater than the differences.

Despite these cautions, the notion of ethnicity does have a material referent, unlike that of 'race', a concept devoid of the biological basis it assumes, usable only in racist discourse (Miles 1989). As Phil Cohen (1988: 24) puts it, ethnicity 'refers to a real process of historical individuation – namely the linguistic and cultural practices through which a sense of collective identity or "roots" is produced and transmitted from generation to generation', adapting and changing as it goes. People really do catch best the subtleties in the play of meanings exchanged within the collectivity in which they were reared, compared with one they enter as strangers.

That having been said, ethnicity seldom exists without ethnicism – the deployment of cultural markers to differentiate the group from others, and usually to flag up superiority over them. Nira Yuval-Davis suggests that ethnic phenomena are never just cultural: they are always also political. They *construct*, she says, the collectivity and 'its interest' (1994b: 193). Clearly, promoters of ethnic culture are often in the business of including-in-order-to-exclude. There may be innocent *differences* (an ethnic group's cuisine may typically make use of ingredients that grow well in its habitual locality), but there are also political *differentiators* (such as culinary taboos that define those who are us, and clean, and those who are not us, and are unclean). When ethnic distinctions are stressed, it is always possible to detect a political project. Often it is galvanized by injustice – domination or marginalization by another 'people'. And often, though not always, its engine is a class elite. Culture can be politicized through a variety of elements in the social formation. Religious apparatuses (some with a global reach, all with male priesthoods) often serve as powerful agents of ethnic projects and use them in their own. The ethnicization of religious affiliation is something Ireland, Israel/Palestine and ex-Yugoslavia have in common. On the other hand in none of them has ethnicity been significantly racialized and language differences are salient only in Israel.

A second question, among women of the projects as in the wider world, is whether ethnic belongings, distinctions and movements are desirable or disastrous. A culture-based movement for survival seems fair enough when a minority culture is under threat. And some feel it is quite possible to garner all the riches of belonging to a culture, even a religious culture, without being a slave to tradition and without feeling superior to outsiders. At Mijas, for instance, Nudžejma, a practising Bosnian Muslim, said she felt well able to challenge the validity of repressive traditions imposed by clerical authorities and to assert new ways from within the belief system. But Rada, Joy and Yehudit, coming respectively from Bosnian Serb, Irish Protestant and Israeli Jewish backgrounds, wanted instead to break out of the boundaries of ethno-religious community and reach for a belonging that was secular and more fully social, that minimized difference: 'humanity' perhaps. Ethnicity, it seems, is neither good nor bad but problematic, and the relation between our sense of self and ethnic identity is bound to be an unsettled one.

The women of the three projects often asked each other what is the difference between ethnicity and *nation*? It is a question academics ask too. Jan Nederveen Pieterse suggests that ethnicity refers to similar processes as nation but 'in a finer print of history'. He sees ethnicity as taking several forms. 'Domination ethnicity' is where an ethnic group (such as Israel's Jews or Northern Ireland's Protestants) has sufficient advantage and momentum to control the state and subordinate, even invisibilize, other ethnic groups within it. Their ethnicity, by contrast, is what he terms 'enclosure ethnicity', confined and inward-looking, with little sense of nationhood. But change, especially modernization, may stir an ethnic consciousness so that dormant ethnicities become 'competition ethnicities', struggling (like those of Palestine or Catholic Northern Ireland) with the dominant ethnocracy for advantage and recognition (Pieterse, 1997).

It is in these circumstances that the concept of nation is brought into play. An element within an ethnic collectivity mounts a resistance against oppression or exclusion, and becomes fired with ambition for greater community autonomy and potentially for state sovereignty. While ethnic cultures may in certain periods of their history be laid-back, barely differentiated, what Pieterse terms 'optional ethnicities', the notion of nation always suggests a project of power. Ethnicity may exist without ethnicism, but nations necessarily involve nationalism – indeed 'it is nationalism which engenders nations and not the other way round' (Gellner 1983: 55).

Nation has to be distinguished from state – which is the term reserved to the machinery for control and administration of a given territory, the source of citizenship and rights, and the agency with the sole legitimate use of force. A nation may be looking for exit from a state, for more respect or autonomy within a state, for unification across state borders, for control of an existing state, or (witness Palestinian aspirations today) to create a new one (Gurr 1995). A nation-state is a 'successful' national project – though many of its nationals may continue to live outside it. In turn, there is usually residual ethnic diversity within, and ethnic minorities may be denied rights. Certainly the three histories just presented will be recognizable in such an account of nation. They are clearly instances of interrupted, incomplete or failed state-making.

Nationalism, like all ideologies, is catching. Sometimes, as in 1980s Yugoslavia, the resurgence of one national movement may be read as a threat to another ethnic collectivity, sparking a rival nationalism. And the national uprising of one oppressed people may inspire another. The national struggle of the Irish against Britain earlier this century encouraged the leaders of other anti-colonial independence movements. Interestingly, the Bosnian and Palestinian women at the Mijas workshop remembered being inspired by Bernadette Devlin, Irish civil rights leader, while the Irish and Bosnian women said that as young women their imaginations had been fired by the Palestine liberation movement. But dominant peoples also embellish their power with national symbols – think of Britain's bombastic John Bull, in his Union Flag waistcoat. Threatened loss of power can be even more galvanizing – witness the national loyalty of Jews in the State of Israel when the Arab alliance looked likely to put an end to it.

Two further questions about nation/nationalism preoccupy theorists: how to understand the phenomenon in relation to history, and what value to place on it. Some stress the foundation of national movements in pre-existing ethnic collectivities and their enduring cultures (Smith 1995). But on the whole theorists of the nation do not take at face value 'nationalism's own account of itself, as an awakening of the slumbering but primordial nation through the kiss of nationalist Prince Charmings' (Smith 1996: 372). Most stress how the histories evoked by nationalist movements are at best selective and at worst falsifications. They understand nations as modern phenomena, brought into being by capitalism and industrialisation and their new class relations, the curtailment of the rights of traditional aristocracies, the growth of bureaucratic structures of administration, the potential for democratic government (Gellner 1983; Hobsbawm 1990). The invention of print and printed news distribution seems have been particularly important in generating a sense of national identity (Anderson 1983). The discursive factor in nationality is often stressed today: nations are seen as constructed unities, imagined (though not illusory) communities. Imagined, 'because the members of even the smallest nation will never know most of their fellow-members, meet them, or even hear of them, yet in the minds of each lives the image of their communion' (ibid.: 6). And community can be imagined in different ways. In some movements, like the blood nationalism of the Serbs, the bonding is around common origins. In others, typically settler societies drawing together people from different pasts, the stress shifts to common destiny (Yuval-Davis 1997).

Should nationalism be seen as a creative or a destructive force? The women found it hard to deny the value of a collective sense of nation-hood to contemporary Palestinians or Northern Ireland Catholics, the self-respect it generates, the hope it offers of ending subordination and winning rights. But what of Serb and Croat nationalisms, in which people have been whipped up by an influential minority into a frenzy of fear and hatred, swept into a deadly project to create a nation-state 'clean' of all other ethnic groups? Or the ambivalent and violent local brand of British nationalism among Northern Ireland Protestants reduced and cornered between a nationalistic Catholic community and the UK state (with its own national agenda)?

Clearly a potential for both good and ill resides in nationalism. Indeed, a single movement may embody both, with progressive and regressive factions each dwelling on its own reading of history, each struggling to create national identity in its chosen mould. All we can do is evaluate the many movements that mobilize a sense of nationhood, applying to each one several tests. How essentialist and exclusionary is its rendering of 'the people'? Does it show promise of ethnic opening or threaten more ethnic closure as it approaches power? Is this a bourgeois project, or a movement of workers and peasants promising class revolution as well as national liberation? Is it authoritarian or democratic? religious or secular? Finally there is a criterion seldom yet introduced into the evaluation except by women: does this national movement perpetuate a regime of male dominance, or does it prefigure a transformation of gender relations? This is something to which I return below.

Meanwhile, what of '*land*'? If time (an evocation of the past and of future destinies) is an important dimension in ethnicism and nationalism, so too is space. Ethnic cultures reflect the territories the group inhabits, but in turn they also always actively constitute place in representing it to themselves and others as 'our country'. In processes like this, space and place can be recognized as social constructs (Massey 1994). They are constituted through social forces and social relations that change and mark the lands we inhabit. The Jezreel Valley across which Bat Shalom members journey to meet each other looks and feels different today, under the mechanized agriculture of the Jewish kibbutzim, from earlier this century under Palestinian tenure and farming practices. At the same time, land structures and inhabits our thoughts. We feel very emotional about landscapes, especially the kind we call 'home'.

National projects often evoke a mystic bond to place (Jackson and Penrose 1993). They draw boundaries, and when they achieve state control over their claimed territory they designate it 'the homeland'. As Doreen Massey points out, maps are social products and reflect the power of the people who draw them up (Massey 1995). And the histories of Northern Ireland, Bosnia-Hercegovina and Israel/Palestine are nothing if not claims and counter-claims concerning the mapping of homelands. So there is visualization involved in national geographies as well as in national collectivities. As Michael Billig says: 'a place – a homeland – also has to be imagined'. Whether by official map-makers or by ordinary inhabitants who seldom lay pen to paper, it is imagined as a unit, the sum of our homes, and that special quality 'continues without dilution right up to the borders' (Billig 1995: 75). Often the political borders are geographical ruptures of space: rivers, shorelines. If they are not, they come to seem so. The line that separates Northern Ireland from the Republic of Ireland wanders along lanes and hedgerows. But one Protestant woman told me that as she grew up, so great had been her community's alienation from the South, 'I saw the border as being like a great river.'

It is more difficult to recognize danger in an attachment to land and home than in the belonging associated with ethnicity and nation. It seems harmless enough to afford ourselves a love of this 'green and pleasant land', our 'home town', our 'homely' flat/cottage/house. Who would blame a Bosnian refugee for homesickness? But often the feeling of belonging to place is mobilized competitively as a source of ethnic or national cohesion.

The German word *Heimat* refers to both home and homeland. A Heimat movement was popular in Germany in the social and economic chaos of the 1930s. It glorified the patriarchal family and valued nature and countryside (Applegate 1992: 67). Heimat was a comforting fantasy of stability, changelessness, harmony and purpose, while all around was in turmoil. Recently Nora Räthzel set out to learn how today's middle-class Germans see Heimat. She found that attachment to Heimat involves an evocation of simplicity and peace, repressing and denying the unwelcome reality of difference, division and tension within both 'home' and 'homeland' (Räthzel 1994). The fact that Heimat ideology was easily exploited by Nazism signals dangers, then, even in a discourse of land/country/home/homeland.

Women, feminism and nationalism

In the three histories I sketched earlier in the chapter women were not visible, but they were not absent. Gender structured those social movements, their goals and the national identities they forged. And there is evidence, unearthed by feminist historians, of women active (though seldom in the leadership) in all those processes.

To consider only Ireland, the women's organization Cumman na mBan was formed in 1914, as part of the nationalist uprising against British rule. It had 43 branches in 1916, and had grown to 800 by 1921. In the Anglo-Irish war the women were scouts, despatch-riders, intelligence workers and nursing aides, often in danger zones (MacCurtain 1978: 55). The Irish Suffrage Movement, by contrast, saw a number of conflicts and splits between those favouring nationalism and internationalism (Ryan 1997).

But women's commitment to the Irish struggle gained women little as a sex. When at last sovereignty was won, they were not rewarded with equality, and the Irish Free State proved no less patriarchal than the one it displaced. In Northern Ireland 75 years later women were still absent from power. The journalist Suzanne Breen wrote in the *Independent* newspaper soon after the Docklands bomb:

> The Northern Ireland peace process has been run by men. Men in republican and loyalist paramilitary groups called the ceasefires eighteen months ago. Men in the British and Irish governments talked to men in the unionist and nationalist parties. Men in the IRA then decided to end their ceasefire (*Independent*, 29 February 1996: 6).

The women in the three projects had their own experiences as women in relation to contemporary national movements. Their proximity to them varied from one country to the other and according to the stage and political nature of the struggle. For instance, given the nature of the recent wars, the Bosnian women had nothing good to say about nationalism and certainly did not call themselves nationalists. But nationalism could look different to a Palestinian woman. Suad Abd el-Hadi sometimes felt driven towards nationalism against her will: 'I feel nationalism when I feel discrimination against me.' Some of the women hoped they could reinterpret nationalism in a way they felt comfortable with, ridding it of exclusiveness, militarism and masculinism. Marie Mulholland, of Catholic background, had resigned from the Irish Republican party Sinn Féin some years before because of its position on women. Now she said:

> the kind of nationalism related to land and who owns the land has always been violent and savage. But I still believe there is a nationalism which allows sharing. Different people who live in the land bring in their cultures and arguments and you create a mix of all the different cultures. This could be a form of nationalism we haven't seen yet.

So are nationalism and feminism compatible? It depends of course on what *kind* of nationalism and what *kind* of feminism you are talking about – for both of them are plural movements.

Feminist historians documenting liberatory moments in national movements do not hesitate to write of 'feminist nationalisms' (West 1992, 1997a). In Europe such moments have been few and far between. Gisela Kaplan writes: 'So extraordinary and unusual is the alliance between feminism and nationalism in Europe that I was able to find only two examples: nineteenth-century Italy and twentieth-century Finland.' These were rare instances in which, as she puts it, 'nationalism was capable of functioning as a force of an *ascending* citizenship' (Kaplan 1997). Certainly the programme of German National Socialism of the mid-twentieth century included a reversal of women's progress towards emancipation after the First World War (Koonz 1987). This is the kind of nationalism which, as Cynthia Enloe puts it, 'springs from masculinized memory, masculinized humiliation and masculinized hope' (Enloe 1989: 44).

Positive examples are more common among anti-colonial movements. Kumari Jayawardena documents Asian independence movements of the late nineteenth and early twentieth centuries when the struggle was against both pre-capitalist patriarchal social structures and Western imperialism. Then, 'capitalism brought women into the social sphere and into economic production, nationalism pushed them into participating in the political life of their communities' (Jayawardena 1986: 257). Male elites sometimes back 'women's rights' as a signifier of modernization. But such histories show that women can be simultaneously actor and hostage to nationalism (Kandiyoti 1993). Even in liberatory national movements women are driven to a double militancy, organizing 'in and against' the movement to give a contrary spin to its prevailing gender relations. If women in the movement organize in the interests of women as women, and more so if they form anti-militarist and cross-ethnic women's projects, they are quickly cast as traitors.

As anti-imperialist movements win power they commonly lose whatever socialist class ideology and progressive gender dimension they may have had in the early stages of the struggle. Turning to later twentieth-century developments in the Asian independence struggle, Jayawardena records a decline in women's movements. They had never been autonomous and were marginalized as power came within reach (Jayawardena 1986: 259). And Valentine Moghadam, concerned with late twentieth-century Islamic revolutions in which the nation is conceived as a religious entity, finds that 'feminists and nationalists view each other with suspicion if not hostility, and nationalism is no longer assumed to be a progressive force for change' (Moghadam 1994a: 3).

The relation between national and gender identity is seen more analytically in the work of Nira Yuval-Davis. Constructions of nationhood, she points out, 'involve specific notions of both "manhood" and "womanhood"' (Yuval-Davis 1997: 1). The more regressive the rendering of national community, the more does nation involve reproductive and familial imagery (birth, blood, sons) and the more profoundly is gender differentiated and essentialized, man as warrior, woman as nurturer.

Yuval-Davis and others have shown how the discourses and policies

of nationalist regimes position and exploit women in relation to reproduction, in a double sense of that word (Yuval-Davis and Anthias 1989;
Yuval-Davis 1997; Kandiyoti 1993). The leaders urge population growth
(often with eugenicist overtones) to ensure that the collectivity will
survive and outnumber its rivals. So women's prime duty becomes
motherhood. We shall see how the demographic balance in Northern
Ireland strikes (variously) hope and fear into community leaders there,
and we shall find evidence too of pro-natalist policies in Israel. Second,
women are defined as the 'reproducers' of the nation's culture. As
children we are supposed to learn tradition 'at our mother's knee'.

So woman is, in a sense, highly valued in nationalist discourse and
often symbolizes the spirit of the nation – Britannia, Marianne.
Sometimes she is its ultimate sacrifice, that brave woman with a child
on her arm and a gun in her hand. But, though she may look strong up
there in the nationalist imaginary, this woman is not autonomous. As
men's lives are at the disposal of the nation, women's bodies are at the
disposal of men. Bosnian women have reason to know how extremist
national movements transfix women as living boundary-markers of the
collectivity (Anthias and Yuval-Davis 1989; Mežnarić 1994). The patriarchal family, microcosm of the nation, governs women's behaviour,
because only their sexual containment guarantees the purity of the
bloodline and the honour of the family. When men are sent to war to
protect hearth and home, one of the things they will be told they die
for is to keep their womenfolk safe from defilement by enemy men.
Rape of 'their' women is the most effective way of penetrating an
enemy nation's defences, destroying its property, hurting its morale.

But if it is important to discriminate carefully between national
movements, it is equally important to distinguish rigorously between
one kind of feminism and another. For a start, not all women's activism
is feminist. Movements of women defining themselves as mothers, for
instance, may be constructing the identity 'mother' biologically, not
questioning the ideology of the patriarchal family. Or they may be
constructing it socially, as primary caretaker. It matters which. The
former movement may be conservative, even fascist. It is certainly, as
we shall see, readily co-opted by nationalist projects.

Further, we need to question even feminist movements as to their
practice and discourse on gender, democracy, class, ethnic and national
difference. A minority of feminists, while they recognize women's oppression, remain within essentialist thinking. When they invoke 'woman'
as collective social actor she is given a primordial meaning, someone
'naturally' different from (and better than) men. This is an ideology
every bit as immobilizing and divisive as essentialist constructions of

the nation. The majority tendency in feminism, by contrast, is anti-essentialist. It recognizes gender identities as socially constituted. From this perspective, when 'women' are invoked as collective social actor they are (like nation) an *imagined* community, a concept it is understood will take different shape in different minds, and be used for different purposes. And the blame for women's oppression then lies not with men 'being' men (natural-born rapists and killers) but with gender and other power relations.

On the whole women's movements have set great store by democratic process. When democracy has failed it has usually been less for lack of democratic intent than lack of organizational skill. But one important failing has been white, middle-class Western feminists' blindness to the inequalities inherent in class and ethnic difference. In reality, working-class women's organizations and struggles have been an important strand of the Western European women's movement of the last 30 years. Trade union women, for instance, were active on issues of equal pay and women's working conditions long before 'new wave feminism'. Ethnic minority women in the metropolitan countries and women in Africa, Asia and Latin America also have a long history of generating their own demands and actions, and are arguably the ones with most to teach today. It has taken time for authoritative Western feminisms to respond to critiques and abandon their universalizing discourse. But the more they have done so, the more feminism has matured and pluralized.

We need, then, to define our terms quite carefully, taking for granted the progressive quality neither of 'feminism' nor of 'nationalism'. When I use the word feminism in the remainder of this book, I mean by it an anti-essentialist, democratic feminism, inclusive of women differently situated in ethnic, class and other structures. When other kinds of women's activism are involved, I make this clear.

Feminism in this sense does tend, I think, to immunize women against regressive constructions of ethnic and national identity. If you pick a non-primordial gender card you are less likely to reach for a primordial nation card. A gender critique strips the myths away from notions like 'community', 'country' and 'people' invoked in nationalist discourse. A feminist is likely to see community and people as seductive words that hide gender and class inequalities within. Because she has seen how the innocent notion of 'home' conceals confinement, divisions, oppression and violence, she is the more likely to be sceptical of 'home-land'. If you see home as a 'golden cage' you may suspect that homeland too has its contradictions. A feminist analysis is not a bad place to stand to get a perspective on violence as a continuum – from domestic violence (in and near the home) to military violence (patrolling the external boundaries against enemies) and state violence (policing against traitors within). It makes women question the pursuit of political movements by violent means.

This is what gives importance to the quiet struggle over 'feminism' and gender ideology that, as we shall see, goes on within the Women's Support Network, Bat Shalom and Medica. What is the significance of our being *women's* projects? the women ask each other. Why is it we don't include men (even working-class men, even non-sexist men, even democratic men)? How do we justify gender separatism if we condemn ethnic separatism? Are we organizing separately as women because women 'are' – peaceful, nurturing? Or precisely to evade this kind of determinate position in relation to men? These questions continually take on new implications as the projects' circumstances change. As we shall see, they are never conclusively answered but they never lose their urgency.

Northern Ireland: Women's activism in a divided city

At first encounter, Belfast has an air of mundane normality. There is something rather pleasing about its small-grained texture, the mauves and rust reds of its terraced housing, the pebble grey of housing estates, seen always against the soft green folds of Black Mountain and Cave Hill that shield it from the north-west winds. There are some memorable features: the gracious precincts round Queen's University, the derricks and gantries of the docks. The city faces eastward over the grey waters of the narrow sea that separates Ireland from Britain, and the waterfront gives the place a breezy lift.

It is not until you get down to walking its pavements that you see the city for what it is: the most militarized and war-torn of Western Europe. Belfast is not shocking in the way that Beirut in 1975 was shocking, great buildings pocked by shell-fire, or sunk into heaps of rubble. It is not like Mostar in 1995, with a single ethnic hate-line seared through its centre, one side smashed, the other standing. What is appalling about Belfast is the neat, municipalized, everyday apartheid drafted on the drawing-board of its streets. Belfast has 51 administrative wards. At the last census, 27 of them had more than 95 per cent Protestants or 95 per cent Catholics. Taking a less stringent measure, a 90 per cent majority of one or other religion, three-quarters of the city is ethnically segregated (McKittrick 1994: 40). Along the borders between the particularly conflict-prone districts the authorities have erected long high fences to keep people apart. They call them 'peace lines'.

British soldiers in Belfast used to carry a colour-coded map of the city pasted to the butts of their rifles. Perhaps they still do. Residents of the city carry the map in their heads. But they are assisted in remembering which zone they are in by colour-coded streets. Loyalists have painted the kerbstones of many of their pavements the red, white and blue of the Union Jack. In Catholic areas lamp-posts are often ringed with the green, white and gold of the Irish tricolour. Adjacent communities mark up the tally of deaths on local walls as though the war were a darts tournament. There are, besides, Belfast's famous, unequivocal murals. Gable-ends in loyalist districts feature balaclava-hooded men bearing Armalites. Republican walls tend to Gaelic resonance and memories of British repression. The murals, and the graffiti ('Fucking Fenians', 'Remember Bobby Sands') shout: this is our patch, keep out! It is important knowledge. Many have died as a result of being in the wrong bit of Belfast.

It is the acceptedness of Belfast segregation, its embeddedness, that is disturbing. Daily life incorporates the divisions in a way that practice has made seem effortless. People step deftly through the intricate mesh of ethnic boundaries without making a big deal of it. A complicated system of black taxis runs two parallel cheap collective transport services, one through Protestant, one through Catholic areas.

Separation induces mutual ignorance, from top to bottom of society. David McKittrick quotes a senior Catholic civil servant who, asked whether his Protestant colleagues lacked insight into local life, answered: 'With some of them their ignorance is total, absolute and complete. You have people determining housing policy who have never been on the Shankill Road or the Falls Road' (ibid.: 42). Down in those very roads the locals too are foreigners to each other. A social worker I met takes women in mixed groups to a café for a snack, now on one side of the war line, now on the other, 'teaching them that the food in the Falls is just as tasty as in the Shankill'. And in a sense they are not even fully acquainted with themselves or their own past. A youth worker said of her Protestant youngsters: 'They see themselves as British. Yet ask them why they're British, they've no idea. Ask them what they like about being British, they've no idea. Ask what they're frightened of, what would happen if we had a united Ireland. They don't know.'

Two areas of Belfast stick in my mind, two tiny ghettos, one Catholic, one Protestant. They are mirror images one of the other, a mile or two apart by one measure, several light-years by another. Bannside is a vulnerable Catholic parish of a couple of hundred houses, encapsulated in a large Protestant area, out along the Shore Road. Pauline Y, a local community activist, showed me around. The neighbourhood has that desperate air of a place lost in the blind eye of whatever municipal powers should be watching over it. The housing is in poor shape. Rubbish accumulates on derelict sites. A report by the local community centre says: 'a foul smell emanates from the nearby sewerage works ... There has been unplanned commercial and motorway development which has resulted in serious deterioration in the quality of life for residents.' And of course Bannside's location leaves it hostage, wide open to sectarian violence. Twenty-five people have been killed here in as many years. Among them were two of Pauline's brothers.

Belfast. Urban life fenced and mutilated by military and
paramilitary control.

Hawthorne has a chirpier look to it, a neat little Protestant enclave of terraced houses and squares, built not so long ago. There's a sliver of grass, a few bushes, and a garden seat. There are Protestant neighbourhoods far more decrepit than this one, but it is a ghetto for all that. The children have to run the gauntlet of surrounding Catholic areas to get to their Protestant school each morning.

Five hundred people live in Hawthorne, surrounded by 'peace lines'. Karen and Kim, 13 years old, told me: 'We know them all.' Hawthorne inspires their love and loyalty. They want to live here when they grow up. The way they talked about their world, it was like football culture turned murderous. Us and them, our team and theirs, but instead of sport on the pitch it is manhunts over the peace lines. And the score is in dead and wounded. The 'wee boys' Karen and Kim like to hang around with will soon be in street-gangs, being groomed for membership of the UVF or the Red Hand Commando. A boarded-up house: what was the story? I asked the girls. An isolated Catholic family used to live here. They were put out one night. 'What did you feel about that?' 'It was right.' 'Why?' A pause for thought. 'The wee girls were cheeky.'

The degree of ethnic segregation in Belfast has, by certain counts, more than doubled in the last two decades. Older women I spoke with, able to recall the days before the Troubles recommenced, had childhood memories of greater mixity. Patricia X, a Catholic, said: 'When I was growing up there was none of this "hate the Catholics", no way. Yes, on the Eleventh of July they burned the Pope. We could smell the bonfires. But we were never brought up to *hate* Protestants.' Many described relocations their families had made since. Some of these, especially in the stories of Catholics, involved violence: threats, broken windows, arson. Some were simply the result of hard decisions. It is a dilemma. If you live in the 'right' area you may see your children grow up to join the paramilitaries; if you live in the 'wrong' area you put their lives at risk. It is the sum of thousands of little words of warning, underlined by threatening gestures, thousands of little safety-minded choices, that has made the map of Belfast what it is today.

So, people say, it is harder to feel comfortable in a mixed marriage now. There are fewer pubs where you can drink together. The likelihood of your children meeting 'theirs' in the swimming pool is less. Today you don't go to the nearest baths. You take a bus into town and another out again to reach a pool in a safe area. The closeness of the boundaries is like a band around your brow. You yearn for wider horizons. Fear weighs on you. Little fears: Protestant kids who pelt screaming past the church door, too fast for the Catholic priest to sprinkle holy water on them. 'It's really *his piss*. We all know that.' And the big fear: Pauline

Y, who has seen death at close quarters and whose judgement I would trust, says, 'Sometimes I have visions of us being slaughtered all around these streets.'

Different cultures, different classes

If it is important to know the ethnic colour of the ground beneath your feet, it is equally important to know to whom you are speaking. People straight away want to put a tag on you. Up here, said Tina McCrossan, who comes from the South, first, 'They have to decide whether you're Catholic or Protestant. And *then* they can relate to you, after that.' It isn't done directly. They listen for your name, where you went to school, how you pronounce the letter that comes after 'G' in the alphabet (Catholic schools teach children to pronounce it 'haitch', Protestant schools 'aitch').

Can't you tell by looking? Protestants think they know a Catholic. What are the markers – dark hair, perhaps? Can you be sure? 'Oh, *I* can! It's their eyes, it's like they're looking straight through you' (O Connor 1993: 324). And some Catholics think they can tell a Protestant by fair hair or blue eyes: 'She's a Hun!' Or by that nose in the air. 'They think they're sort of, what would you say, a cut above you. Sort of "Look what we've done for you, we've given you them jobs, built you that estate. Isn't that awful good of us." As if like, they're higher up than we are.' (This was the way Patricia X put it, in interview.)

It is true enough that there are two contrasted cultures in Northern Ireland. They call them 'the two traditions'. Irish Catholics' culture is ornamental, articulate, with a strong Celtic/Gaelic trope. They are a people who readily give voice to their oppression in song, poetry and dance. They dwell on history, they romance it. From the French Revolution to Montgomery Alabama, they feel, surely the tide is running our way.

The culture of Ulster Protestants resists the flow. It is defensive and insecure. Confidence was badly shaken by the abolition of Stormont. Their political project is riven by ambivalence: loyalty in the bosom of the Union with Britain? or go it alone, and to hell with those who would sell us out? To be British, or to be Irish our way? Protestants celebrate climactic moments of their history too, but are often ignorant of the political facts of where they came from and why they are there. Aspects of Protestant culture, epitomized in the triumphalism of the Orange Order, are unpleasant. But as Geoffrey Bell points out, the different mentalities of the Catholic and Protestant militants are 'not due to the fact that Catholics were somehow "nicer" people, but because the different politics of the two communities produced different practices; one community was fighting to maintain a system of privilege, the other was fighting to overthrow it' (Bell 1978: 128).

The separation of the two cultures is increased by distinct religious traditions. (Not always by *belief*. Sometimes it is a matter of experiencing a similar religious oppression in a different ethnic context.) They differ in their sports, their music, their political parties – each side to his and her own. They are held in a place apart by each other, for the identities are mutually defining: Protestant is what is not-Catholic, Catholic is not-Protestant. The gulf has its uses to the Northern Ireland Establishment, whose control is guaranteed by Protestant and Catholic disunity. And the British of course, from way back exploited Protestant fears as a tool against the national independence movement.

It is always difficult to be sure, of course, how much such differentiating cultures come 'from below' and how much they are embellished and promoted institutionally 'from above'. Certainly individuals slide messily between them, and some of those I talked to were uneasy with any stress on cultural difference. They pointed to a presence of trade unionism and other manifestations of a political left in Northern Ireland, stronger in some periods than today, as unifying factors.

Class too is a complicating factor. The reforms prompted by the civil rights movement have benefited some in the Catholic community, who have risen socially, moved out to desirable suburbs. In doing so, like the Black middle class in the USA, they have become more conservative. Many young middle-class Protestants choose to go to university in England or Scotland, and often do not return. Meanwhile the Protestant labour aristocracy, the male manufacturing workers and the white-collar employees, have suffered steady reversal, first in the Depression of the 1920s and 1930s, more recently through recession and Conservative economics. 'The overall picture is of a confident Catholic group, young and growing very rapidly, faced with nervous and retreating Protestants: a middle class in the making watching another in flight' (O Connor 1993: 190).

The bottom strata of both communities feel abandoned by a world their televisions show to be undergoing a series of technological and social revolutions without them. And it is down here that the war has its most brutal expression. As a taxi-driver told me, 'The middle class stirs it. The working class do the fighting.'

Shared disadvantage

There are, however, three things the two working-class communities share: *poverty*, *violence* and *political neglect*. And women of those communities experience all three in a distinctive, gendered, way.

The Catholics of Northern Ireland are accustomed to *poverty*. The recession of the 1930s was deeper and lasted longer in Northern Ireland than elsewhere in the UK. The post-war boom was shorter-lived. And by 1970 consumption per inhabitant was only three-quarters the UK average (Rowthorne and Wayne 1988). In the period from Partition to the resumption of direct rule from Britain, Ulster Protestants used their predominance as capitalists, property-owners and administrators in the public sector to assure that what opportunities there were went to Protestants. Even in the early 1990s, on all major social and economic indicators, including income, employment, qualifications, housing and health, Catholics were worse off than Protestants (McKittrick 1994: 21).

It was mainly Catholics who told me of real hardship in their childhood, 'born in the wee houses, the dump houses, not much furniture, not much food' (Pauline Y). And it was Catholics who today talked about trying (like the 217 families of Bannside) to keep warm with one coal fire, going short of food at the end of the week, never having enough money to enjoy shopping in downtown Belfast. Unemployment in some Catholic areas of North and West Belfast runs at 80 or 90 per cent. 'Honest to God', said Janis Quinn, a community worker in Ardoyne, 'I don't know many people that *are* working.'

Pride often keeps Protestants from admitting similar poverty. But some Protestant areas are in little better shape than Catholic areas of Belfast. The manufacturing industry and public sector jobs from which their men were accustomed to draw their steady pay-packets have both been drastically eroded by economic recession and by Conservative policies. Take the Lower Shankill. It was built for the labour force of engineer works and shipyards. Today in appearance and socio-economic standing it is scarcely distinguishable from the neighbouring Catholic Falls Road. The people with jobs have moved out to the suburbs. With such dim prospects of employment there is little enthusiasm for education or training. These people know what 'pockets of deprivation' means. Ballybeen, a Protestant estate in East Belfast, has newer housing stock and a few lucky men have jobs in manufacturing. But the community has a clear sense now of being only a little above the bottom of the heap, alarming to an ethnic group trying to sustain an edge over an insurgent minority.

Women, as everywhere, do the most unpaid domestic work, take most responsibility for managing family poverty and have the worst choice of jobs. Claire Keatinge, who runs Belfast Women's Training Services, says the characteristic jobs for working-class women (Catholic and Protestant alike) are low-paid, part-time and 'unskilled'. Usually it is casual work, local to their homes. 'It would be shop work, hospital work, school dinners, all those things. You go and work for somebody in the home, a bit of cleaning, collect the kids from school.' She explained: 'Women with those kinds of jobs, for it to be worthwhile, must have a partner who's working. Or you must "do the double".' Doing the double means claiming state benefits (which are very mean) while supplementing them with undeclared work on the side. Unscrupulous employers hold wages at a low level, which in turn drives many people into illegality.

Violence is a second reality of life shared by Protestant and Catholic working-class communities. First there is state violence. From 1969 West and North Belfast became militarized zones, studded with barracks and watchtowers, boxed up in peace lines and roadblocks, encrusted with barbed wire. People got used to encountering arms-bearing soldiers everywhere, in the park, in the hospital ward, in the front garden. (And on your roof: the British army installed a helicopter pad on top of the Divis flats.) Nor were the weapons mere show. Six children, to say nothing of adults, were killed by the state's rubber bullets between 1971 and 1981 (Edgerton 1986). The Catholic communities have borne the brunt of military and police action but when Protestants have been in conflict with the state, as in the Ulster Workers' Council strike and resistance to the Anglo-Irish Agreement, they have felt it too.

Second, both sides experience sectarian violence. Many of the women I met in Belfast had witnessed violent events, seen blood, stumbled across dismembered bodies. In some districts there is scarcely a street corner that is not scarred by a bad memory. The experiences begin in childhood. Úna ní Mhearáin, now a community worker in the Falls Road, remembers being strung up from a tree at primary school because she refused to join in the chorus of 'Kick the Pope'.

Wives and daughters of (mainly Protestant) policemen live in constant fear at home. Finally, both communities suffer from the attentions of their own paramilitaries. These take two forms. One is intimidation. For example, a Protestant community centre innocently started exploring Irish culture in language and dancing classes. The UVF came in the night and stencilled threatening insignia on the wall. The other is punishment beatings, a self-policing within the communities to inspire discipline and conformity. The IRA uses picturesque forms of torture:

shaving women's heads, tarring and feathering. On both sides there is 'knee-capping'. A surgeon in a Belfast hospital described its methodology this way.

> The so-called knee-capping is a very barbaric form of punishment, with a sort of severity scale to it. The most common is being shot in both knees, then there's being shot in both knees and both ankles. And then most severe is both knees, both ankles and both elbows. We haven't had very many of these, probably no more than two or three (quoted in McKittrick 1994: 145).

In Northern Ireland justice, fair laws and trusted order are in failure, and many men carry arms, on active service for one illegal force or another. 'Armed patriarchy', Lynda Edgerton calls it (1986: 76). In such situations personal violence erupts easily. So even more than elsewhere, women are dealing with battering men. At a meeting I attended of a women's mutual help project two of the five women came in that morning with bruised faces, and women in interview too told me of violent marriages they had been compelled to escape or withstand.

Living in violence as in a magnetic field, people make working adaptations. A woman will make sure her sister is in the house when 'he' is likely to come home drunk. People install steel gates, bars and shutters in homes where the risk of paramilitary attacks is high. And people trying to organize political or trade union life become sensitized to indicators of trouble. 'You adjust your schedule,' said Patricia McKeown, an officer in the trade union UNISON. You put off the meeting till tomorrow, choose a different venue.

People become so used to ducking and diving that only when the ceasefires came in 1994 did they realize what a distorting effect violence had been having on their lives. After initial disbelief, the relief was universal. Pauline said, 'I just felt: *thank God* there's going to be nobody else killed, murdered or maimed in Northern Ireland. People who've never felt that fear, and that feeling when you lose someone, can't understand to the same degree as a person that it's happened to. What we went through – I wouldn't want that to come to anybody's door.'

All at once there were fewer security checks. The soldiers shed some of their hardware. People began to put a cautious toe over the geo-political lines criss-crossing the city, to visit a relative or friend. People in mixed marriages, living in the 'wrong' area, breathed a little easier. Women active in the community felt they could now get away with a little more self-assertion. While the war was on, the community's men could argue for conformity in the name of loyalty. Anne McVicker, a community worker in the Shankill, says: 'Before, I just had to do the job, keep my head down, rock the boat as little as possible ... It's not to say that men were out in the street saying "don't you women do this, don't do that". But the ceasefires have created – it's almost like you can take a breath.' The cessation of violence was beginning to shift just a little the perception among politically minded men of what and was not 'politically correct'.

Of course, people didn't trust the ceasefires altogether. 'Something in the back of my head', remembered Pauline, 'said "Wait!"' Nevertheless, when the London Docklands bomb was exploded, and even more when it became clear that the IRA really was renewing its campaign, not merely nudging the British government into honouring its commitment to a peace process, it was a devastating disappointment.

The third common experience of the two working-class communities is *political exclusion*. People often speak of the 'democratic deficit' in Northern Ireland. Direct rule created an anomaly, a region neither really inside Britain nor fully detached. Political direction comes from a senior minister of the British government, but the administration is effectively in the hands of the Northern Ireland Office, a branch of the civil service, and *ad hoc* boards and trusts. London is distant, and local government in Northern Ireland has reduced powers.

'The place', says Patricia McKeown, 'is run by unaccountable, un-elected people, who do nothing at all to make the decision-processes, the ordinary ones that govern our lives like about health and education and housing, open and transparent.' Instead, policy tends to emerge from many informal networks, 'cosy relationships' between civil servants, local politicians, church leaders and non-governmental organizations. (NGOs are influential in Northern Ireland and are sometimes criticized for being overly self-important.) There is evident scope for patronage and the abuse of discretion.

The major political parties in Northern Ireland are organized on sectarian lines. They seek votes not on the basis of social or economic policy, but purely on their stand on the constitutional future of the region. 'All politicians in this area', said Susan Brown, who lives in Ballybeen, in the DUP-controlled Castlereagh District, 'always have and always will fight elections on the Orange and Green thing, you know, and ordinary social issues don't come into it at all.' It is not the habit of local politicians to hold surgeries for their constituents: 'They have no interest in responding to our needs.'

The great majority of local councils are controlled by the Ulster Unionist Party or the Democratic Unionist Party, whose only interest is in keeping the nationalist parties out of power, by fair means or foul. For some years the nationalist parties, Sinn Féin and the Social Democratic and Labour Party, undertook a boycott of electoral politics, with

NORTHERN IRELAND / 59

the effect of diminishing yet further the democratic quality of Northern Ireland's structures. When Sinn Féin did begin to enter local councils the majority Unionist councillors manipulated procedural rules to limit their effectiveness. Sinn Féin brought successful legal cases against them on more than one occasion.

Unsurprisingly, dissatisfaction with local government is widespread. Pauline says: 'I don't think ordinary people get a chance to think and express how they feel about what's happened in the past 25 years, the fact that there's an awful lot of hurt and an awful lot of heartache ... What I would hope for is that those people can go to their parties and say, "Listen, we don't want it any more. We've had it up to here. We want you to speak *for* us and say what we want. Not to sit there and put your own agendas first."' Catholics like Pauline suffer most from this failure of local democracy, because Unionist councils have behaved with extreme partiality in funding policy, disfavouring Catholic areas and Catholic projects. Nevertheless, Susan is not the only Protestant constituent to have become more and more aware of being ill-served.

If the working class is deprived of democracy, women are doubly excluded. At the time of my research in 1996, all Northern Ireland's members of the British and European parliaments were men. Men held 88 per cent of local council seats. Indeed, men rule all institutions of power – church, state and quango. The old Unionist parties have no apparent interest in either women's votes or women's political energy. Women are there to make the sandwiches. The nationalists are little better. Sinn Féin has more women activists than other parties, but on women's issues it needs continual prompting. The social issues women are normally deemed competent to deal with have no relevance for the parties. And in the political context of Northern Ireland, conflictual as it is, women are held to lack the toughness needed to fight and win (Roulston 1996).

Women often discuss the pros and cons of joining the parties, standing for a council seat. Some, like Susan, find the politicians 'so *childish*! Honestly, I wouldn't waste my time!' On the other hand, there are signs of flux and change that may be opening up spaces for new voices to be heard.

Grassroots activism

The Women's Support Network is an expression of working-class women's projects in Belfast. These projects are the outcome of two relatively new processes in the political life of Northern Ireland. Community development on the one hand and the women's movement on the other have signified politics with a small 'p' mobilizing and challenging big-P Politics as it is normally done.

The outbreak of violence in 1969 prompted a Community Relations Act, under which a Community Relations Commission and Department were set up and community development officers appointed. It was accompanied by a Social Needs Act, making available money for local community centres in designated areas. Inevitably the community groups fanned to life by these measures quickly came into conflict with the state. Official commitment to community relations (CR) thereafter fluctuated. In the mid-1970s community work was made the responsibility of the District Councils, a small compensation for the other powers withdrawn from them. These authorities had little interest in nurturing grassroots discontent, and played their role without enthusiasm. But it was too late to put the genie back in the bottle. Community centres and projects were here to stay, and during the 1980s they made full use of resources available through a community job-creation scheme and special programmes targeting social need in Belfast.

In 1991 a community relations structure was re-established, and in 1993 the British government affirmed its commitment to community development in a new official strategy. Nationalist areas were quickest to see the mileage in small-p activism, so that community work experience accumulated first in Catholic hands. But it was not long before Protestant communities began to demand funding too, complaining to their district councils that community relations expenditure was being used to 'reward' Catholic areas for rioting. To Protestants, as a study of Protestant community development points out, 'to go against the state on social issues meant siding with the people who wanted to bring it down' (McCready 1993: 16). So while Catholic communities readily leapt into campaigns against the authorities, Protestants were at first disinclined to rock the boat. But it was not long before Protestant activism too took a step beyond bingo and pensioners' outings.

More or less simultaneous with this community development movement came the second-wave women's liberation movement. Women had been active in the civil rights marches of the middle 1960s, and in the early 1970s women began to get together in groups and campaigns. Feminism has been a powerful influence for change in Northern Ireland, as it has been around the world. But the differences that bedevilled the movement everywhere, generating tensions between socialist and radical feminists, between lesbians and heterosexual women, between women's rights activists and those who wanted a more far-reaching transformation in gender relations, were all evident within the small community of Belfast. And here of course the national political conflict compounded the rest. 'The attempt to build a broad-based women's movement has repeatedly foundered', says Finnuola O Connor, 'on the clash of political identities' (O Connor 1993: 355; see also Evason 1991 and Roulston 1997).

At the risk of over-simplifying, one could say that there was one women's movement that would have been recognizable to the contemporary movement in Britain at this time, a movement of mainly educated, mainly middle-class women concerned centrally with women's issues, in which women (of varied ethnic background) were mainly present as individuals. Beginning among university women, it had overlapping membership with the Northern Ireland Women's Rights Movement and the Communist Party of Ireland. A divergent left-wing tendency, the Socialist Women's Group, opposed its reformism, while sharing its opposition to the IRA's military campaign. Some of these women went on in the 1980s to form the Belfast Women's Collective (Roulston 1997).

There was another movement, of mainly Irish Catholic nationalist and republican women, committed to the struggle against British imperialism, many of them pursuing a second front against male dominance in the nationalist/republican political arena. Many became active in Women Against Imperialism, in the Relatives Action Committee and in other campaigns in support of women prisoners during the prison protests and hunger strikes of 1981–82. These activists were closer to the women of local working-class communities (Roulston 1997).

But there was a widespread feeling in the 1980s that new-wave feminism, especially its 'leadership', was largely failing working-class women. It was never so easy for women whose men were involved in armed conflict, whose young were in prison and who had few sources of support other than 'the family', to stand clear and condemn male power in political parties, paramilitary formations and marriage. In the 1980s working-class women began to organize on their own account, and the form their movement took was distinctive, focused around local women's centres in both Protestant and Catholic areas. It answered their own needs and took account of their own constraints. Úna says, looking back, 'I think the emergence of the community-based women's centres really challenged that leadership, it challenged that mode of thinking.'

Belfast women had always been the backbone of their communities, and naturally they became the mainstay of community development as it developed in the 1970s. Community development was about tackling inequality, and it was about countering the social work ethic of 'helping victims' with an alternative ideology of empowering the disadvantaged. As such it opened a door for women. Doing *women's* community development enabled them to look to their own interests as women while also furthering the interests of their impoverished working-class families and communities. Susan says of the dozens of women's projects and women's centres that have come into existence in Belfast since 1980 that it has been 'women like us, who didn't give a damn about politics, who were, every one of us, concerned about the price of bread, the price of coal, the price of electricity'.

The women's centres

One of the first Belfast women's centres was the Downtown Centre, established in 1985 by 'women's rights' feminists, without any particular community or political allegiance. It set about campaigning and lobbying, serving individual women from all over the city. Other centres, given the segregated nature of Belfast, tended to have either Catholic or Protestant users, but not both.

The centres in Catholic areas had widely different origins. The Footprints Centre in Poleglass, for instance, was prompted by the local Catholic priest. By contrast, the church was positively unsupportive of the Falls Road Women's Centre. Founded by republican women active in Women Against Imperialism, it arose out of an action by women organizing against army harassment. The centre in the strongly nationalist Ardoyne area, where the workers described themselves to me as 'a cluster of very militant women', was begun by a group of ex-prisoners and prisoners' wives. From the start it made no attempt to hide that it was a resource for battered women.

The Protestant centres differed too. The Ballybeen Women's Centre was formed earlier than the others, in 1983. It was inspired by a local neighbourhood community worker, alert to the desperate dearth of communal facilities on this vast estate. She went to the local council to seek premises. The Shankill Women's Centre was sparked to life by a survey of local need carried out by women of a tenants' association. The 'Women Too' centre in Windsor began with a series of public meetings from which concern emerged about the poor health profile of the area. A key actor here was a student from outside the community. Together, the women squatted a local house as a base for activities. Cregagh women got together and took over a snooker club, the domain of local paramilitary men. They recall how they spent weeks on hands and knees scrubbing away the smell of beer and cigarette ash before the place blossomed as the Greenway Women's Centre.

Once under way, however, the centres tended to develop along similar lines. The logic of local need everywhere dictated a certain range of activities. There had to be a management committee, a meeting space, a crèche for the children of workers and users. The centres soon began women's self-development courses, building confidence, improving ability in reading, writing and maths, doing what the schools had failed to do. Information was made available about health, welfare rights, local institutions. Training was begun in carpentry, computing and other job skills. The centres also set up youthwork, childcare and community work training courses so that the jobs created in the centres would be within the grasp of local women. A lot of the staff today are former users.

The women's centres are mid-scale organizations, not so far-reaching as the NGOs of Belfast-wide or Northern Ireland scope, but an important part of their localities' community development effort, capable of stimulating and providing space for many smaller single-purpose groups: young mothers, teenage girls, cooking and keep-fit enthusiasts, women pensioners. They usually exist alongside, but independent of, a mixed-sex community association.

The women's centres face three problems. They have to establish democratic structures and processes capable of reconciling internal differences. For example, in Catholic and Protestant areas alike, women users will differ in their attitude to contraception and abortion. How do you decide on a position on these divisive issues? Second, they have to steer a skilful course to maintain on the one hand a relationship responsive and responsible to the wider community and on the other their autonomy as women's projects. Powerful external forces are always seeking to control them: central and local government, churches, quangos, parties. And the paramilitaries of both sides, whose organizations are very active at community level, exercise a pervasive and at times threatening surveillance.

The third big problem for the centres is funding. They vary in the scale of their budgets. The Ardoyne Women's Centre, for example, sees political merit in independence, surviving on a shoestring without paid workers. The struggle for funding of 'Women Too' in Windsor has paid off in a £300,000 purpose-built centre, five or six staff and more temporary 'job scheme' workers. All these women have become adept at making grant applications and have won support for different purposes from a wide range of bodies: various government departments, regional boards and trusts, local councils, the European Structural Funds, charities, the Lottery, the Northern Ireland Voluntary Trust. 'Every time a new source of funding comes on stream people are staggered by the over-demand,' says Judy Seymour, of the Women's Resource and Development Agency. 'Everybody has twenty new project proposals up their sleeve.' But project money for temporary staff is one thing, core

Women's community centres are an important resource in Belfast.

The women's centres provide crèches, classes, advice and meeting space. They mainly serve neighbourhoods that are demographically Protestant or Catholic. But there are (it's sometimes forgotten) other ethnic groups in Belfast.

funding for permanency is another. The centres have never been able to be sure they will exist tomorrow, and in late 1996 several were in danger of closing.

Crossing communal boundaries

Once the centres were well established and local women routinely dropping by, some of them began, without exactly trumpeting it about, to bring women of the segregated communities into contact. They were not the first to have done this. While politicians had been shying away from the political risk of being seen talking to each other, numbers of quite ordinary and much braver people had been taking the physical risk of doing this.

For instance, action committees of relatives of IRA and loyalist prisoners had got together to campaign for prisoners' rights and against the daily humiliations of prison visiting. The trade unions too had been operating cross-communally. The National Union of Public Employees (NUPE, now UNISON) had workplace branches, such as that in the huge Royal Victoria Hospital, that spanned across communities. Many of its shop stewards' committees and branch committees were of mixed Catholic/Protestant composition. It was also the union's practice to appoint branch 'community officers' to develop contact between the union and local community groups, which together would mobilize against hospital closures and other public sector cuts. Often they would organize demonstrations whose routes took them across community boundaries, relying on their credibility as a union to give them immunity from attack.

The most sustained cross-communal activity by women has been the Women's Information Group (WIG), which has organized monthly meetings without interruption since 1980. The information days began with twelve women; meetings in 1996 were fetching 150. The WIG bus would go the rounds, picking up women and taking them to a venue (now in one commmunity, now in the other) where there would be a crèche, a speaker and a social lunch. WIG has been wary in its choice of discussion topics, avoiding religion and big-P politics and focusing on shared issues of everyday life: health problems, rent rises, juvenile delinquency.

The establishment of a Central Community Relations Unit in the Northern Ireland Office in 1987 and a Community Relations Council in 1990 marked a revived official commitment to funding activity to reduce sectarian animosity. There had long been projects, mostly ecumenical religious and pacifist projects, organizing 'reconciliation' work. Now community organizations could request money to pay for cross-communal work. But sceptical community workers and activists saw 'official CR' as cosmetic, in the spirit of 'Let's get 25 Catholics and 25 Protestants and bring them to the Icebowl and they'll have a lovely time skating around.' It seemed to them depoliticizing, a refusal on the part of the government to take on the structural reasons for the war in Northern Ireland, and instead, as Úna, coordinator of the Falls Women's Centre, put it, 'to put the problem back on the doorstep of the victims: if only you could be *nicer*!'

Worse, this kind of CR is manipulative. Roslyn Y told me the following story. A certain Irish cultural association in Dublin, doing their bit for CR, invited Shankill women to send down a group for a cultural visit. When the hosts found out that one of the Shankill women would be a Catholic, they wanted to veto her inclusion. 'The whole point was to have a group of Protestants,' they complained. The visitors were also to be featured performing the unionist song *The Sash*, in Gaelic, in the fishmarket. 'We felt we'd be like goldfish in a bowl,' said Roslyn. Shankill Women's Centre turned down the invitation. A study of Belfast women's organization at this time said, 'Some women in local groups see CR as the soft end of the Anglo-Irish agenda; other see it as the British agenda' (Rooney and Woods 1995: 7). Certainly nobody recognized it as theirs.

The women's centres had reason to look twice before jumping on a CR bandwaggon being rolled out by the government and 'the Great and the Good' of the province. First, incautious cross-communal activity could endanger people's lives. Even though women are less at risk than men, the number of women victims of sectarian attack and punishment meetings had increased over the years. Second, that approach was unlikely to produce enduring effects. One thing the community development principle had instilled in community workers was a step-at-a-time approach. And the first step had to be educative work within the centres to break down misconceptions and myths about 'the others'. The second step should be working on acceptance of the many *other* differences, internal to the communities, thereby creating a mindset ready to approach external differences. Third should be building up women's own confidence as individuals and their group confidence and effectiveness as women. As Anne McVicker said of women of the Shankill Women's Centre: 'They're starting to make their mark in the Shankill ... and their paths and their routes are going to lead outside the Shankill.'

It was generally understood that Protestant women in particular needed time and resources invested in 'single identity work'. Research was suggesting that the Protestants of Northern Ireland were alienated,

Transversal politics: young women from Protestant and Catholic areas of Belfast meet for the first time in a cross-community network.

experiencing a crisis of identity (Dunn and Morgan 1994). They felt themselves a 'misunderstood and much maligned entity'. They needed to 'get to know and "like" themselves as a people' before they would gain the confidence to make creative cross-communal links (McCready 1993: 85). Catholic women were confident that when Protestant women had been organizing for a while in local centres they would readily find common cause with themselves, and see how they were being hood-winked into believing they were well looked after by their politicians.

Cross-communal working by the centres has had its ups and downs. There is genuine fear – 'If she's from Crumlin Road/Turf Lodge she might know some UVF/IRA men who maybe want to try and kill me.' Contact has dwindled in the aftermath of violent incidents, when you might feel: 'I'm sorry, I just can't bring myself to go there at the moment.' But it has always been sustained in the long run by women's irrepressible wish to reach out, to recover some of the mixity the older ones among them had once enjoyed and the younger ones wished they had. And the ceasefires of course helped for a time.

A good example of this kind of activity is a particular young women's network. Tina McCrossan works with young women at the Shankill Women's Centre. She took me along with a handful of her youngsters to the first night of this network, an initiative of women community workers from North and West Belfast. There were around ninety young women, average age fourteen or fifteen. You couldn't hear for the chatter, and you could hardly see across the room for cigarette smoke. A very cautious approach was being taken by the adult women to encouraging interaction: no artificial requirement to mix, no enforced talking about 'our prejudices', no lectures about sectarian language. (Indeed a scribble-board on the wall seemed to invite uninhibited com-ment, and by the end of the evening it carried one or two collective insults.) Positively, as social cement for the occasion, the community workers had invited women of a *third* 'community', Chinese living in Belfast, to come and teach the young women how to fry prawn crackers and make festive paper cut-outs. The evening was generally held to have been a success. There had been no fights, the youngsters had learned that the other side didn't have two heads, and they seemed to want a repeat. Tina's Protestant young women were now asking 'When can we meet some of the wee boys?'

That evening of course illustrates 'the price you pay for getting people into the room' (Patricia McKeown): certain areas of silence. It was a theme that women I spoke with returned to again and again. Tact, knowing when to keep your mouth shut, is a valued sign that 'people have learned to hold a complex identity' (Joanna McMinn).

The strength of working-class women's self-organized cross-communal work has been that their everyday lives and needs have provided a solid common interest. 'We talked about our kids, employment, education, health, all these things. And we recognized that each of us was getting up in the morning to the same problems' (Mary X).

It had often been links between the women organizing the centres that had led, in time, to links between their various groups of users. As each new centre was set up, it had looked to the ones already up and running for help – deciding on management structures, putting in grant applications, handling wages. 'I'd have been lost without help from Anne at the Shankill,' said Joy Poots, one of the coordinators of the Windsor Women's Centre, thinking back to the early days. Between older and newer centres there was 'almost a kind of mothering' going on.

Another factor that made cross-communal activity between the centres both more likely and more possible was that (in a way that still astonishes me and that I have found no way of explaining), several centres had appointed as coordinators women from the 'other' com-munity. We shall see in Chapter 3 more of these individual cross-working women and the significance of the choices they and their women's centres made. Certainly, they were risky choices. No publicity, either inside or outside the centres in question, was given to the anomaly. There were times at the height of the Troubles when approaches had to be made to paramilitary commands to seek guarantees that these anomalous community workers would not be targeted for assassination. There were always contingency plans 'to get you out the back door'. But even through the years of greatest carnage these appointments survived well.

Changes in women's lives

The women's centres, supported by other Belfast women's projects such as the Belfast Women's Training Services, the Women's Resource and Development Agency and the *Women into Politics* project (of which more in Chapter 3), have brought solid gains to women working in them and using them. Joy Poots of Windsor says: 'What I hope our centre does is give women some sort of space or forum to reflect on what they want to hold on to and what they want to challenge or change in society and in their own community.'

There are effects for the individual too. Kate X remembers when Footprints opened. 'We were excited about having somewhere in the parish where you could go and do things, not be stuck at home. We were nervous, anxious too. What a big change it would make to me coming here.' A lot of the women I met said getting involved with the centre had profoundly altered their lives. Some had broken out of repressive family roles. Mary said: 'When we first opened up I was just a housewife. You kept saying, right, "I'm just a housewife", and "coming out to help in the wee community centre". I've *grown*!' And she felt she'd broken out of class confines too. 'Years ago I would have, you know, seen a difference between me and someone from the Malone Road, and maybe been afraid to talk to them because of being ashamed of what I am. But not now. I've totally turned around, and changed. I'm just as equal as anyone on the Malone Road now.' Some women had, in learning assertiveness, been able to renounce violence. Where they'd once only been able to defend themselves from a violent partner by hitting back, now they could find words to stop him in his tracks.

The loss of 'real' employment for women, the companionable jobs of factory and shop, have meant a whole generation of young women growing up with a very narrow range of friendships. The activities of the centre had made them social people. Getting involved had given them a better idea of themselves and made them braver. I had to believe this when I went to join some of the Footprints women on a day's 'team-building' exercise in the woods. There, with skilled help and a lot of encouragement from each other, these not so young, not a bit athletic, previously house-bound mothers of many children were in turns walking (albeit secured in a safety harness) along a narrow plank spanning between two trees, 30 feet above the ground. I felt dizzy just watching. Their pleasure in the achievement and the bonding was memorable.

But women often take a while before they walk through the door of their local centre, and many (the great majority of women in any community) never do so. Some are afraid it is only 'women with problems' who go to those places. It is easiest for older women. 'Women's centres seem very feminist, almost radical, when you're young,' says Joy. 'You've got to keep in with your boy at that age.' It's a fact that a lot of men don't like their women going there. They label the activists 'lesbians' and 'women's libbers', ascribing nothing but bad to those terms. As everywhere, the women are asked to justify doing something that excludes men. Some men just like keeping their women indoors: 'I'd like to come, but he says I'm going out too many nights a week.'

Conventional gender relations in working-class Belfast are heavily subordinating of women. The Catholic Church exploits the political situation to retain a firm grip, instilling fear of sexuality, inhibiting women from questioning tradition. The Protestant churches and the Orange Order and similar loyalist institutions are oppressively patriarchal. Shirley Black described the typical marriage in Ballybeen. 'There would be a very conservative attitude so that the women would be put down, basically second-class citizens. The view would be that the man would be head of the household and any decisions regarding money would be the domain of the man, and on politics however he decided to vote the woman would follow suit.' The crunch comes when children are born. 'When I worked I never got treated badly. But once I had children I was undermined as a person,' said Donna Davis of Greenway Women's Centre. 'There's not many women got off their knees here, if you know what I mean,' said Janis Quinn, speaking of Ardoyne. 'Not many *strong* women.'

The political violence of Northern Ireland gets transmitted directly into the family. Mary said of local men, using a curious metaphor: 'They can go out and *feed* on the violence, and they can come home, and they can batter their wives.' It is often assumed that women in working-class families are close, that they support each other. That is true in some regards. But women I spoke with gave clear evidence that shame, fear and religious inhibition keep women from confiding in each other on matters like violent men, like sex and sexuality, pregnancy and abortion. Here in the women's centres those matters quickly come into the open and women find they are not any longer alone, drowning in silence.

These women are now much tougher than they used to be on their partners and sons. There are more men around today who go hungry if they will not knuckle down and cook a meal. But it is an uphill task. 'I think men are programmed,' Mary says. 'There's no movement with them. They're static ... Men aren't prepared to change like women.' And they will not let their communities shift either. 'They're the ones who want to keep it a Protestant community, a Loyalist community,' said Joy (she could just as well have said a Catholic community, a nationalist community), 'and who has the control and the power and the authority? It's the paramilitaries, and they're men.' Ailbhe Smyth, the Irish poet, said it in a way many of these women would recognize:

The ex-colonised oppressors colonise. (Habit of centuries.) They don't listen. Theirs is the Republic, the Power and the Discourse (Smyth 1995).

3
Women's Support Network, Belfast

It is out of this environment that the Women's Support Network developed. In the early days of the women's centres the local councils of Greater Belfast had supported them with small seeding grants. But as the centres gained the confidence to challenge council policies, the councillors became suspicious and hostile. These were women with attitude. The British government had meanwhile laid down a policy that any community group in Northern Ireland that had links with paramilitary organizations should be barred from state funding. The grants received by Downtown, Shankill and Falls Women's Centres from Belfast City Council became due for renewal in 1990. The women decided to lobby the council together for continued support.

The council meeting approved grants to two of the three, refusing the application of the Falls Road centre on the grounds that its management committee, workers and users were well-known republicans. All the women were angered by the frank unfairness of this political vetting, and by the apparently casual way the council was willing to risk the safety of the Falls women by such finger-pointing. They challenged the decision and went public in their condemnation of the council's sectarianism. In a cross-communal move that astonished the media, the Shankill Women's Centre hosted a press conference in the Falls Women's Centre.

It was journalists asking 'Where will you take it from here?' that prompted the creation of the Women's Support Network. The Network's first action was to form cross-communal sub-groups to meet the Belfast councillors of each political party, one by one, calling them to account for their decision. The women did not rebut the council's claim that the Falls women were republicans. They simply said: 'So what if they are? They have a feminist outlook, they have a commitment to women. When did you become judge and jury over people's political affiliations?'

The Women's Support Network concluded that the political parties (with the exception of Sinn Féin, the only one that had spoken up for the Falls women) were patronizing about women's activity and lacked any vision on women's needs. They were in fact shockingly ignorant about women. Maybe some facts would help. The Network now raised a substantial sum from the Equal Opportunities Commission to carry out a thorough survey of women's grassroots organization throughout Northern Ireland. The report of the research, which identified 200 women's groups, rural and urban, fuelled the Network's campaign for an adequate policy response by state and voluntary sector to the needs of women in the community (Women's Support Network 1992).

The women next came up with the idea (its *chutzpah* startled even them) to invite Mary Robinson, president of the Irish Republic, to visit Belfast as the guest of the Women's Support Network. Marie Mul- holland was working for the Network on a voluntary basis at this time. She remembers, 'All of us were inspired, you know, by this woman. She was just something special.' Mary Robinson was known to be supportive of women and would certainly value their cross-communal structure, but no president or prime minister from the South had visited the North for 30 years. When she accepted the invitation (it was issued jointly with the Northern Ireland European Women's Platform), the Network was plunged into a nightmare of protocol and security that made them feel that 'this was a bigger ballpark than any of us had ever experienced before'.

But the success of the day itself, the president's genuine warmth and the very public endorsement she gave them, made the gamble worth- while. Valuable contacts with the South flowed from the event, too, with Mary Robinson hosting a meeting at her official residence, Aras an Uachtarain, where the Network met with over seventy women's groups from South and North. Patricia McKeown, who has played an active part in the Network, said afterwards that the most impressive thing for her had been that the president had chosen for her first visit not just women 'but working-class women of the most beleaguered areas, women who are given recognition by nobody, who'd spent most of their lives being demonized by the people in power'.

So the Network became better known and it also grew in substance, with funding from the Northern Ireland Voluntary Trust and several private charitable bodies. It clarified its purpose as a linking mechanism between women's groups, a support network for the coordinators of the women's centres and several Belfast-wide projects, and a 'collective feminist voice' of organized working-class women in the city. Its activ- ities included liaison, lobbying, consulting, researching and campaigning. It set out to win the attention of the most powerful sources of influence on women's community development: the Northern Ireland structures, the Irish government and the European Community.

Two developments in particular are worth citing because they throw light on the main interest of this chapter: the nature of the Women's Support Network as an alliance. One of the projects whose coordinator, Joanne Vance, is a member of the Network has more than ordinary significance for its overall ideology and aims. This is the Women Into Politics project. Northern Ireland, as we have seen, is endowed with neither a properly democratic structure nor responsible political parties. Its politicians, almost all male, display the worst in masculine combativeness towards each other and disdain towards women. Policy change would not be a possibility without a new kind of policy *maker*. Women, perhaps? But women active in the community had seen little to attract them in political engagement.

All the same, even at the height of the violence, while sectarian killings seemed to be occurring every week in Belfast, women were talking to each other about next steps. Joanne found that: 'What came out of the discussions very strongly was that women felt frightened to speak about their politics. They felt they didn't have the understanding they maybe would like to have.' The 1980s had produced in Belfast a cohort of women with well-honed activist skills and a growing confidence. If the peace process were to roll and talks about the future constitution of Northern Ireland begin, a profound shake-up of local democracy was bound to follow. 'We'd got to be in there with the new ways,' said Joanne. So the Women Into Politics project offered a series of workshops. They began in the segregated communities but ended as cross-communal and Belfast-wide. They opened by simply breaking the silence, in workshops called 'Let's Talk Politics'. They culminated boldly with preparation for 'Making the Leap' into more active engagement.

But could women's engagement in big-P politics be achieved without women either abandoning their cooperative way of doing things or getting destroyed by the power system? 'It's a gamble,' said Joanne. The hope lay in giving women confidence, ensuring a vocal constituency of women behind them, and, ultimately, in seeing change coming about in the political parties as a result of fresh political realities – one of which, of course, would be the eruption of women's issues into the arena. At the very least, women might feel they had a little power in deciding for themselves how to cast their vote. And, in any case, as one woman said to Joanne, 'Whenever our husbands tell us to shut up we want to be able to turn around and say "well, look, I know a thing or two as well".'

A second initiative that characterizes the Network was Women Working For Change (later called Making Women Seen and Heard). From the start the intention had been that the Network would not 'take' leadership or credit, but rather would aim to be a catalyst, spinning off other dedicated projects and initiatives. And this was a successful example. With the ceasefires, a flurry of meetings seemed to break out all over Northern Ireland. Talks about a new democracy, talks about economic development, talks about a peace dividend. 'There was a process taking place and we felt excluded from it,' says Marie. In particular, the European Union now committed a large fund to a Special Programme for Peace and Reconciliation in Northern Ireland. Would women get their share? The Network and the trade union UNISON together used their many effective contacts to mobilize a forceful lobby to ensure that decision-making concerning the distribution of the very large aid budget from the European Union would include women and observe equality criteria. Now they are determined to win a similar commitment within British government policy in Northern Ireland: the long-term guarantee of an infrastructure to enable the survival and growth of women's community development projects. Without a coherent policy of public spending on people and areas in greatest need, groups like the Shankill and Falls Women's Centres, like Ballybeen, 'Women Too' in Windsor and 'Footprints' in Poleglass, will be for ever toting their begging-bowl round the charities to avert the continual threat of closure.

Differences and commonalities

The Women's Support Network has its offices in the city-centre Downtown Women's Building. The phone and fax lines are continuously busy. The kitchen is a place where you will always find two or three women thrashing out problems over the instant coffee. In Chapter 2 we met some of the women who come together from their jobs as co-ordinators of the various community-based projects to form the active core of the Women's Support Network. There are around a dozen, though the number is growing. They are typically aged between thirty and forty-five, and most have higher education qualifications of some kind. They are quick-thinking, well-informed, busy, wry and without illusions. Hard-smoking, some of them, too.

The group includes women of Catholic, of Protestant and of mixed background, with varying degrees of attachment to community and religion. Some are representing projects in areas of the same ethnicity as their own, others are cross-working. In 1995 Marie Mulholland became full-time coordinator and increased funding enabled the addition of several support staff. Marie adds a further dimension of difference in the Network by being a lesbian whose sexual identity is an important, clearly stated component of her political identity.

What permits this disparate group to hold together? One thing is that, as individuals, they are precisely similar in being different, a bit out of line. Marie says: 'All of us are misfits in our own communities – and yet sometimes we're very typical of them. But there *is* a non-conforming streak in all of us.' A high proportion of the women are in marriages or partnerships with someone from the 'wrong' community. This of itself puts them out of step. Most have rebelled against conventional family backgrounds. These individual qualities explain the personal chemistry, perhaps, but there is something much more important. This cross-communal working (just as in the women's centres) is a *functional*, not an *emotional* choice. Patricia McKeown says they came together not out of friendship, but 'because a common goal or common cause was stronger than the fear of personal risk involved in moving out of safe familiar territory and across onto enemy terrain'. So the women of the Network and the projects they represent hold together around a short string of commonalities: the high value they ascribe women, and a concern about women's poverty, both individual and collective, and about their political marginality.

Everyone in the Network, after all, was coming from a women's project of some kind, a place where, in contrast to the world outside, women are put first. The Network itself was just one more link in women's solidarity. 'The bottom line for us, surely, was "together you're strong",' said Judy, of the Women's Resource and Development Agency. And Anne of Shankill Women's Centre stressed the advantage that lies in numbers, in making a women's discourse widely heard, normal: 'You'll not just be seen as ... you know, like mad women.' Beyond that, probably most of the women would agree with Marie that 'women' is a good starting point for a wider politics. 'Women all experience marginalization in society. So we have something to say about other inequalities that exist in the world. As a feminist I believe that the basic inequality between men and women, if addressed, could lead to a lot of changes in other inequalities.'

One of these of course is 'class'. The women continually describe their communities as working-class. Does this mean the Network is socialist? Its members don't say – or at least I didn't hear them say – 'We're on the Left'. It comes much more easily to speak a language of 'poverty', 'the working class' and 'equality'. But on the iniquities and inequities of class oppression, and on its palpable reality in Belfast, they are in absolute agreement. And, as we have seen, the Network formed around the urgent need to get women's contribution in the working-class communities recognized and properly funded, and finds a further source of coherence in tackling women's invisibility in the political system.

A shared analysis that underpins the Network's strategic choices is the proper response to rhetorics of 'peace' and 'reconciliation'. These are not the Peace People. They do not seek peace at any price. They believe peace thrives only in democracy and justice. Patricia McKeown says:

> All these frustrating years of listening to the condemnation of violence, when what they should have been doing was addressing the root causes. Violence was only a symptom of what was wrong with the place ... [We need] some semblance of democracy, some fair treatment for our people, and I mean all of our citizens, some commitment to equality as a central issue. Because it wouldn't have taken too much analysis to have figured out that the people most likely to engage in violence on either side were the people with the least to lose, the ones who didn't have any kind of real hope for the future.

As to 'reconciliation', the women of the Network are also agreed that the Community Relations Council, the churches and other official and unofficial agencies, are too ready to pursue the government agenda, putting the blame for violence on prejudiced and ignorant people, and therefore favouring projects that bring individuals and small groups into conciliatory postures. This is what Claire Keatinge of Belfast Women's Training Services calls 'the politics of avoidance ... "Let's all be nice about it, let's meet in the middle".' 'Everybody's experience of death is tragic,' she says, 'but there are fundamental issues to do with the structure of the state where I'm going to disagree with that person, and if you're going to understand each other's position, then those issues have to be on the table.' The Network delivered a critique of Community Relations Council policy in 1994, and argued that their funding priority should be community development not community relations. So sensitive are they to the corrupted currency of 'community relations' that they can hardly bear, I felt, to give credit to themselves for anything called cross-communal working.

Handling disagreement

On these things the Network can speak with one voice. But the ethno-national difference its members embody is continually subject to mobilization in the communities they live in. It is like a wedge between them, sometimes barely felt but now and then rammed home by the public statements of extremists, by inflammatory government policies and incidents of violence. Of course ethnic belonging is modified by lived circumstances (what education you received, where you work, whom you marry) and is stressed more or less, according to choice. And in any case political opinion can never be read off from ethnic belonging. Nevertheless the women do also have quite marked divergences of political position – if by political we mean constitutional and party politics, politics with a big P.

I will cite just two examples – although others would do just as well. Marie Mulholland is an Irish nationalist. She finds it hard to envision a future that is not a united Ireland. She is not the only one in the group who feels this way, but her anti-imperialist nationalist/republican point of view is particularly significant given her high profile as co-ordinator and spokesperson. Gillian Gibson, by contrast, is an instance of a Network member who feels herself to be British. Growing up she felt she had more in common with people in Scotland than with those living in the South of Ireland, across the border. She indeed is the woman I cited in Chapter 1 saying 'There might as well have been a great river dividing the North from the South.' She comes from a Protestant family in the unionist heartland town of Portadown. Until recently she would have aligned herself unhesitatingly with unionist politics. As with Marie and the other women, experience has matured her political opinion and added new dimensions to it. She says: 'There's been a shift for me. But I wouldn't like to lose a sense of being British. I'd want to hold on to my identity, albeit in Ireland.'

There are, besides, differences within ethno-political groups as well as between them. There would be those on the nationalist side who would be closer to, and those who would be more distant from, Sinn Féin and the IRA. On the unionist side there would be a difference between, say, a woman with her heart still in the Union and Protestant culture and a woman who has shifted away from both and would now more readily identify as socialist.

So the political differences were marked. But they are not extreme. And in this respect it is interesting to look to the perimeter of the Network, to the women who might have reason to play an active part in it and for some reason do not. There I found women on both unionist and nationalist sides who were more sharply defined in their positions than those within. They were not dissociating themselves publicly from the Network: on paper their projects were members, as individuals they shared its aims and affirmed its uses for women. But they perhaps felt less able than some of the more central women to accept the exigencies of the day-to-day processes of cooperation. Conversely, the women central to the Network were prepared to tolerate this holding back, not demanding total immersion as a condition of membership. These perimeter women perhaps exemplify the outer limits to the possibility of an alliance. And, acknowledging the existence of limits, the Network has always been scrupulous in calling itself not 'the' but 'a' collective voice for women.

Within the active group, how are the significant differences handled to avoid animosity and disintegration? It seems to involve two processes that are in a degree of tension. The first is to go one step beyond acknowledging, being public about and inviting respect for diversity among members and projects within the scope of the Network: they *actively affirm and value difference*. They do not celebrate the fact that differences so profound as those between nationalism and unionism exist in Northern Ireland. But they do find pleasure in the fact that forms of those differences can and do find a place within the Network without destabilizing its inner equilibrium in the way that Northern Ireland's polity is destabilized.

The difference between acknowledging and suppressing differences had to be clarified when a Women's Coalition formed in Northern Ireland to field candidates in the post-ceasefire election. Should the Network give public support? After much deliberation it was decided not to formally endorse the Coalition campaign. In fact, they felt no confidence in the fairness of the Constitutional Forum, the new official structure the elections were held to fill. But more interestingly the Network reasoned that, to hold together in the context of big-P elections, a woman's party representing women as women would be obliged to adopt *neutrality* on issues that were at stake in the constitutional debate. This was different in their view from seeking tactical *common ground* while maintaining political differences. All the same, it was a difficult decision and quite a few of the women individually cast their votes for the Women's Coalition candidates, just glad to see women standing up for women's interests.

The second process is one of *elective and selective speech and silence* on potentially divisive issues. This appears at times conscious, at other times intuitive. Some choices prove judicious, others risky. In 1996 in Northern Ireland the big issue on which the peace process was snagged was: should Sinn Féin, as political representative of the republican movement, be allowed to join the talks before the republican para-militaries (the IRA) had handed over their weapons? In the Network, no such precondition was being imposed. Nobody needs to drop their political holsters by the doorpost when coming in to do Network business. 'Our role as a Network has not been to test those loyalties, but rather to give each of the individuals support to examine them for herself,' says Marie. A distinction is being made here between being different and being divisive.

Women's Support Network, Belfast.

The women clearly enjoy being able to be 'themselves' (not suppressing a part of the person each senses herself to be). It is a narrow but a really felt line that divides 'leaving your politics at home' from bringing them to work albeit without actively debating them there. Perhaps the Network has a special importance for some of the cross-working community workers, who during their daily work may find it productive to minimize their difference from the majority of women in their centres. They might, for instance, not wish to let on there how they vote. In the localities, as Gillian says, 'the implications of talking out of turn have real consequences'. By contrast the town-centre Network office and its activities constitute an environment where it feels OK that someone whose father you know to be a member of an Orange Lodge should know in turn that your menfolk are in the IRA.

The comfort is built on the knowing use of silence. To some women at some moments the practice is satisfactory. For instance, Anne says: 'I've no doubt that if we all started talking constitutional politics we certainly would never reach accommodation or agreement. There's absolutely no doubt … there would be some quite extreme views. But I think we all maybe know that, and that's why we keep off it.' In this way the Network remains, as she puts it, a safe place where you can be 'just a bunch of individuals'. It can seem a test of judgement and tact. 'You judge the times when it's appropriate,' says Gillian. 'We're very skilled at that here. We know our own timing. It's not that you're ignoring a thing, or avoiding it. You just know when it's right, and when it's not.'

When friendships flower in the space of silence, confidence gradually grows and allows a play of difference in jokes. The judgement and tact become a real expertise: we're flying. During the social evening at the Mijas workshop the Belfast group, Catholic and Protestant together, delighted everyone else by acting a skit featuring the Pope of Rome and the Reverend Ian Paisley, fundamentalist loyalist leader of the Democratic Unionist Party. Each is fully capable of laughing at a caricature of her own community. But, at other times and to some women, the silence can become an avoidance, a passive lie. Several women remarked to me that, in their view, the Network had not really sufficiently become a place where differences could be expressed, explored and worked through. They had an uneasy feeling that unless political differences were explored more fully, the alliance might prove to be meaningless or vulnerable.

Gillian Gibson felt (and I think she was not the only one) that for a moment the ceasefires had seemed to allow the Network's agenda to broaden from women's issues to big-P politics. But that moment had gone and they had again lost the habit of honest discussions on and around their political differences. Partly it seemed to be lack of time. (Away from day-to-day work, at the Mijas workshop, they had certainly not held back from exploring their differences.) Here in Belfast, though, 'The agenda's all business now. It's been a long time since we really talked … The people who sit on the seats are all different, but there's never any debate or discussion now about that difference.' Joanne agreed. To get its work done the Network had had to leave a lot unexplored. Of course, in a way, the fact that they could simply choose to set difference aside and get on with action was a strength. 'But it can also be a stumbling-block,' she said. They felt that mutual tolerance had become a kind of taken-for-granted thing. The differences lay buried now, and this too-pervasive silence was potentially destabilizing. But Marie saw it differently. You can't safely raise big-P political antagonisms at just any time in any place. The Women Into Politics project was precisely and thoughtfully designed to create such a safe space. The new discourse it was engendering would break the political silence not only among women in the communities and in the centres, but in the core of the Network itself.

Multiple bridges

To this point in my account of the Women's Support Network I have tended to simplify by showing a few deep areas of difference and potential division, pre-eminently ethnic histories and attachments and big-P politics, offset by a string of commonalities where agreement is unproblematic in the Network. In reality, the negotiations that now weave and now unravel the web of internal cohesion are more complex than this.

The complexity struck me only when I was already well into the research. I had called my project 'Women Building Bridges' and in my own mind I was clear that the bridges in question were simply (simply!) ethno-political bridges. In the case of the Women's Support Network I saw *the* bridge as being one that could bring Catholic/republican and Protestant/unionist women together. Now I was beginning to understand that these particular women found *this* span relatively unchallenging. As we saw, many live in mixed relationships, their post-school education had lifted them out of sectarian environments and involvement in the women's centres had furnished experience of cross-communal contacts.

What actually stretched the Network more was building and maintaining a whole system of bridges across a landscape chasmed by many less obvious dimensions of difference. It was often harder to work with the differences *within* community identities than between them: the gap between, for instance, radical and moderate nationalism (or unionism), or between secular leftism and cultural orthodoxy. And, given the Network's self-defined political role in Belfast and Northern Ireland, the main purpose of establishing any one arch across an internal difference was in any case only to establish a footing for a bridge reaching across the even wider space separating the Network from an external constituency. We could consider three bridging exercises on which the Network was active: *abortion*, *violence* and *feminism*.

On *abortion*, Northern Ireland lacks Great Britain's moderately liberal legislation, being closer on this matter to the Republic of Ireland, where the established Catholic Church is renowned for its rigidity. The women's centres are often approached by women for advice and for contacts to enable them to get pregnancies terminated. Each centre responds in the way that feels comfortable to its management committee, within limits determined by the climate of opinion among users.

'Anti-abortion' and 'pro-choice' opinion is not, as one might suppose, polarized on a Catholic/Protestant dimension in Belfast. 'I think the thinking on abortion, and on divorce, is very similar between Catholic working-class women and Protestant working-class women,' says Anne McVicker. 'I've seen Catholic women who've been totally against abortion under any circumstances, but I've seen Protestant women likewise.' The Protestant churches, while stereotyping the Catholic Church as repressive, are equally intolerant of abortion. And of course many Catholics quietly ignore (and some loudly contest) the ruling of the Catholic Church on reproductive matters. Probably none of the women's centres fails to create an environment in which women feel safe to raise reproductive problems, but they in turn are managing bridges between women in desperate need of help and deeply conservative elements within their communities. Among the centres serving Catholic communities, one may have a policy to inform and advise while another will go much further, ready to give practical help in securing an abortion. Probably the same differences exist between centres in Protestant areas.

If there is such difference among its constituent parts, how does the Network evolve an agreed position for public presentation? Here a decision has been taken to depart from the usual consensual decision-making and fall back on majority opinion. A formula as been evolved whereby the Network is authorized by all its members to speak pro-choice, while one centre, of a contrary view, has agreed to disagree, abstaining from this aspect of Network business. Marie says, 'They recognized that it was fairer to do that than to impose their minority will on the Network as a whole.' Not ideal but, so far, workable.

As to *violence*, the Network does not engage in a public discourse of peace and non-violence, preferring one of justice and equity. But violence is a matter that no alliance in Northern Ireland can very well ignore: the victims of military, sectarian, disciplinary and misogynist violence bleed too near and too visibly. Again the women's centres are building bridges between women who are opposed to violence for any reason, women who deplore but understand violence, women who accept a need for violence in certain circumstances, and women who positively support men and organizations involved in both armed struggle and the violent enforcement of discipline.

I asked Marie whether there was agreement on violence among the women actively involved in the Network. She said, 'I wouldn't be sure on that. We've always given each other a lot of leeway on that.' And indeed when I had a chance to interview women I did find a range of positions. Of course everybody longs for violence to end: it is the shadow that darkens every aspect of life in Northern Ireland. The experience of the ceasefires, and their interruption, had only served to make that more achingly clear to everyone. Some women would say with Patricia McKeown: 'I suppose I make a distinction. I *understand* why so much of it has gone on. I can't *condone* it.' Or with Joy: 'Violence has so many ripple effects, it spreads outwards, and so how can you use it? Because someone else's child can be made parentless by your actions.' Others, with Úna and Anne, would make careful, reluctant distinctions: between war and murder, between civilian and military targets, between casual and political violence. In particular, some found disciplinary violence difficult to condemn out of hand. For instance, where the authorities refuse to act how do you restrain men who habitually batter their wives? Should local paramilitary force be enlisted to deal with them? One woman said, 'I think an awful lot of it's necessary. The police do nothing about it. And you have to understand you're dealing with some bad bastards who just won't be told.'

In the autumn of 1996 Windsor Women's Centre, of which Joy Poots is joint coordinator, was the target of violent assaults by extremists in the local community. It is situated in a Protestant and strongly loyalist area where paramilitary organization is powerful and often threatening. The Windsor women decided to invite President Mary Robinson, whose support for Belfast women's projects was by now well known, to visit their centre. They were encouraged in this by the ceasefires. But by the time the visit became a reality, the atmosphere in Northern Ireland had subtly deteriorated in a summer of violence and instability. When Robinson arrived at the centre she faced a noisy crowd on the pavement outside, waving Union flags and protesting against this 'head of an

enemy state' intruding on loyalist terrain. That night the Windsor Women's Centre was set on fire, apparently at the behest of a local paramilitary organization: a kind of punishment beating.

Joy felt that until then the locally powerful men had largely ignored the cross-communal activity of the Women's Centre, which after all was only women talking to women. 'And now suddenly they realized, big shock, this had been going on. And now they were saying, "You have to stop! And if you won't stop, we'll stop you."' The centre's opponents clearly meant business. The arson was repeated on two subsequent nights, along with the smashing of the reinforced glass of the centre's windows.

A problem that underlay all the women's community organizing and networking in Belfast was dramatically highlighted by these incidents in Windsor. How can you be 'representative of' the community when that community contains some who espouse violence and some who reject it? Joy and Gillian both stressed the difficulty of bringing women together on issues of this kind. 'I don't know how you can build bridges between these different ways of thinking,' said Joy. So the issue of violence is continually unsettled and unsettling in the Network.

Finally, *feminism* is something that calls for negotiation and bridge-building skills. There may be a parallel between the way the minority prefers to turn a blind eye on the abortion issue and the way a not-totally feminist collective permits the Network to take a feminist public stance. In both cases the women who attend Network meetings and share in its decision-making have not merely to make up their own minds, they are also busy sustaining a bridge back to a community-based women's centre or project which has its own internal divisions and balance of opinion. And in both cases there may be women who 'are in two minds', personally adhering to cautious or even conservative positions while seeing political advantage in being part of the Network with a radically challenging public face.

The Network made a decision without too much difficulty to call itself 'a collective *feminist* voice of women in Greater Belfast'. But we saw in the last chapter that some women in the environment of the women's community-based centres dislike the notion of 'feminism', which they associate on the one hand with man-hating and stridency, on the other hand with middle-class arrogance. There are others who have deconstructed feminism to their own satisfaction, qualifying it (or strengthening it, depending upon your view of these things) in a way that articulates it to some other aspect of themselves, some other belonging, in a way they can feel comfortable with. So Kathleen Feenan of the Women's Information Group talks of 'family feminism', while Janis

Quinn of Ardoyne Women's Centre prefers 'street feminism'. The term 'rights feminism' seems more appropriate to Úna, of Falls Women's Centre, locating women's rights firmly in a context of human rights.

Joanna McMinn, an early Network member with experience in community-based education, says, 'Feminism is alienating to the women within community groups if it's just presented coldly on a plate. But if it's actually addressed on a one-to-one basis, on a particular issue, as a discussion, it's not like that.' The coordinators (even ones who may hesitate or qualify the term before identifying with feminism) are in fact continually encouraging their centres along a spectrum of what others would call feminism, doing it woman by woman and issue by issue. And the way that the lesbianism of two Network members is not merely accepted as an important part of their own sense of self, but welcomed as a valued dimension of identity within the alliance, is an indicator that the feminism of the Network is not just skin-deep.

There are, of course, as we noted in Chapter 1, feminisms and feminisms. This is a feminism that, although the centres and the Network organize separately as women, is not 'separatist'. Most of the women go home to men, and the Network as a whole seeks to be effective in a mixed-sex world. Women's oppression, the gender-specific violence women experience and women's characteristic strengths are acknowledged, but the prevailing philosophy is not an essentialist celebration of 'women'. The Network continually links a discourse about women to a discourse about class power and economic inequalities. It has a vision of a changed society – transformed families, communities, parties and national structures.

Maintaining an alliance: a democracy of differences

The Network sees itself as an organization of women's projects in deprived and oppressed communities, coming together the more effectively to achieve space, voice and impact for working-class women in the Northern Ireland polity. But my first interest in it is as an *alliance* for those purposes. Any alliance, by definition, is characterized by distinctive elements in its membership – they have to cohere across or in spite of *something*. To sustain the association and take effective external action, an alliance must therefore evolve a practice for dealing constructively with its defining differences. As we have seen, the Network's significant differences include (and I am not ranking them by importance) differences deriving from ethnicity, such as culture, religion and sense of national belonging; differences of big-P politics, including ideology and allegiance; differences concerning violence; and a cluster of differences on a gender dimension – contrasting sexual orientations, a range of opinion on reproductive rights, and on feminism.

The women were proud of the group's achievements. It was a long and ambitious journey they had made together since 1989. The record of output spoke for itself and by the end of 1996 the search to increase funding was beginning to bear fruit, so that the coordinator (Marie Mulholland) and the administrative assistant (Rosanna Holmes) were about to be joined by several other members of staff. What had enabled it to survive? The stability and endurance of the alliance seemed to depend on two things: an area of common ground and a practice of internal democracy. The Network's common ground will by now be apparent. We have seen that it does not mean neutral ground, but rather involves subject areas where sufficient shared interest exists to make it worthwhile and possible to negotiate agreement for action. But what of *democracy*? The issues here seemed to be those of inclusion and equality.

In any alliance, of course, there are limits in respect of inclusiveness. Hard decisions have to be made as to whom to make efforts to hold in, whom to let go. There will always be a 'difference too far', to include which would run contrary to the main political aim. But everyone whose presence will increase the likelihood of achieving its aims ought to find it possible to participate, and to participate on equal and equally satisfying terms. Was this happening? I wanted to probe deeply for the points where failure would be most likely to occur. Because unless I were able to see this I could scarcely hope to emerge from my engagement with the Network bearing knowledge of use to other women's alliances in other equally difficult situations. So I asked, frankly, does it always work? does it live up to its rhetoric? do your feelings get hurt? do you always feel fully a part of this thing? do you always come back? Or, of those at the edge: why are you not more involved?

Most of the time, relations were good within the Network. But not always. At moments in its life some members had felt peripheral. A woman just outside the Network (who wanted to remain anonymous) described it as made up of women who were different from the average community member or centre user in being professionally qualified community workers, essentially *managers*. 'It's a particular perspective that doesn't represent all women,' she commented. Judy, of the Women's Resource and Development Agency, had also felt reservations about the Network. Its members, she said, sometimes gave the impression of having 'known each other since the beginning of time'. So it was not easy for a woman 'to come in and feel "I'm part of this, what I say counts"'. She felt that: 'networks can be beautifully anarchic and creative when they are working well. But they can be cliquey – unless there are lots of points of entry, unless you're very aware of that [danger] and ensure in your working practices, in the detail of what you do, that you're constantly inclusive.' In its early days the Network had lacked that good practice, 'saying hello to people, sending out notice of a meeting in time for people to get it in their diary'. She felt more comfortable once the Network had formalized a little, establishing an effective management structure.

Some had felt the exclusiveness as a question of style and language. For example, the Greenway Women's Centre is run by volunteers. Two key women in the centre are working-class women of Protestant and unionist background. Donna Davis originally attended the Network for Greenway, but she had felt out of place among women whom she perceived as being more highly educated ('they've got their degrees'), and using unfamiliar language. She said: 'It was above my head some of the time. I'm just an ordinary housewife.' She went on: 'All this talk, the language. Sometimes they were using all these initials for things and we were, like, "Oh god, what's happening?" It was very elitist to me sometimes, which I hate.'

The Network is a series of concentric rings of women, at its heart a group most of whom have community work skills and share a set of competences and a language. In a sense, the bridge the Network builds back to the constituent centres and projects has to be an arch linking one language to another, an equalizing of discourses. It was not only Donna and Greenway that felt the difficulty. The individual co-ordinators were also sometimes aware of how their own centre's members would feel alienated by style and language, and the consequent burden of interpretation and equalization that they themselves carried.

A second tendency to inequality in the Network seemed to be a cultural imbalance between Catholic and Protestant. In community and feminist politics generally there is a curious inversion of the general dominance of Protestants over Catholics in Northern Ireland. This is partly because of the early gathering of community work skills and qualifications in Catholic hands. As a result, in the Network there is a subtle Irish/Catholic hegemony. It derives not from a wish to dominate, more from an exuberance in that culture. An example: when a banner needed to be made quickly for the Network's Development Plan launch, the job was given to Falls Women's Centre who have plenty of experi-ence with these things. The image they produced to hang above the speakers' table on the day was a handsome black-and-white design featuring a Celtic knot and 'Women's Support Network' in Gaelic-style lettering. In the absence of conscious effort to resist it, what results is Irish-Irish, not British-Irish. It reminded me of something I'd heard elsewhere. Thinking of 'Irish language', 'Irish music', a Protestant woman told me, 'It's almost as if they're saying "We have our culture. Join us!"'

By contrast, the Protestant members of the Network are less interested in celebrating their culture. The one they have inherited they tend to subdue in their own lives, because it has historically been domineering – not only over Catholics but also over dissenters within. Catholic women are used to celebrating the many strong women in the history of Irish nationalism. By contrast, Protestant women have only recently looked for feminist role models in their communal history. Women's rights oppositionalism sits comfortably with Catholic rights oppositionalism, uncomfortably with the Protestant defensive posture. For these reasons it is possible to see how even in the Network a Protestant feminist might feel shaky, challenged and vulnerable in face of what seems like a very practised, articulate Catholic feminism backed up by a movement and a literature. You can need it and fear it at one and the same time. And you can perhaps be glad that, in the name of being properly tied back to your community constituency, you can hold it at a distance – making a distinction between the politics of the work you do for women, and the identity you choose to acknowledge as part of yourself.

Gillian spoke more graphically about Irish/Catholic hegemony than other Network members, but I don't think she was the only one (Catholic or Protestant) who felt it. She said to me, 'I would be conscious that the unionist Protestant woman's viewpoint would be very rarely heard at Women's Support Network meetings.' A very committed member of the Network, she feels, all the same, that it is at its best in a crisis. The experience of the Mijas workshop had, she felt, helped Network members discuss fundamental differences normally not dealt with at Network meetings.

An alliance notionally has a number of resources on which to draw, potential supports to the sustainable cooperation it has to build. They include *money*, *networks* and *democratic process*. It was in the nature of the Network that it needed funding. It had had grants in the past and, with 'peace' in prospect in Northern Ireland, more potential sources were opening up. But the women felt that too much of their energy was consumed in just sustaining a cash flow. What they needed was a more democratic environment in which civil society would be nourished. They wanted a political culture that would value autonomous community and women's groups, rewarding them with money without enslaving them in dependency.

The Network was specially responsive to developments that enabled it to do just what its name suggests, 'network'. It thrived when horizons widened, when international borders could be crossed, when it could see itself as part of a feminist universe. Particularly invigorating had been the sheer excitement and pleasure in making links with women's organizations in the South, in Europe and (through participation in this project of ours) with women in other conflictual worlds.

But the third and perhaps the most important resource for an alliance is of course participatory democratic process, the careful and caring management of interaction and decision-making. When things go right, when agreements are easy to reach, when the range and scope of policy is expanding and people are enjoying working together, it is not happening by chance but because somebody is, or more likely somebodies are, fostering good communication, good listening, inclusive activity and supportive relationships. When things go wrong it is because these processes are failing.

The Women's Support Network is formally conscious of the importance of good process. In her coordinator's *Report* for 1995/6, Marie Mulholland dwelled on how it needed 'to create structures and processes of management and organization which allowed women to become involved at various levels, provided for their varying interest, skills and experience and ensured that the life-course of the Network was continually regenerated'. By late 1996 the Network had changed from a loose gathering to an organization structured as a plenary, a management committee and working groups. A commitment to inclusion and equality was subsequently built into the Network's *Development Plan*, which reads: 'How we work is as important as what we do ... Every woman participating, in a voluntary or paid capacity, should feel valued, involved and included and this should be the basis of constant, thoughtful analysis and review' (Women's Support Network 1996: 20). And in talking to a meeting in London in 1996 Marie thought aloud about the way women can change the nature of power in and through their own organizations. 'Do we exercise power with love, with honour, with justice and with equality? That's the criterion for me. Process is really important. Partly it's in process the solution lies. If the process is fair, accountable and democratic the product will be accountable, democratic and fair.'

The principle was therefore in place. Members of the Network were satisfied that mostly it was applied. But now and then it ran into trouble. I witnessed some deep disagreements that threatened to split the alliance. One of the issues at stake had been the quality of the internal democratic processes of one of the member projects. How representative were they of their community, how well were they ensuring inclusion and equality through their management structures and processes? Failure to resolve amicably disagreement over *their* democratic process had left women painfully wondering if there had been a momentary failure of the Network's *collective* democratic process. Views were expressed for instance, both before and after this event, that some women's unhappiness had at times not so much been 'dealt with' in the Network as evaded, that issues had sometimes 'been handled messily, badly', leaving the impression that if you failed to concur with the main line in the Network you could be ostracized.

So the Women's Support Network, like any real live alliance, had made mistakes and misjudgements. But it was showing a capacity to learn from them. None of the member centres or projects had withdrawn. Indeed, as more centres and initiatives had started up in Belfast, the Network had grown. The project had survived some extraordinarily turbulent times, times of war and times of peace that seemed little different from war. And in contrast to louder political actors in Northern Ireland – male-led parties, male-led paramilitary forces, male-led government agencies – the Network was consistently heard as an ethical, intelligent, reasoned feminist voice for change.

4
Israel/Palestine: Across an abyss

The Bat Shalom group of Megiddo, Nazareth and The Valleys in northern Israel, like the Women's Support Network in Belfast, is an alliance of women drawn from two ethnic groups caught up in inimical national projects. Like Northern Ireland's Protestants and Catholics, the two Israeli communities live largely segregated lives. But in the case of Bat Shalom the contrast between their economies and lifestyles is much sharper.

On the one hand there are women from the dominant Israeli Jewish culture of this area, that of the kibbutz. The kibbutzim they live and work in, intermixed with cooperative farming villages, the moshavim, are spread out across the fertile plain and the surrounding low hills of this region. Their partners in Bat Shalom are Arab women, some Muslim, some Christian, who live in villages and towns, quite ethnically and physically distinct, situated here and there amid the Jewish farmlands. They are Palestinian Arabs who have become Israeli citizens, a remnant of the former majority population of the region, the ones who remained and survived in the cataclysm of 1948.

To understand the significance, and the difficulties, of Bat Shalom as a working alliance one needs to know something of the contrasted societies its members inhabit. An important factor in the group's relationships is, in fact, how incomplete is the knowledge that each community has of its neighbour, the rigid identities each normally ascribes to the other.

Jewish women of the kibbutzim

Only a small proportion, around 3 per cent, of Israel's population are members of a kibbutz. Nevertheless, kibbutzim occupy more than a third of the country's agricultural lands, and moshavim a further third (Davis 1987: 62). Beyond its significance in the agricultural economy, the kibbutz as an institution has had enormous importance in the ideology and political structure of the Israeli state. The first, Degania, was founded in 1905 by Zionist pioneers inspired by early Russian revolutionary ideals. It became a model for many of the communities established in the later wave of immigration during the period of the British Mandate. The kibbutz system reflected both the socialist principles of the pre-state Zionist movement and the desire of many Jews at that time for a 'normalization' of the Jewish people through physical labour and closeness to the land. The primary work was farming, and the land and its product were held in common. Mental and manual tasks were shared. Labour was not paid, but each member's shelter, food and other needs were met by the collective. Management and decision-making were participatory.[1]

Some of Bat Shalom's Jewish members live today on old kibbutzim founded in that pre-state period. Others live in kibbutzim established on land expropriated during and after the hostilities surrounding the creation of the state. And it is these post-war kibbutzim that are the most troubling expression of Labour Zionism, a deeply contradictory philosophy exemplified in the policies and personality of the state's first prime minister, David Ben-Gurion, and still an important current in Israeli politics today. Labour Zionism's in many ways revolutionary, down-to-earth, sharing ideals have a flaw at their heart: it lies in the matter of who is counted as a member of the community of equals. In the concern to put right the disadvantage of Jews, equal human value and equal human rights were not accorded in Zionist thought to Palestinian Arabs and other non-Jews. Nor indeed in practice has Zionist democracy been extended equally to all Jews.

The kibbutz was used by the first government of the new state of Israel as a practical means of rapid deployment onto evacuated Palestinian properties. Much as the Zionists wanted control of this land, they were few and the effort needed to realize ownership was daunting. Yossef Weitz, head of the Jewish National Fund Colonization Department, recorded in his diary on 18 December 1948 his thoughts on a journey through this land where Bat Shalom's women now live, then newly emptied of its Palestinian inhabitants.

> The whole day we rolled over Galilee and we saw all the agricultural wealth that they have left behind them. And the heart is heavy. Shall we have enough strength to continue all these crops, to improve them and extend them? Shall we be capable of settling here thousands of Jews to repeople the human desert, and make Galilee flower again? (cited in Halevi 1987: 192).

Sending out experienced 'kibbutzniks' to establish new settlements

---

1. In the above and following material on the history and significance of the kibbutz in Israel I draw mainly on Davis 1987, Flapan 1987 and Halevi 1987. I cite them individually only where quoting specific data.

was part of an unconcealed strategy to pre-empt any move by Palestinians to return. But taking control of the land was not, in mainstream Labour Zionist thought, held to be in any way incompatible with an ideology of equality and sharing, the humane principle of 'from each according to ability, to each according to need' by which the kibbutz communities lived.

All kibbutzim and moshavim were incorporated as companies of the Nir Cooperative, constitutionally established for the settlement of Jewish workers and owned by a holding company of Histradut, the General Federation of Jewish Labour (Davis 1987: 53). In this sense, the kibbutzim were not incidentally Jewish, they were and remain specifically Jewish, and it is doubtful whether there has ever been a case of a Palestinian Arab being admitted as a member – although kibbutzim have for some time employed Arabs as wage labourers. Besides, kibbutz agriculture is also subsidized from official sources, since, despite intensive methods of production and prices protected by a Jewish boycott of Arab produce, it has seldom been fully economically viable.

Most kibbutzim belong to one of two associations. The larger is related to the Labour Party, the smaller to Mapam, the United Workers' Party, which is likewise Zionist and non-religious but to the left of Labour. There is also a small minority of religious kibbutzim. Of the Jewish women in Bat Shalom, the majority are members of kibbutzim of the Mapam group, the Kibbutz Artzi Hashomer Hatzair. Mapam and the Israeli Communist Party (Rakah) were the only parties to protest consistently against Labour's policy of expelling Palestinian Arabs from Israel. A one-time national secretary of Mapam has described the inconsistencies in the party's politics and the hypocrisy with which it was charged, both from within its own membership and outside, for attempting to reconcile opposition to expulsions of Palestinian Arabs with subsequent colonization of their land (Flapan 1987: 115).

There is a second matter on which, for all its collectivist and egalitarian principles, Labour Zionism was from the start retrogressive. If the relationship to Palestinian Arabs raised a question of what was meant by community and membership, gender relations raised the question of just what was meant by equality. Jewish women were considered formally equal with Jewish men. But natural sex differences were stressed and there was no intention to change relations between the sexes, and in particular male authority.

Among the Jewish pioneers early in the century there were far fewer women than men. The work in this hard terrain and hot climate demanded great physical stamina and, as resistance from Palestinian Arabs increased, the life became dangerous. Many of the women who

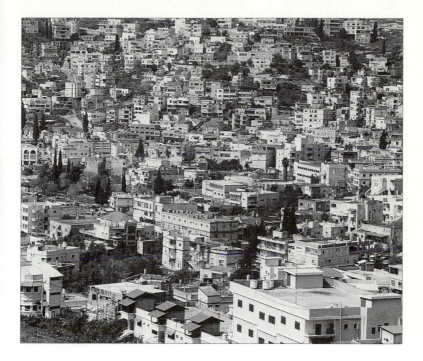

Adjacent, different, unequal. Jezreel valley, Jewish agriculture (left). Nazareth,
Arab city (above).

did join the kibbutzim proved themselves tough and brave. But from the start they had difficulty in establishing a principle of sex equality in the distribution of work. Whenever emergencies permitted a modicum of normal life, as soon as domestic arrangements began to develop beyond mere survival, and especially when children began to be born, women were expected to retire from production and defence and attend instead to the collective's food and housing, clothing and childcare (Bowes 1986; Safir 1993b).

Domestic arrangements on the kibbutz did indeed constitute a clear break from traditional family life. The collective ate together, food was cooked communally. Clothing was made, laundered and mended collectively. There was no cash, no shopping, no spending. Vehicles and other equipment were owned in common. Private quarters were minimal. In particular, the kibbutzim became famous worldwide for instituting collective child-rearing practices. The children would spend their days in communal care, graduating from the kibbutz nursery to its kindergarten and then its school. At night they slept in the children's house, watched over by adult workers. Parents, all of whom shared in the daily work of the kibbutz, were encouraged to spend 'quality time' with their children in their own quarters after work and on the Sabbath (Palgi 1993). It was a system justified in part by the needs of security, for the children could be better defended from attack this way. But it also reflected the Labour Zionist ideology that favoured collective upbringing, for the purpose of reshaping human nature.

However, the reshuffling of domestic arrangements was not accompanied by a new deal in the matter of which sex did what work. Kibbutz nursery workers and teachers have almost always been women. If within childcare there was a further division, between labour and love, it was the woman as worker who performed the former, the woman again, as mother, who provided the latter. The sexual division of labour was never inscribed in tablets of stone, but it was always informally understood in the kibbutz system that there was men's work and women's work. Men worked in construction, agriculture or factory, and few women, even if they wished it, were welcomed into the more skilled, heavy or responsible tasks in those environments. In the administration's statistics, as well as in everyday language in the kibbutz, this was classed as 'productive' work, and highly valued. Domestic and service work, to which women were deemed naturally fitted, was termed 'unproductive' work and accorded secondary importance (Bowes 1986: 140; Safir 1993b: 256).

Over the years, in fact, many kibbutzim have returned to more conventional family relationships, women's work schedules have been modified to allow them to spend more time with their newborn babies, and often today children sleep in their parents' accommodation. Changes in this direction were first introduced by Takam, the United Kibbutz Movement, in 1966 (Palgi 1993: 262). Childcare, it must be said, has never failed to be accorded social value – children are recognized as the lifeblood of the nation. But it is uniquely to women the system ascribes value for doing it. So a shift back to familism had little bearing on women's working lives. Cooking in a canteen or a kitchenette, tucking a child into bed in a dormitory or a bedroom, are much of a muchness. And in a system where one is paid not by cash but in kind, the difference between private and public work is anyway of reduced importance.

Little concern was shown either among the management of kibbutzim or in the national kibbutz organizations about the persistence of this profound sexual division of labour in the system. It was a convention passed from the pioneers to their successors. A study of second-generation kibbutz members, using figures from 1975, showed that even of men born on the kibbutz, 91.0 per cent as against only 15.5 per cent of women were working in 'productive' occupations (Ben-David 1975 cited in Silver 1993: 271). In 1980 Kibbutz Artzi did respond to such figures with a decision that 20 per cent of workers in education and service branches should be men. But if general conclusions can be drawn from the comments of Bat Shalom women, by the mid-1990s the policy had had only limited influence. The women dairy workers shown in the photographs overleaf are unusual in breaking the mould. The problems continued to be those familiar far from the kibbutz, a vertical and horizontal occupational sex segregation combined with an undervaluing of women's activities.

The life of a kibbutz member, like that of any Jewish Israeli citizen, is interrupted by spells in the armed forces. The relationship between the army and the kibbutz has been more than occupational, it has been symbolic. These have been the twin pillars of Israeli society: the sword and the ploughshare, both imbued with masculine meaning. Men in uniform are often seen around the kibbutzim, both kibbutz members on leave and other soldiers stationed there while serving away from home. Women too are seen in uniform, because they also perform military service, doing both an initial stint as youngsters and annual service afterwards as reservists. But the terms of women's military service are different from those of men. They are called up for a shorter period. They do not have to serve if married, pregnant or mothers. They are more readily exempted on grounds of insufficient education or fitness and are enlisted in a special women's unit. Women often remark, un-comfortably, on the name of this unit, the acronym CHEN – which

Kibbutz: collective production, collective consumption.

means 'charm'. Their role in combat units is limited to that of in-structor. Mainly they serve in administrative, domestic or educational posts. Sharing militarization with men therefore does little for women's equality (Yuval-Davis 1985; Bloom 1993).

Because of the work women mainly do and because of their greater involvement with children, they are under-represented in the responsible roles in the kibbutz management system and are less involved than men in decision-making. Through the triad of kibbutz, military and Zionist organizations, the leading figures in the kibbutz movement have always played a disproportionate part in the Israeli state (Bowes 1986). But it has been mainly men who by stepping up into the kibbutz national bureaucracies have achieved connections with the powerful para-state Zionist organizations and become key actors in the political parties.

So the women of kibbutz society in Israel today continue to live in a male-dominated system, despite the many advantages they un-doubtedly have over their Arab sisters, and the quality of their lives compared with those of their own mothers and grandmothers. Of course, there are radical differences between life on an Israeli kibbutz and conventional Jewish life as it is lived in New York, Tel Aviv or even the local town. Women are not isolated in the home. They are never economically dependent on a husband and their children are maintained by the collective. A woman suffers scarcely any social penalty for remain-ing or becoming unmarried. Yet kibbutz women do not have sex equality. The traditional patriarchal family has gone, only to be replaced by a modernized form of collective male dominance.

The prestige and popularity of the kibbutz lifestyle has in any case waned. Akiva Orr writes, 'in 1964 anyone who left a kibbutz – or the country – was considered a traitor, nowadays the leavers are envied by those left behind' (Orr 1994: 54). And women more than men may have reason to think of leaving. They talk of being torn between the un-deniable merits of this uniquely collective form of society, an ideal they are reluctant to betray despite its betrayal of them, and the appeal of finding a different, more mobile identity as a woman, in the more open, if more competitive and consumerist, urban world.

The unknown neighbour: Palestinian Arab women

In 1949 the Arabs of Palestine, scattered far and wide by the fighting of the previous two years, found their separation from relatives and friends had been sealed by a new state boundary. Four-fifths of them at least (the exact numbers can never be known) were now refugees outside the Green Line drawn on the map by those who negotiated the armistice. Inside the state of Israel remained around 150,000. Many of these insiders too were adrift, detached from their land and homes, sheltering in temporary accommodation or packed in with friends and relatives. By far the larger part of Israel's residual Arabs were located in Galilee, in the north, and an area somewhat to the south of it, known as the Little Triangle. Neither of these areas had been intended under the United Nations partition plan to be part of Israel – they were captured by the Zionist forces during the fighting and never relinquished.[2]

These Palestinian Arabs were not only severed from those now outside Israel's borders, they were separated from each other too. Under military rule they were largely restricted to the localities in which they were registered as residing. Special permits were issued to males wishing to travel to work beyond these confines. Their lives had so changed that they scarcely recognized themselves as the people they had been. Arab city culture was largely destroyed. Farmers, uprooted from the land, and with expropriations continuing, began, to their own surprise, to be a distinctively small-town people. Umm El-Fahm, Ara, Nazareth, Iksal – those places that were villages quickly became towns, towns in turn burst at the seams. And each was an island in an ocean of Jewish state agricultural land. The men were no longer traders, subsistence farmers and stock-rearers. Those lucky enough to find work had become day-labourers. They were a new commuting male proletariat, subject to many security restrictions, at the rock bottom of the Israeli job market. For women, who had gardened and farmed family land, it was difficult to replace this source of income and they found they had lost status in the family. The fabric of the economy had been torn apart and new dependencies created.

Under the founding declaration of the state and later legislation by the Knesset, the Israeli Palestinian Arabs were granted citizenship of Israel. As citizens they were formally guaranteed equal rights. But the state, through structures assured by its Zionist founders, was a Jewish state in which non-Jews could never in practice be equal. And there was particular caution with regard to Palestinian Arabs because they were seen as a potential fifth column, likely to put loyalty to the Arab cause before loyalty to Israel.

Israel has been called by one of its tougher Jewish critics an apartheid state, comparable to South Africa before 1994 (Davis 1987). In fact the

---

2. In this account of Palestinian Arabs in Israel I draw mainly on Jiryis 1976; Lustick 1980; Davis 1987; Kretzmer 1990 and Ashkenasi 1992. I cite them individually only where quoting specific data.

separation and inequality that structure the Israeli state have their basis in two uniquely Israeli constitutional devices. First the Law of Return, together with later legislation, gives Jews worldwide the right to claim Israeli citizenship while denying that right to exiled Palestinian Arabs, recently inhabitants of the country. Second, important aspects of Israeli society and economy are devolved by the state (bound to treat its citizens equally) to the para-state Zionist organizations (not only free to discriminate against non-Jews, but in many cases bound to do so). Besides, many rights have been made dependent on having served in the Israeli armed forces, from which the majority of Palestinian Arabs are barred. In such a system, with limited rights, mobility and job choices, the Palestinian Arabs were bound to become a disadvantaged underclass.

Even in Galilee, the quite numerous Palestinian Arab minority living around them was little seen and largely forgotten by the majority of Jews. Haifa city's shopping centre, the housing estates of a town like Afula, the gardens of a kibbutz or moshav, these were places where Arabs seldom set foot. Some Arabs were even more invisibilized than others, for there were some who stayed illegally on their land or later returned to squat it. Half a century after losing their property rights, these communities remained outcasts from society, unrecognized by the state, denied access roads, electricity or state services.

Much of the Palestinian Arab political and professional leadership had left the country, and for the remainder a low profile and compliance with the regulations that governed them seemed the wisest route to survival in this alien state. Israeli officials enmeshed community elders, mukhtars and religious leaders in a web of collaboration. The rivalry they encouraged by favouring Druze over Arab, Christian over Muslim, Bedouin over Sunni, undermined solidarity. Although the more progressive Jewish political parties gave token support to Arab representation, autonomous political organization was suppressed. A movement in support of land claims was quickly put down by the state.

Then came the Six Day War of 1967, in the course of which Israel seized those parts of Palestine that had until then remained outside its control. It was a serious setback for Arab interests in Palestine but, curiously, a moment of renewal for those locked in Israel. Suddenly, a population of a million or more Palestinian Arabs had been swept in to join them within the new expanded boundaries. The occupation awoke in Israeli Palestinians a new collective self-awareness, problematized old identities. Nabila Espanioly remembers:

As a result of the 1967 war, Palestinians living in Israel started to ask

nationally motivated questions such as 'Who are you?', 'What is the relationship between us and the Palestinians under occupation?', 'What is the
connection between us and the state of Israel?' (Espanioly 1994: 112).

Coming soon after military controls over the Palestinian Arab population were lifted, the occupation also prompted a new political activism.
The Israeli Communist Party, Rakah, had been the moderate party
favoured by middle-class Palestinian Arabs, especially the Christians.
Now more began to join it and to formulate a cautious political
programme. There were also more radical stirrings in movements that
rejected the legitimacy of the Israeli state, such as 'Sons of the Village'
and, among the new generation gaining higher education, the Progressive National Student Movement. Organizations linking the local
councils of Palestinian Arab municipalities, and Arab Members of the
Knesset, among other initiatives, began to build an infrastructure for
Palestinian Arab society inside Israel. Twenty years later the intifada
(see p. 26) in the West Bank and Gaza would give a second kick-start
to confidence and activism. It carried one step further the process in
which the Israeli Palestinian Arab dual identity was evolving: one the
identity of a subordinated ethnic minority aspiring to citizens' rights
within an oppressive state; the other that of a nation adrift in place-less
limbo, dreaming of statehood.

So different is the life in Nazareth or Iksal today from that on the
kibbutz that it is sometimes difficult to recognize that these cultures exist
in the same country, let alone the same locality. The Arab towns are
clearly bounded, their white and cream painted houses packed along
dusty, treeless streets, in sharp contrast to the shady watered lawns of the
kibbutzim. State expenditure on street maintenance, drainage systems
and refuse collection is deficient, giving an impression of deprivation and
'under-development'. The houses are mainly family-owned properties,
showing signs of being continually extended to accommodate the up-
and-coming generation, with the effect that the constructions grow ever
taller and will soon cover each available square yard. Mixed in among the
houses are shops, mosques, churches, garages, schools, small factories.
Near the centre are the municipal offices, the focus of political life.

Whereas cash is scarcely in evidence on the kibbutz and individuals
are barely distinguishable from each other in clothing or consumption,
in the Arab towns there are economic and social class distinctions: there
is a little new money and there is (even more visibly) an entrenched
poverty. Where on the kibbutz the notion of 'family' is reinterpreted
through the ideology of the commune, here it retains a traditional form.
The family is everything. It looks after its own, educates for survival

Demography counts. Palestinian Arabs bear more children. Their
daughters have ideas of their own.

and shares resources as a form of social security. When it gets a foothold in the economy it invests for security, spends (on jewellery, clothing, furniture) for self-respect, competes fiercely, gives generously.

The traditional Arab *hamula*, or clan, has been maintained into the modern period, partly in communal self-protection. Manar Hassan, who grew up as a girl in a Muslim Palestinian Arab family, suggests that the values of the hamula became even more sacrosanct among the Palestinian Arab remnant in Israel 'as a distorted response to the cultural oppression of the Israeli regime' (Hassan 1993: 70). These values were readily exploited by the Israeli rulers and the combination of the two authority systems was disastrous for women. Hassan has angrily denounced in particular the lenient treatment by the state, bowing to community values, of the murder of women by family members 'in defence of family honor' (Hassan 1993: 71).

Demographic competition between the Jewish majority and Palestinian Arab minority has also adversely affected women. To avert the threat of Arab population growth, the Israeli state uses administrative devices that channel free contraception in the direction of Palestinian Arab women, subsidies to encourage a high birthrate in the direction of Jewish women (Yuval-Davis 1987: 80). Even so, Palestinian Arab women spend twice as much of their lives and energies bearing and rearing children as do their Jewish counterparts (Abdo and Yuval-Davis 1995: 307).

Despite traditional patriarchal controls on women, economic need and women's own willpower has brought many more out of the home, into education and employment. At the end of the Mandate period only one-third of Palestinian Arab children of school age were in school. Of these only one-fifth were girls (Espanioly 1994: 109). The Israeli law of compulsory school attendance for both sexes rapidly increased the number of Palestinian Arab girls in school, so that they shared in the rapid expansion of education (Abu Rakba 1993). Many of the new generation grew up bilingual in Arabic and Hebrew, and this included many young women, particularly Christians.

In the 1970s Palestinian Arab women began to follow the path into the formal economy taken by Palestinian Arab men ten or twenty years earlier, seeking jobs in industry, particularly Jewish food and clothing factories. The numbers of Arab women in industry had been a mere 400 in 1965. By 1984 there were 63,000 (ibid.: 189). They did not, in the main, compete directly in the labour market with Jewish women, since even manual occupations were as clearly segregated on ethnic as on sex lines. Young women from middle-class Arab families increasingly passed from school to higher education, and by 1989 women accounted for around one-fifth of Palestinian Arab students in higher education (official statistics cited by Espanioly 1994: 115). Jobs held by reluctant families to be least unsuitable for their unmarried daughters were in white-collar and social occupations within the Palestinian Arab community, so that large numbers became schoolteachers and health workers (Abu Rakba 1993; Espanioly 1994).

So modernization has been pulling the Palestinian Arab women of Israel away from traditional Muslim and Christian family roles. Younger women are more reluctant to play the role of reproducer and enforcer of a culture that oppresses them and their daughters. Escaping the authority of fathers and husbands, they have carried some men with them. They have been described as the principal change agents in Israeli Palestinian Arab society (Mar'i and Mar'i 1993). But simultaneously a political religious movement has been growing, particularly a revival of Muslim consciousness, which threatens women's gains. The growth of support for Hamas and Islamic Jihad in the Occupied Territories has been accompanied by the emergence of Muslim political organization in Israel, especially in the Triangle towns and villages. It is embittering to women that something they have long looked for, a renewal of resistance to the Israeli state and its Western supporters, has brought with it a strictly conventional religious code that calls for women to be covered and confined in the home under the control of men.

Meanwhile Israeli Palestinian Arab women's hopes of liberation were inescapably tied to those of the men who shaped their family and community belonging. Anton Shammas, interviewed by David Grossman in his profoundly moving study of Israel's Palestinian Arabs, *Sleeping on a Wire*, told him:

> My real ideological war will come the morning after the establishment of the Palestinian state. Only then will I have the absolute moral right to demand complete social and political equal rights. ... In the meantime, I wait patiently for the big conflict to end, and then my conflict will begin. Then I'll open my mouth. I'll shout for a year, two years, and if it's not solved, I'll make an intifada (Grossman 1994: 264).

Thinking along these lines, to many Palestinian Arab women living within the Israeli state it seems likely that not one, but two, buses will have to pass by without taking them aboard. Only when the struggle for a Palestinian state in the Occupied Territories is rewarded with success, and only, after that, when the voices of the men of the Palestinian Arab community in Israel have been raised and been answered, will equality for women become thinkable. But this does not, as we shall see, stop women hailing all three buses at once.

Women's disadvantage and the rise of feminisms

Women of both communities had good reason to chafe at their position in Israeli society. Although the Declaration of the Establishment of the State of Israel in 1948 had proclaimed sex equality as one of the founding principles of the state, and although the state-building process that followed included a Women's Equal Rights Law (1951) and subsequent legislation on equal pay and maternity rights, women's freedom was in practice limited by a powerful familial ideology, shaped and sustained by religious authorities and backed by law (Raday 1993: 18).

The Zionist movement that colonized Palestine was mostly a secular socialist movement. But in the formative years of the Israeli state, Labour Zionism secured its political and social hegemony only by forging an alliance with Jewish religious authorities, establishing conservative Orthodox Judaism as the state religion. This was more than a tactic to enlist a majority of voters into the governing bloc. The legitimacy of the Zionist project in speaking for Jews all over the world and in claiming Palestine as a homeland depended on a religious definition of both people and land. Likewise, to substantiate itself as a state 'for Jews' Israel depended on moulding a national culture around religious ritual. The year is patterned by the celebration of Jewish festivals, even if, for those who live in the socialist environment of a kibbutz, these have acquired a cultural rather than a devotional slant.

So Jewish Israeli women are caught in a contradiction between the secular discourse of equality and the religious discourse of Jewishness (accompanied always by its Other, non-Jewishness).

> At the most fundamental level, the level of constitutional principle, the Israeli legal system reflects basic conflict between a conviction that the religious Jewish nature of the state does, and should, inform our concept of womanhood and a commitment to the principle of equality (ibid.: 28).

We saw in Chapter 1 how in political movements stressing ethnic and national identity women tend to be positioned in relation to the family in such a way as to guarantee the integrity of the invoked community. As Nira Yuval-Davis says of Jewish women in Israel, they 'are being incorporated actively in the Zionist endeavour, not only in supplying humanpower to the national collectivity, but also legally and symbolically, as markers of its boundaries' (Yuval-Davis 1987: 67). Because of the elision between the national and religious identity of Jews, the Jewish national project depends more than most nationalisms on religious as well as patriarchal sexual control of women – for children born in relations that in any manner defy religious law are termed bastards and cannot be considered part of the Jewish collectivity.

It is certainly with this function in mind that the Zionist architects of the state conferred on religious authorities – whether Jewish, Muslim or Christian – control of the courts dealing with matters of personal status (Yuval-Davis 1987). In Israel you may consider yourself atheist yet can be married, divorced or buried only as an adherent of an officially sanctioned religion. There is no provision for a person of one religious backgound to marry someone of another. And if Orthodox Halakha Law confines and controls Jewish Israeli women, Muslim Shari'a Law is equally constraining for Muslim Israeli women.

Employment inequalities have also played a part in prompting a movement for women's rights in Israel. It has become the norm for Jewish Israeli women now, those outside as well as inside the kibbutz system, to seek employment. By the end of the 1980s they constituted 38 per cent of the civilian labour force (Izraeli 1993: 168). Like Palestinian Arab women they have become increasingly proletarianized. But the disadvantage women experience in this dimension of their lives has been less aggravational than personal status issues. In response to the inauguration of the United Nations Decade of Women, Prime Minister Yitshak Rabin appointed a committee to examine the status of Israeli women. It included recommendations on equality in the workplace, but it did not even address changes of policy in relation to personal status law, and the one area in which not even one of its 241 recommendations was accepted was 'the family' (Abdo and Yuval-Davis 1995: 309).

Beyond religion, other factors reinforce the cultural identification of Israeli women as wives and mothers. The threat to Palestinian Arab ethnic and national survival puts familial and community pressures on women to fulfil these roles. In the case of Jewish women the pressure comes from state natalist policy, due to the national anxiety to supplement unpredictable rates of inward migration to Israel (Sharoni 1995). Kibbutz women respond most obediently to appeals to bear children, with an average of four, against 2.8 for Jewish women in general (Safir 1993a: 58). A further factor bearing on Jewish women is the security situation, which tends to institutionalize them in the role of 'primary caretakers of a nation of soldiers' ready to fight and die in defence of the collectivity (Sharoni 1994: 130).

Bat Shalom has its antecedents in two oppositional movements that arose within Israeli society in the 1970s and 1980s, the women's movement and the peace movement. Both of these involved a different experience for Palestinian Arab and Jewish women.

In the 1950s and 1960s few women, whether Jewish or Palestinian

Arab, were publicly active on women's issues. Palestinian Arab women who had been active in branches of the Palestine Arab Women's Union and in local resistance under the Mandate were now scattered and reduced to tactics of everyday subsistence (Sharoni 1995). Many of the Jewish veterans of the Women's Workers Movement and the women's suffrage groups that had characterized the pre-state period had become part of the new ruling elite of Labour Zionism (Swirski 1993). For both ethnic groups, national viability was at stake, and as Yvonne Deutsch notes, in times of 'tension between national and gender identities, national identity tends to assume the greater importance' (Deutsch 1994: 103).

Palestinian women's activism did not begin again until the mid-1960s. In 1965, a year after it was founded in Jordan, the PLO set up its General Union of Palestinian Women. The occupation of the West Bank and Gaza followed in 1967, bringing a more intimate form of oppression as the occupying forces entered homes and harassed even women and children. As Tamar Mayer puts it, this 'intensified Palestinian nationalism in gendered ways by provoking a politicized response to the invasion of the private sphere' (Mayer 1994a: 63). Women became central to the strategy of *sumud* (steadfastness) that was the Palestinian's response to their new situation (Gluck 1997).

In the late 1970s women's committees were formed in the Occupied Territories, soon differentiated by their allegiance to the several factions of the PLO. And when the intifada broke out in 1987 it brought women of all ages onto the street and into practical organization: distributing food, teaching classes, supporting prisoners. Educated and middle-class Palestinian women were drawn into closer contact than before with grassroots activists in villages and refugee camps, and the contact fired a new expression of autonomy among women, leading to the beginnings of a critique of gender relations within the national movement. The rise of Islamic political movements, besides, with their unambiguous attack on women's autonomy, reinforced the understanding that women could not afford to defer their struggle till the PLO had achieved national liberation.[3]

Although this nascent women's movement in the Occupied Territories slowed down after one or two years, and was further disempowered by the male-managed peace process the PLO embarked on in 1991 (Gluck

---

3. Since the focus in this study is on Palestinian Arab women in Israel, I do not detail here development of the women's movement in the Occupied Territories. For this history see Warnock 1990; Young 1992; Strum 1992; Augustin 1993; Dajani 1994; Mayer 1994a, b and c; Abdo 1994; Sharoni 1995; Gluck 1997.

1997), it had a lasting effect on women's consciousness. Palestinian Arab women within Israel were also energized by events across the Green Line. Israel's transgression of the border had the effect of renewing contact between Palestinian Arab women either side of it. It provoked self-questioning among many of those within Israel about their identity in relation to the Jewish women among whom they lived and the Arab women from whom they had been separated for so long. The women's movement within the intifada made them more conscious of the way their mothers' generation had been submerged in the catastrophe of 1948, while they themselves had so far failed to forge a new identity and sense of direction (Espanioly 1994).

The hopes of that minority of Israeli Palestinian Arab women who were politically active had been invested in political parties, especially the accommodating Rakah and Hadash, the associated Democratic Socialist Front. At the same time, the energies of many of those more socially inclined were absorbed into the co-optative structures of Zionism, particularly Na'amat, the national women's organization of the Histradut to which an estimated 100,000 Palestinian Arab women belonged (Pope 1993). Now they began to look for an escape from this political conformity. The feminist group Al-Fanar, The Lighthouse, exemplifies the start of a new and autonomous feminist organizing among Israeli Palestinian Arab women (Abdo and Yuval-Davis 1995: 316).

Feminism among Jewish women had a different origin and trajectory. Barbara Swirski pinpoints the beginnings of the modern women's movement in Israel to seminars given at Haifa University around 1970 by women lecturers recently arrived from the United States (Swirski 1993: 294). Certainly it was inspired by 'new wave' feminism in Western Europe and the United States in the late 1960s and early 1970s, and was introduced mainly by Ashkenazi women with links to those countries (Sharoni 1995: 102).

As in Western Europe and North America, the approach was small-group discussion and consciousness-raising. The Haifa women formed a group they called Nilahem, standing for Women for a Renewed Society. The society they had in mind was Jewish Israeli society – for at this point they were concerned exclusively with their first-hand experience of the oppressiveness of gender relations, their own disadvantage relative to Jewish men. Similar groups soon followed in Tel Aviv and Jerusalem. The period was characterized by many small projects: women's centres, bookshops and publishing ventures, refuges and rape crisis centres, and a campaign to protect abortion rights. A series of feminist conferences attracting women from all over the country (and outside) began with one in 1978 in Beer Sheba. But they did not lead to the creation of a national organization (Swirski 1993; Sharoni 1995).

Quite early in the movement's life an uneasy association began with party politics and the formal representative system. Some feminists chose the route of contesting elections for the Knesset in alliance with non-feminist civil rights candidates and later through a short-lived Women's Party (Swirski 1993: 294). A tension between women dealing 'feminism from above' and those suspicious of such tangling with power has continued until the time of writing.

Just as the white women's movement in the United States and Britain angered black women by its easy ethnocentric assumptions, so in Israel the Ashkenazi women's movement (for such it really was at the start) was alienating to Jewish women of Misrahi or Oriental background. And as in those other countries, this exclusiveness involved a class dimension, for Misrahi women on the whole came from a social stratum that was economically disadvantaged relative to the Ashkenazim. The difference was that by the 1980s the Misrahi Jews had become a majority in Israel. In 1987 a group of Misrahi women university students formed their own organization, which began an exploration of the connections between gender and ethnic oppression (ibid.: 298).

When in 1991, after an interval of five years, there was a further feminist conference in Israel, Misrahi Jewish women demanded equal representation. Some Misrahi women felt they shared an oppression with Israeli Palestinian Arab women, for they are themselves Arabs in one sense of the term. Most Palestinian Arab women for their part saw Misrahi women as unambiguously part of the Jewish majority. Nevertheless, the two relatively disadvantaged groups both pressed for and obtained a guaranteed representation at the 1991 feminist conference, with a three-way sharing of participants, workshops and speakers. Although the innovation was controversial among Ashkenazi women, Misrahi Jewish and Palestinian Arab women felt that the two dimensions of their oppression in Israeli society had gained expression for the first time (Safran 1995: 24; Shiran 1993).

But the women touched by feminist ideas were a tiny minority of Jewish Israelis, and they were mainly in the cities. Women in the kibbutzim, and even more those of the moshavim, were slow to respond to feminism. Civil society in Israel in the 1970s was largely nationalist, its activism a 'recruited' activism. In any case the kibbutz system more than any other of the Israeli sub-cultures was socially homogeneous and unselfcritical. It was also closely tied to the major Zionist organizations like Na'amat that were widely seen as the proper vehicles for Israeli women's interests.

The results of a survey by women members presented to the General Council of the Kibbutz Artzi as early as 1958 had demonstrated that many women were dissatisfied with their status in the movement. The council had responded with recommendations for change, but could not oblige its kibbutzim to comply and there were few improvements in the next 20 years (Bowes 1986: 149). In the early 1980s a small group of women from the Artzi and Labour kibbutz groups persuaded their respective federations to create 'departments for the advancement of sex equality'. Staffed by coordinators with modest budgets, these became a focus for the energies of those women who wanted to be active on women's issues (Swirski 1993: 298). But the majority of kibbutz women were reluctant to acknowledge, indeed were shocked to hear it suggested, that 'positive action for women' might be needed in these communities purpose-designed for equality and sharing (Bowes 1986: 148).

Women's activism for peace

What proved a more effective vehicle for engaging kibbutz women was the peace movement. Israel's stunning defeat of the combined forces of the Arab world in the Six Day War was followed by a mood of triumphalism that was not conducive to opposition movements within the state. But national confidence and the national consensus was dented by the Israeli Defence Forces' poor showing in the Yom Kippur War of 1973, and peace-making became thinkable. We have seen that in 1978 Israel signed a peace agreement with one of its neighbours, Egypt, in exchange for the return of the Sinai Peninsula.

This same year an extra-parliamentary pressure group of both men and women, Peace Now (Shalom Ashav), was founded. It had the support of 'doves' in the Labour Party (suddenly in opposition for the first time since the founding of the state) and of Zionist parties to the left of Labour, such as Mapam and Ratz, the Citizens' Rights Movement. Many of its most active members were in one or other of the two secular kibbutz systems (Davis 1987: 89). Despite the fury it provoked on the right, Peace Now was by no means radical. The founding group were senior IDF officers. The writer Amos Oz, among the best known of its members, was at pains to emphasize that they were not 'pro-Palestinian'. He wrote:

> One can't compare Peace Now with the European peace movement. We are 'peaceniks' but we're no pacifists: most of us involved in Peace Now have at one time or another been on the battlefield – and if the worst were to happen and we found ourselves with our backs to the wall, we might fight again (Oz 1994: 47).

A more radical and left-wing Israeli peace movement had existed in a small way from the late 1960s, but in response to the Lebanon war in 1982 it began to take on a national significance, outflanking Peace Now in its content and its style. This movement was closer to the anti-Zionist parties supported by many of Israel's Palestinian Arabs, including Rakah/Hadash. Two initiatives within this 'progressive peace camp' that powerfully challenged the Israeli consensus were the Alternative Information Centre, prepared to break the law to contact and work with politically active Palestinians across the Green Line (Warschawski 1992), and Yesh Gvul, an organization supporting soldiers in the selective refusal of orders to carry out actions in the Occupied Territories that they considered contrary to human rights (Menuchin 1992).

The distinction between the two camps of the peace movement was not Zionism versus anti-Zionism, since membership on this score was inconsistent. They were more clearly distinguished by their different reasons for wanting withdrawal from the occupied Palestinian lands and peace with the Arab world. The mainstream movement was motivated primarily by Israeli self-interest – it saw the occupation as threatening to undermine security and/or the Jewish demographic majority. The progressive camp stressed human rights and was more consistent in support for an independent Palestinian state. The mainstreamers were wedded to US policy for the region. They remained unwilling to jeopardize an annual aid handout of $4 billion by approaching the PLO unless and until the USA itself was ready to do so. The progressive camp was more inclined to see the USA as part of the problem (Hurwitz 1992). It is doubtful whether even a small minority would have welcomed the amalgamation of Israel and Palestine into a single democratic state of mixed ethnicity, reaching from the Jordan to the Mediterranean.

Women's separate peace activism began in 1982. As Israel's wars began to seem a matter less of national survival than of military adventurism, so some women, like some men, began to feel less constrained by national loyalty, more ready to voice their doubts. Separate organization by women was prompted in part by women's dissatisfaction with the male dominance and masculine style of the existing peace movements, partly by women's perception of their gender-specific interests in peace and war. In the Yom Kippur War of 1973 Israel had clearly been fighting in self-defence. Far from resisting mobilization, some women had expressed anger on sex equality grounds at their exclusion from useful roles in defence of the country. But the Lebanon war of 1982 shifted perceptions. Many saw it as an aggressive and unjustified invasion by the Israeli Defence Force. It triggered powerful anti-military feeling both within the army and without. Women were involved in two initiatives, both demanding withdrawal from Lebanon but diverging markedly in their gender analysis. The group Parents Against Silence (mainly but not only women) campaigned for withdrawal from an unjust war and the return of their sons. They were popularly represented in the media as 'mothers', and the familial discourse they employed played into conventional women's roles in a patriarchal society. Certainly they were at pains to dissociate themselves from feminism. They folded in 1985 when Israel pulled out from most of Lebanon (Sharoni 1995: 107).

By contrast, the second group, Women Against the Invasion of Lebanon, proved to be just the beginning of a growing sequence of women's peace initiatives. Where Parents Against Silence had drawn the sting of reaction against them by playing the 'motherhood' card, Women Against the Invasion of Lebanon were women who had already been active in the women's movement and now began to develop a feminist analysis of militarism. They were viewed by both right and Zionist left as foolish extremists (Sharoni 1995: 108). The Lebanon war over, the group only lived up to its unpatriotic label by shifting its critique to the Israeli presence in the West Bank and Gaza, reshaping itself as Shani, Women Against the Occupation.

It was the outbreak of the intifada that turned women's pioneering peace initiative into something that, even if it remained a minority movement, was visible country-wide. The Israeli soldiers' brutal repression of stone-throwing Palestinians – and many of the insurgents were only children – was shocking to Israeli Jews, for whom the IDF, in which most of them had served, was a 'people's army' engaged in necessary defence. Simona Sharoni recalls:

> It was women, in small groups at first, who confronted these images and grasped the message that ending the Occupation was the primary issue and challenged the general climate of passivity and denial within Israeli society (ibid.: 111).

One subversive action involved women from the feminist magazine *Noga* installing a generator and a slide-projector on a Tel Aviv city-centre street to project disturbing photographs taken by journalists in the Occupied Territories and banned by the military censor.

In the same way as the change produced by the intifada in the nature of the conflict awoke a feminist consciousness among some Palestinian women, it also led many Jewish Israeli women to apply a feminist analysis to the gendered nature of their own state. It made some of them look for more contact with Palestinian Arabs, both in Israel and

Jewish women join Palestinian Arab women in an International
Women's Day march in Nazareth.

in the Occupied Territories. And as Jewish women proved themselves more committed to an open stand against the Israeli state, Palestinian Arab feminists on both sides of the Green Line felt more able to cooperate in their actions, or even join their movements. Shani began to organize house meetings between Jewish and Israeli Palestinian Arab women and visits to Occupied Territories (Deutsch 1994).

Women's peace actions took imaginative non-violent forms. One mobilized hundreds of women up and down the country in sewing embroideries for assembly into a huge Peace Cloth symbolically intended to cover the table on which, one day, a peace agreement would be signed. If such things had resonance with the kinds of women's anti-war protest seen in many other countries, this was no accident, because international links and conferences were all part of the process (Deutsch 1994).

One day in January 1988 ten Israeli Jewish women from the radical left took a decision to demonstrate together on the pavement of a Jerusalem square in solidarity with the Palestinian people. They wore black, and stood in silent vigil. Yvonne Deutsch describes what followed.

> Women in Black demonstrations spread to Tel Aviv and Haifa, and from there to kibbutzim, moshavim, and other villages around the country. By July 1990 participants counted some thirty women's vigils involving both Jews and Palestinians from Israel who demonstrated in black against the Occupation every Friday, at the same places and times, often to cries of 'whores!', 'traitors!', 'Arafat's whores!', and similar expressions. As the popularity of Women in Black grew throughout Israel, these protest groups provided a model for women's protest groups in other parts of the world. Within a short space of time women in the USA, Italy, the Netherlands, Australia, Germany and England had organized similar solidarity vigils (ibid.: 90).

Some Israeli Palestinian Arab women joined Jewish women in Women in Black vigils, notably in Haifa. But the majority continued to work separately, and put their energies into collecting food and medical supplies for the Palestinians under occupation (Espanioly 1993: 151).

For three years women's peace activism held the high ground in Israel, capturing media attention. In December 1988 a national Women and Peace Coalition was formed, involving many of the Women in Black groups. Campaigns, conferences and exchanges were organized. A parallel initiative, the Israel Women's Peace Net (Reshet), set up the following year, involved prominent women from the political mainstream of Zionist centre and left parties. In December 1990 6,000 Israeli and Palestinian women, together with women from Europe and the USA, joined in a march for peace in Jerusalem.

This 'Women Go for Peace' march was the peak of the Israel women's peace movement and the last major event before the Iraqi leader Saddam Hussein invaded Kuwait and retribution was dealt by the USA with Western and Arab allies. The new alignment of forces in the region produced by the Gulf War, the enforced passivity with which Israel was obliged to suffer attack by Iraqi missiles, and the PLO's pro-Iraqi stance, threw the Israeli peace movement into disarray. Jewish and Palestinian Arab women were disillusioned by each other's reactions to the war. Palestinian Arab women were disappointed by Jewish women's failure to take a stand against Western intervention. Jewish women were shaken by Palestinian women's failure to condemn Saddam Hussein. Joint demonstrations almost came to a halt for a while (Deutsch 1994).

As we saw in Chapter 1, international moves to resolve the Israel–Palestine dispute followed from 1991 as part of the USA's post-Gulf War strategy for the region. They culminated in the 'Oslo Accords', which led to the creation of a Palestinian Authority and steps towards a sharing of power in the Occupied Territories. The masculinity of the top-level peace talks was not lost on women (Sharoni 1995). Hanan Ashrawi's prominence on television screens did not disguise from women that on both sides the negotiators were men and that it would be men's priorities that any peace arrangements would enshrine. That cloth the women's movement had so diligently stitched was not on the table.

But perhaps, in retrospect, it seemed better not to have shared authorship of such a compromise. What ensued was yet more repressive violence in the Occupied Territories, in which this time the PLO's new police forces were implicated. Then Arafat's most ferocious Palestinian critics, the militant Islamists Hamas and Islamic Jihad, turned to terrorist killings in Israel. Political reaction and religious fundamentalisms threatened women of both communities and on both sides of the line, but they did so in such different ways that fear and demoralization immobilized all but a few of the former women's peace activists.

There were, however, two things the women's peace movement had achieved between 1988 and 1990 that could not be thrown into reverse. One was a three-way process of dialogue between Israeli Jewish women, Israeli Palestinian Arab women and women in the occupied Palestinian lands. Political events might interrupt but could not end the solidarity work, the visits, joint demonstrations, working groups and conferences. Of particular symbolic importance had been the commitment of Israeli women to maintain contact with Palestinian prisoners and monitor their treatment in Israeli gaols in the group called Women for Palestinian Women Political Prisoners.

The second ineradicable achievement flowed directly from this cross-communal contact and provided the common ground on which the alliance could develop and grow. It was a new insight, a genuinely new knowledge, created in women's practice on both sides of the Green Line: men's sexual violence against women and the military violence of the state were inextricably linked. Women for Palestinian Women Political Prisoners were getting clear evidence that what Palestinian women had been telling them was true. When women were its objects, Israeli military repression in the West Bank and Gaza took unmistakably sexual forms: molestation, harassment and on occasion rape (Strum 1992; Young 1992). Jewish women started asking themselves questions about what their own partners, fathers, sons and male friends might be guilty of in the West Bank, and questioned their own relationship with these men in a new way. Israeli women demonstrating for peace could not mistake the violence in the sexualized insults they received from male patriots on the streets. There were reports of a sudden increase in incidents of domestic battering by Jewish men during those weeks of the Gulf War when they were reduced to impotence as Scud missiles fell, required to sit passively at home while other men in other armies exulted in retaliation (Sharoni 1992: 459). If gender identities are formed in such violent processes, then the gender relation had to be a key political issue. And if a militarized society was a disaster both to women of the oppressing community as well as the community of the oppressed, an alliance between women would help both groups.

Simona Sharoni recounts a story that made newspaper headlines in 1991. A Jewish man, Gilad Shemen, 23 years old, shot and killed his Jewish girlfriend, Einav Rogel. Two years before, during military service in Gaza, Shemen had shot and killed a 17-year-old Palestinian girl, Amal Muhammad Hasin, who was reading a book on her porch at the time. A military court convicted him of 'carelessness' in causing Amal's death, but he was released after appeal. Einav Rogel, it later transpired, had been suffering violence at Gilad's hands long before he killed her. She had told nobody. Sharoni says: 'she was not able to make any connection between the death of Amal Muhammad Hasin and her own life in the shadow of fear and violence that Gilad brought to their relationship. Einav lived in a society that refuses to address such linkages' (ibid.: 447).

But it was stories like this that led feminists to make those very links. By late 1996, when this account ends, the women's movements in Israel and Palestine had a clearer analysis of violence as a continuum from the intimately personal to the national and military. Whether you are struck by a man's hand or by a laser-guided missile, gender power, they were saying, has something to do with the matter.

5

Bat Shalom: A women's group
for peace

The busy road-junction at Megiddo is more than just a bus-stop on the
highway from Tel Aviv to Nazareth. It is an ancient crossing at the
heart of the Levant that armies have trodden for millennia. On one
corner is the hill of Har-Megiddo, an archaeological site with excava-
tions from the First and Second Temple periods. This is the biblical
Armageddon where the battle between the forces of Good and Evil will
be fought in the Last of Days. In the present of days, too, it is a site
of confrontation – though a non-violent one. This is where women
protesting Israel's occupation of the Palestinian territories often choose
to hold their vigils. The target of their protest stands across the road
from Armageddon: a barbed-wire prison camp where 2,000 Palestinians
from the Occupied Territories are detained.

The network of peace activists called Bat Shalom of Megiddo,
Nazareth and The Valleys is not an easy project to describe. In fact,
they have difficulty describing themselves. For a start, many of the
members live an hour's drive from Megiddo junction, and as many live
in the surrounding hills as in 'the valleys', so that not everyone who
belongs to it would even recognize the name. And there is incomplete
agreement as to who may be in and who may be outside this group. In
some ways the membership is simply a matter of who turned up to the
last meeting, protest or event. But despite its blurred edges and stop–
start character, the project does exist, had a three-year history by the
time I visited it in 1996, and proved extraordinarily instructive in the
profound differences it spans and its relationship to the conflict that
surrounds it.

When the Israeli women's peace movement faltered during the Gulf
War and the Madrid–Oslo peace initiatives that followed soon after,
Women in Black in this area persisted longer than most. Even when the
vigils finally ended, some of the local women kept up their momentum
and transferred their energies to a new project in Jerusalem. It comprised a women's centre in Jewish West Jerusalem, with the name Bat
Shalom, in partnership with a similar centre established by Palestinian

women in East Jerusalem, an alliance they called 'The Jerusalem Link'. But travelling 150 kilometres to Jerusalem for meetings was just not practical and in 1993 Lily Traubmann and a handful of others decided to start a local group for the area they lived in, the southern part of Galilee and the northern part of The Triangle.

The boundaries of this provincial Bat Shalom are indistinct, determined by how far you feel it worth travelling to get to an evening meeting or a midday demo. It draws in women from a dozen kibbutzim around Megiddo, the fertile Jezreel and Beit She'an valleys, and the forested Menashe Hills. At its geographical centre is the Jewish town of Afula, while on the edges of the circle lie the Arab towns of Nazareth and Iksal to the east, and Umm El-Fahm and Ar-ara to the west. If you stand in the cotton and wheat fields of the plain as dusk falls, the twinkling lights of these towns around the skyline more or less delineate Bat Shalom's territory.

As well as continuing to press for those still elusive goals, a serious peace process, an end to the occupation and the creation of a fully independent Palestinian state, the new group decided to work on relations between Jewish women and Palestinian Arab women living *within* the state of Israel. This was partly in reaction to the fact that, now it was no longer dangerous to meet women from the Occupied Territories, even elite and politically middle-of-the-road Jewish women were getting in on this act. It seemed time to reassess strategy. Partly it was a wish to make a politics that 'begins where we are' – in other words to reach out to *local* Palestinian Arabs. Lily and the other Jewish women who had stood on the roadside as Women in Black in the 1980s had been surprised and pleased when some of these women, uninvited, quietly began to join the vigils. Now they wanted to deepen this partnership for peace and widen it to touch more local women from both communities.

The core group of the new local Bat Shalom established what they termed a 'forum', not so much a committee as a regular open meeting. They drew in women through the kibbutz network on the Jewish side, and on the Palestinian Arab side they relied partly on the Na'amat grapevine, since two of the core members worked for this Histradut women's organization. The forum set up activities of several kinds, choosing a dual focus of peace protest and 'coexistence'. They saw the former as their most urgent responsibility and they tried to respond to political developments promptly, with whatever actions seemed appropriate. They issued press statements and supported national protests. But their most characteristic form of action was roadside vigils in the style of Women in Black. Standing with placards in Hebrew and Arabic, they were often the target of abuse and insult.

To carry their gendered peace politics to a wider circle of women, in the three years between their formation and my visit in 1996 Bat Shalom Megiddo had organized a string of cultural and educational events. They were held alternately in the Jewish kibbutzim and the Arab villages and towns. The Palestinian Arab women would for instance mark International Women's Day with a joint discussion or other event in a centre such as Nazareth. And each year the Jewish women were hosts during the festivity of Succot, the Feast of Tabernacles, as celebrated in a secular way by the left-wing kibbutz movement.

Bat Shalom's focus on coexistence of course meant addressing Palestinian Arab disadvantage in Israel. The group had been particularly pleased with two evenings of drama improvisation around themes of Jewish discrimination against Israeli Palestinians. They had dealt with acutely divisive issues of identity, oppression and prejudice, in a way that allowed for laughter. But the most sustained effort of Bat Shalom of Megiddo, Nazareth and The Valleys had been running weekly workshops, drawing a regular attendance of around fifteen women, both Jew and Palestinian Arab. These were led by professional facilitators. The first, which ran for two years, addressed 'coexistence'. The second, still current when I was with them in 1996, was dealing with 'leadership' from a women's point of view.

The distant Bat Shalom in Jerusalem was valued by the local women as a source of national and international connectedness and also of small grant funding (to pay facilitators or hire a bus). But the relationship was not without friction. The Jerusalem project was seen as too much in the pocket of establishment women, including key Knesset members. 'A bit yuppy', some said. And there was annoyance when they refused requests for funding because they judged the Megiddo group insufficiently 'organized' or insufficiently 'feminist'.

My first difficulty on arriving at Megiddo was to understand just who comprised the membership of the group and whom I should be getting to know, working with and ultimately interviewing. I began to understand that the project was a series of overlapping circles, each defined pragmatically. I should begin with the women who normally attended the organizing meetings of something they thought of as 'Bat Shalom', gradually shift to the somewhat larger circle committed to turning out on political demonstrations, thence to women attending the current workshop and further still to those attracted mainly by the social events. In fact, some of the women in these last two circles, although the organizing group thought of them as being 'in' Bat Shalom, were not themselves so sure that they 'belonged' to such a thing. While I was in Israel I attended all Bat Shalom activity and interviewed 25 women, including most of the core and others from the various circles. I also chose to interview one or two women of the old feminist peace community of the region who had positively chosen not to be 'in' this current local version of the movement. Their observations on Bat Shalom helped me to understand its nature more clearly and to define its outer edges.

Handling identity difference

The Catholic and Protestant women of the Women's Support Network in Belfast, despite community segregation, at least share their inner-city working-class experience. And in Medica, as we shall see, there are many graduated shades of belonging to the different Bosnian ethnicities. By contrast, the Bat Shalom group is deeply fissured down the middle, comprising two clear 'sides', Jew and Palestinian Arab. We have seen that they come from sharply contrasted environments, two bounded ethnic clusters without mixed marriages, mixed parentage or shared lifestyles to soften the distinction between them.

The Jewish 'side' of Bat Shalom Megiddo is a strongly homogeneous group in ethnic or cultural terms. They are almost all members of the kibbutz system, sharing a rural existence far removed from the life of the city Jews of Tel Aviv or Jerusalem, or even the town-dwellers of Afula, the local Jewish shopping and business centre. Furthermore, although one or two come from Takam (Labour Party) kibbutzim, the great majority come from the Artzi (Mapam/Meretz) kibbutz system. They are thus all oriented towards a secular socialism.

There are several important internal dimensions of difference *within* the collective identity 'Jewish Israelis' between which Bat Shalom Megiddo does not (yet) attempt to build bridges. The kibbutz population on which it draws is, by a process of informal but effective exclusion, almost entirely Ashkenazi. Unlike Bat Shalom Jerusalem, the local group has so far balked at reaching out to Mizrahim (Middle Eastern Jews), feeling that their greater adherence to religious orthodoxy and right-wing politics would make this, as yet, too difficult a challenge. Nor does the group include any women from the more recent waves of immigrants to Israel such as the Russian and Ethiopian Jews. Since income and resources are shared in the kibbutz system, socio-economic class differences between members are also muted, so that all the women are effectively of a kind within an Israeli middle or managerial class. All live inextravagant lives and have as a matter of principle shared both decision-making roles and menial and manual work in collective kitchens and laundries. If they have particular expertise it is mostly childcare or youth work. If they have trained or worked outside the kibbutz system for periods in their lives they have eventually returned to it.

Within this rather homogeneous community, the main differentiation is one of generation. A minority of the women, the older ones, have memories of life before Israel. They have come from the Jewish Diaspora, before or soon after 1948, some from South American countries, some from Europe. Some, as children, escaped the Holocaust. Nitsa Shapira, for instance, remembered hard early days in Israel, living in tents, gaining their bread with minimal equipment. Pesi Hildesheim came as a child from Romania and grew up in Israel determined to join a kibbutz and be an agricultural worker. She was allocated to looking after chickens – a start that did not prevent her eventually serving as general secretary of her kibbutz. Most of the Bat Shalom Jewish women, though, were second-generation Israelis. Amit Cohen, Yael Ring and Esther Steinberg, for example, are such *sabras*, born on a kibbutz where the cypresses their parents had planted had already grown tall and the avocado and lemon trees were bearing fruit. They were bred to a sense of belonging here and nowhere else.

Both generations feel that recent developments have undermined the transformative ideals of the kibbutz, and few think the kibbutz is as sex-equal in reality as it is in principle. But there is still a loyalty to the ideal and a warm appreciation of the practical sustenance this society gives its members, especially as parents. 'You can put so much energy into the good things, the important things, without worrying about money and business and stuff,' Esther said. The one social gulf these rather similar Jewish members of Bat Shalom have set out to bridge is that separating the kibbutz from the Palestinian Arab villages and towns, so near and yet so far away.

The Palestinian Arab 'side' of Bat Shalom also have some homogeneity as a group, although less than their Jewish partners. None of them belongs to those minorities among the non-Jewish minority: Druzes, Bedouin or Circassians. They are similar in their 'small town' existence, and share the misfortune of being the leftovers of 1948, Israel's second-class citizens. All have long family memories of belonging to this bit of ancient Palestine. Nahla Shedafni, for instance, answered my question 'How long have your family lived in Iksal?' with a precise 'Four hundred and fifty years'.

But the Palestinian Arab women are more internally differentiated than the Jewish group in terms of religion, class and education. The initiating group of Bat Shalom Megiddo are drawn from both the Muslim majority and the Christian Arab minority. And whether Christian or Muslim by background, they vary in the degree of their

A face reveals plenty about the self, little about ethnic or national collective identity.

attachment to church or mosque. The Palestinian Arab 'side' also includes a greater range in terms of income and educational qualifications.
Some are professional women with university degrees from Jerusalem
or Tel Aviv, relatively mobile and connected. Take Amal Khoury, for
instance, one of the community's few women lawyers, or Rodaina Jarisy,
with her doctorate in social work. Others are working more locally in
their villages, typically as education, health or community workers. Suad
Abd el-Hadi is a good example. Discouraged by her father from moving
away to study nursing, she instead became secretary of the village school
in Iksal. She is unusual in driving her own car.

The social geography of Israel, it will be evident from the previous
chapter, gives Jews and Palestinian Arabs little chance to get to know
each other. Those Bat Shalom women who had been active in political
parties or in prior peace initiatives had some firsthand knowledge of
'the other'. But for the characteristic women drawn in by Bat Shalom's
open activities there had been little occasion for meeting and mixing.
Even in Haifa, Galilee's main city, Jews and Arabs live adjacent but not
together. And out in Galilee and The Triangle the kibbutzim have little
interaction with the Arab places with which they share a landscape.

The Kibbutz Artzi Federation stresses coexistence. In its schools, as
Yehudit Zeidenberg remembers, 'We were taught, all of us, that they
are our good neighbours and friends.' But the ideal was seldom substantiated. Sonia Zarchi recalls a rare outing to the nearby village. 'When
we were children we sometimes went there, walked there, it was like a
"walking trip". We visited them, we met children the same age as we
were, we had an event together. Maybe once or twice, it was, not more.'

Most kibbutzim employ a few Arabs as day-labourers. Just a few
unusual kibbutzniks made a point of getting to know them and celebrate
their festivals. But to the majority they were invisible, and better so.
'They eat in the same place we eat,' said Vera Jordan, regretfully. 'You
just don't even see them.' Likewise outside, she explained, the Jews 'go
from the kibbutz to the shopping centre, or they go into Haifa to a
movie, or they go to a seaside resort – places where there's no chance
to meet Arabs'. The lack of provision for secular ceremonies places a
huge impediment in the way of mixity. Not only do kibbutzim make life
impossible for the very few who marry Arabs, they make death difficult
too. Vera's kibbutz not long ago was exceptionally accommodating in
agreeing to bury, since nowhere else would accept it, the body of a
Jewish woman who had married an Arab man and gone to live in his
community.

It is not surprising that for many of the Jewish women of the
kibbutzim, public protest felt 'too sharp'. Esther Steinberg, for example,

admired the demonstrations and said, 'It's important.' But she added, 'I don't like to *do* it. I feel like maybe I'm afraid.' Lily recognized that the majority of Israeli Jews 'will only ever have spoken to an Arab man as his boss – and not at all to an Arab woman'. So the new organization needed to begin with friendship. And there were women who were hungry for that. Sonia was one of them.

> It's very rare, but occasionally I travel in a bus and there'll be an Arab person sitting next to me. I always want to talk to them, to say, you know, I'd like to be your friend, let's get to know each other. But then I say to myself – well, what could I say to them? And anyway it's, like patronizing, like racist even, isn't it, to feel like that, to want to know them just because they're Arabs? Besides, if you want to start talking, you have to ask questions. And maybe ... So I don't do it. I just have the feeling I'd like to.

So, Sonia said, she had signed up for a Bat Shalom workshop. 'I hadn't actually done anything to meet Arab people, but when somebody was looking for me, I immediately knew that's what I wanted.'

The Palestinian Arab women brought with them to Bat Shalom a rather different perception. Oppression sets up a one-way mirror. The oppressed may be invisible to the oppressor, but from the other side of the mirror Palestinian Arabs feel they have a clearer view of Jews. For one thing, while very few Jews bother to learn Arabic, Israeli Arabs learn Hebrew from an early age and are saturated in the dominant culture. 'My children watch TV all the time,' says Amal. 'It's controlled by the Israeli authorities: Hebrew language, Hebrew news, Hebrew mentality, everything.' For another they must deal, inside and outside work, with the powerful institutions of Israeli society. Who could be a better placed observer than Rodaina, for instance, this thoughtful, political Palestinian Arab woman who works in the heart of the Zionist system as local organizer of women's activity in the Histradut?

What the Palestinian women wanted out of involvement in Bat Shalom was, first and foremost, to give muscle to their struggle for a Palestinian state for their nationals in the Occupied Territories and the wider diaspora, and for improved rights for themselves in Israel, by entering into alliance with progressive Jews and carrying their actions onto Jewish turf. But also, as with the Jews, the wider circle of Palestinian Arab women in Bat Shalom had a second motivation that had less to do with regional politics than with coexistence. Samia Shehadna, for example, felt that while Palestinian Arabs in Israel had long since got the message that they had to live with the Jews, Jews hadn't yet 'really understood that they have to live with us. I'm always looking for Jewish people so as to help them know it.' Rowaida Assaid said she herself met

Jews often enough. Her aim in joining Bat Shalom's workshop had been, in a way, *for* Jews, to dispel their fears, 'and show them I'm not a monster'. Suad took particular pleasure in wearing her traditional headscarf out and about among Jews to show them that 'You can be a Muslim without being a terrorist.' They all felt, despite the identity gap between them, optimistic about being able to work with these particular kibbutz women because, as Nahla said, 'They're not extremists, they don't blame Arabs and they've been consistent in working for peace.' A search for political partners among the Misrahi community, the moshav farmers or Afula shopkeepers would, they felt, have less chance of success.

There were misconceptions, of course, and perhaps this was one of them: the Jewish women might have been surprised to find that they were not the only ones who felt themselves to be a touch altruistic. The Palestinian Arab women too felt they had a favour to bestow on their neighbours. In addition there were privately expressed cultural criticisms. Some of the Jewish women complained that 'Some Arabs are too passive, don't take things into their own hands,' while the Palestinian Arab women felt a bit of 'bossiness' from some on the Jewish side, an assumption that everyone sees things their way. Israeli Ashkenazi women are very direct. I found it disconcerting at times. Vera understood it could be a problem for Muslim women, particularly. 'Telling the truth is a value stressed by Jewish and Christian people. But the most important value for a Muslim is something else: it's not to hurt you, your self-respect. She won't tell you something you wouldn't like to hear.' The problem, she said, was 'knowing what's just politeness, what's really meant. It's not just a question of language, it's different codes. I just can't *feel* it, I'm not sure.' And if sometimes the Jewish women in Bat Shalom seemed insensitive to Arab realities, their partners sometimes trampled on Jewish sensitivities too.

So, in my conversations with them I was the recipient of many stories that ended with hurt feelings. But these are not, I think, the things to stress in this analysis, because cultural difference was not the main challenge taken up by Bat Shalom. This was not the hole into which they were most liable to tumble. In the end, affection and goodwill were mostly capable of ironing out such differences. Nitsa wound up a discussion with Vera by saying (it was elliptical but clear enough): 'After all, I don't trust many Jews that I can't stand, and I love one Arab that I trust.' It was political differences that were the complex and costly ones – political (as the Belfast women would say) with a big P.

Peace: another kind of war

Early 1996, when I was with them, was a difficult time not only for Bat Shalom but for all Israeli peace activists. Both Jews and Palestinian Arabs in Israel had placed hope in Yasir Arafat and the PLO. At first some, at least, of the Bat Shalom women had felt something good could eventually come out of the 'Gaza and Jericho first' accord. But Arafat was proving not only weak but undemocratic, even brutal, in the use of his new powers. This was undermining the confidence of both Israeli Palestinian Arabs and Jews, in Bat Shalom and other peace organizations, in their former bold call for respect and validation for the PLO. Some, at least, thought that the Meretz alliance of left-wing parties could push the peace process along through its new governing coalition with Labour, but more and more it seemed that Shimon Peres was talking peace and acting war. So a lot of women knew what Nabila Espanioly meant when she said at a conference in Jerusalem: 'What we're seeing is that their peace isn't our peace. I worked for this peace. But now it's arrived, I still can't dance.'

And even if Arafat and Peres were disappointing to the peace constituency, the faltering steps they had taken towards agreement were quite enough to get each branded a traitor by his own set of extremists. While I was working with the Megiddo women, the media were carrying reports of the trial of right-winger Yigael Amir for the assassination some months before of Peres's predecessor, the peace-broker Yitshak Rabin. Completely unrepentant, he smirked at his fellow Jews from their television screens and warned them, stirring memories of Auschwitz, 'You'll end up soap for Arafat.' He could not easily be dismissed as an isolated freak. Right-wing and politico-religious Jews were demonstrating with placards that read: 'Peres, you're next to go.' And the shock-troops of reaction, the settlers in the Occupied Territories and East Jerusalem, were fuelling violence by making increasingly provocative land-grabs.

Meanwhile, outflanking Arafat, Hamas and Islamic Jihad were frightening ordinary people in Israel and collaborators in the Occupied Territories. In the space of the one month I was there, five bombs took Israeli lives in busy urban centres. In revenge the Israeli government set about exacting collective punishment by wrecking suspects' homes and closing the Green Line, locking out thousands of Palestinians from their jobs in Israel and ruining what there was of a Palestinian economy.

What could Bat Shalom do at such a moment? Women needed to make themselves seen. Increased militarization in Israel was setting back yet further Jewish women's agenda for change, and the new forces

Taking a public stand for peace. Bat Shalom women often choose busy road junctions to display their bilingual message.

in Palestinian society were pushing women back from feminism to Islamic fundamentalism. So the group went out on the roadside yet again. They had no problem in presenting a united face for this purpose and proclaiming, 'Don't let this de-rail the peace process', 'No to violence, yes to peace'. But there was no denying that the suicide bombings made all Jews look fearfully on any Arab face in the crowd, and suspicion gnawed deeper still when it was learned that the Tel Aviv bomber and his explosives had been carried into Israel by a lorry-driver from a Galilee village, known to some women in Bat Shalom. And from the perspective of Fatma Younis living in an Arab village like Ar-ara, it seemed that the kibbutz women could only with difficulty understand the vice in which Israeli Palestinian Arabs felt jammed.

> Yes, all right, you demonstrate against the violence. But you don't hurt like we hurt. We do care about the innocent Jews that are killed. But those bombs kill Arabs too. If we're in a bus when a bomber strikes, we're killed like anyone else. At the same time, if we're in the area near that bus, and they find out we're Arabs, we're attacked by the Jews around. Besides, we also care about our own people in the Occupied Territories, our families and friends. It's very difficult for us: we don't know where we belong.

So no, in difficult circumstances like this, mere cultural difference was not the problem. It was politics, the identification of its members with different political positions on nationhood, citizenship and competing rights to land and property that most challenged the viability of the Bat Shalom alliance.

Dimensions of political division

Bat Shalom Megiddo was clearly putting more weight on friendship and coexistence than the Women's Support Network in Belfast. In the absence of a more experienced constituency there was little choice. On the other hand the women had not shied away from highly public, even risk-taking, political activity. This called for agreed points of political principle. They were generally held to be: the withdrawal of Israel from the Occupied Territories and the creation of a fully independent and sovereign Palestinian state; peace between Israel and the new Palestine; and the establishment of democratic and just regimes in both states. But when I began to ask women to tell me in more detail what these things meant to them, I found that underlying apparently simple points of agreement were an alarming number of ambiguities, alternative readings and potential divergences.

The principal sources of divergence lie in individual and group histories of political positioning and affiliation, where women's sense of self comes from. The stories of two women in the core group of Bat Shalom may help to exemplify this. One is Palestinian, one Jewish, both are in their sixties, both are proud to call themselves feminists.

Samira Khoury was born in 1929 and her first taste of political action was as a five-year-old in a school classroom at the time of the uprising against the British Mandate. Born and raised in Nazareth to Orthodox Christian parents, she grew up a strong, confident young woman and trained as a teacher in Jersualem before getting her first job in the coastal town of Akka (Acre), another centre of Palestinian Arab population.

When the Israeli state was declared and Israeli forces swept across Galilee, dispossessing Palestinians of land and property, she remembers the population of Nazareth 'doubling in a night' as the refugees flooded in. But Nazareth was not exempt from the sacking. 'The Hagganah took people from their beds, beat them, tortured them,' she said. 'They destroyed everything in the houses. They mixed the corn and the flour and sugar.' They rounded up the young Palestinian men and interned them. Samira, then 17 years old, mobilized with other women, steeling each other against running away, demanding the release of the men.

Samira married in 1950. In 1956 a large area of Palestinian agricultural land on the edge of town was confiscated by the Israeli government for the construction of a Jewish twin city, Nazareth Illit. Her husband's family was among those who had land seized at this time. The people of Nazareth camped in the orchards and resisted the bulldozers. She took part in demonstrations of Al-Ard, the Organization for the Defence of the Land, and saw hundreds imprisoned.

Samira had supported the UN partition plan and to this day feels bitter about the betrayal of the promise of a Palestinian state and the brutality involved in the establishing of the Israeli one. But, she says now, 'Life had to go on.' She joined the Israeli Communist Party at an early age, and in the 1970s became involved in dialogue groups with Jews, because she was sure it could only be by allying with progressive Jews that Palestinians would get their rights. She helped found Tandi, the communist-backed Movement of Democratic Women in Israel. She has always been active in Hadash (the communist alliance into which the Communist Party merged in 1965), and more recently formed a system of women's help-lines and refuges in and near Nazareth.

Vera Jordan was born a year or two after Samira, in Berlin where her father was a shopkeeper, a communist. Soon after Vera's birth he was imprisoned by the Nazis and on his release, in 1935, the family emigrated to begin a new life in Uruguay. She recalls how as a child she had pigtgails, something unusual in Uruguay. Another child called after her one day: 'Jewish Polish Nazi'. The words made no sense, but their ugly message was clear enough. She was a foreigner, and detestable. Once a teacher told her off with the words, 'In *our* country, little girls don't sit on the floor.' Vera remembers even now the shock of recognizing, 'So I'm not Uruguayan.' Much later, when she was 16, a Catholic teacher chided her, 'You don't know how to speak Hebrew? Your own language?' 'He told me I should work on my identity,' she says. 'So I did. And in that way I found it.'

But when she came to Israel in 1955, a young woman of 20, it was not because she was a Zionist. That came later. An admirer of the principles of the kibbutz, Vera came first and foremost to put communism into practice. She joined many other South Americans at Kibbutz Ramot Menashe, a left-wing, atheist Zionist community founded in the 1948 upheaval on Arab 'absentee' land. For most of her working life she has been a kibbutz accountant. She married and had one son. Her party has been Mapam, the left-wing Zionist party. 'And in those days,' she says, nostalgically, 'left meant really left.' She helped found and worked in the Kibbutz Artzi's Department for the Equality of the Sexes. When the peace movement began she joined Peace Now, couldn't stand its sexism, and soon became active instead in Women in Black and Reshet, and in a rape crisis centre in Haifa.

Vera is deeply committed to working for peace with Palestinians but never underestimates the difficulties in the way of mutual understanding. 'We want peace and we have to work it out. How. What. On every item, one by one. Because I don't know what is emotionally charged for them, and they don't know what is emotionally charged for me.'

These are the kinds of belongings that have shaped Bat Shalom women's political sense of self. On each side, women peace activists have to be careful not to run too far ahead of their much more conservative and traditionalist constituencies, the kibbutz and the Palestinian community. And they are characteristically supporters of different political parties. Although there is no complete mapping, many of the Jews belong like Vera to left-wing Zionist Mapam/Meretz, while many of the Palestinians are active like Samira in the non-Zionist Communist Party/Hadash. Together these comprise Israel's left-of-centre, so that party affiliations are not a serious source of separation. It is simply that women who give so much time and energy to party organizations sometimes have little left over for Bat Shalom.

From the way women described to me their individual opinions, deeply coloured by ethnic background, I began to map dimensions and distances of political difference. The three major sources of political disagreement that challenge Bat Shalom as an alliance are: the precise arrangements for a Palestinian state, the nature of a future Israel and, most fundamentally, the issue of land.

What kind of 'Palestinian state'? It should not be surprising perhaps that it is precisely those Jewish women who most value the existence of Israel as 'a home for the Jews' (and this is one of many definitions of being a Zionist) who are best able to sympathize with a Palestinian woman's desire for a state of her own. Some non-Zionist (or, as Hannah Knaz termed herself, 'post-Zionist') women, feeling that the Jews were misguided in trying to create an exclusive 'nation' state in the first place, see no value in setting up a second nation-state alongside the first. Hannah is a former Women in Black/Women and Peace activist. She is not a member of Bat Shalom, but rather a sisterly critic on its margins. Talking with her helped me clarify the boundaries of the group. Her constitutional dream would be one of dissolving nation-states into a confederal Middle East, Israel softened into some kind of not necessarily Jewish 'entity' (among others). Most of the Palestinian Arab members of Bat Shalom would agree, as would some of the Jews. Yehudit Zeidenberg, for one. She says, 'I think I'm lacking a "nation bone" in my body.' But the unifying position of Bat Shalom is more pragmatic. Allowing for existing nationalisms and the reality of nation-states, it goes no further than the slogan: 'Two states for two peoples.'

But there are different ways of reading even that. It is possible for a woman who is powerfully motivated by the Zionist ideal to want, at heart, a Palestinian state in the Occupied Territories because it is better for Israel. After all, one reading of 'two states for two people' can be 'a second state to secure the Jewish purity of the first'. If the Israeli Palestinian Arabs had a 'home to go to', they might, perhaps, who knows, *prefer* to go there, or at least stop pressing for Israel to become something other than a *Jewish* state. Palestinian Arab women, too, can be a little equivocal around this issue. They may dearly want to see a homeland for the scattered souls in the Palestinian diaspora, but deep down many have little desire, as individuals, to exchange their stable status as minority citizens (albeit disadvantaged ones) in a rather prosperous and orderly Israeli state for a Palestinian 'homeland' that, on current evidence, may be desperately poor, veering dangerously between anarchy, dictatorship and religious fundamentalism.

Other variations among the group on what the Palestinian state would mean concern policy on Jerusalem and on Jewish settlers in the West Bank. Israel's victory in the 1967 war fulfilled one recurring theme in the Zionist dream, that of gaining control of Jerusalem in its entirety.

Some of the most violent episodes since the Madrid/Oslo peace accords have been over Israel's colonizing strategy on the Palestinian side of the city. Where would Jerusalem stand in a 'two state' future? The Palestinian Arab women would vary as to whether they envisage a Jerusalem divided in two or a unified, but internationally administered, city. But the Jews are more emotionally divided than this.

Lily, in whose socialist and feminist politics Zionism plays no part, has few feelings for Jerusalem, except to despair at the way it represents a block to peace. Vera says of this close friend, 'She'd just like Jerusalem to disappear into thin air.' And she does admit, 'That might be easier. But if it did *I feel I would disappear too*, I just wouldn't be here.' The moment she first set eyes on Jerusalem when she arrived as a young woman in Israel it was a kind of epiphany: 'I felt I'd found my home. I asked myself, where had I been before?' On the other hand Pesi, whom Vera sees as even more wedded to the Zionist ideal than herself, nevertheless never gives up her insistence that cooperation is possible: 'For me, Jerusalem ought to be a normal city. At first two cities perhaps, but gradually becoming one, with the holy places held in common. Separated and together at the same time.'

And what kind of 'Israel'? The Palestinian Arab members of Bat Shalom agree with the Jewish members that Israel has the right to a secure existence. They accept the state as a *fait accompli*. And both Jew and Palestinian Arab in principle want an end to the minority's disadvantage, the anomaly described in the previous chapter whereby they are 'citizens in principle but not in practice'. But for equality to be substantiated what else must change?

Religion is one point at issue. So long as religion can be dealt with as 'culture and tradition', people coming variously from Christian, Muslim, Jewish backgrounds, being believers and non-believers, the women of Bat Shalom are delighted to 'affirm their difference' (as the Irish women would say), even 'celebrate' it. But religion is a vehicle of politics and medium of power. I asked the women: 'How can Muslims and Christians be equal with Jews in a state governed in part by the religious laws of Judaism? For non-Jewish citizens to be truly equal, must Israel not become a secular state, in which all religions are relegated to civil society and accorded equal respect and equal rights?' I received divergent answers. Lawyer Amal Khoury said, 'Yes, of course.' And some of the Jewish women would agree. Esther, for instance, says, 'My dream is that we can all live together in the same country, that Israel can be like other countries in the world, each one celebrating holidays differently, doing traditions differently, but friends, together – normalized.' The problem is, however, that even non-believers like the kibbutz socialists cannot evade the contradiction in which, as we saw, Israel as a whole is caught: Judaism as a religion (given the ethnic diversity of the 'Jews') is essential to the legitimacy of the state, as the only available definer of the Jewish nation.

A second divergence concerns the Law of Return, the right of Jews anywhere in the world to come and live in Israel. For the first generation like Nitsa, who came here prepared if necessary to fight for this home-land for the scattered Jews, a project that has cost her the lives of three children, how can there ever be any question of abandoning this found-ing principle? Most of the second-generation kibbutz women too would be very reluctant to cede the Jewish Right of Return. But Palestinian Arabs and non-Zionist Jews like Lily and Hannah believe this is a historic error that has to be exchanged for a more realistic, non-racist, quota-based immigration policy that distinguishes the need for asylum from actual persecution from other motives.

A third source of disagreement concerns militarism and security in the Israeli state. Just how real is this 'Arab threat to Israel's survival' that legitimates the extreme militarization of Israeli society? Most of the Palestinian Arab women, highly sensitized to the regime of collective punishment continually meted out by the Israeli army in the Occupied Territories, to the disruption of Palestinian life by the arbitrary im-position of curfews and border closures, are sceptical on this score. But Vera says, 'If Arafat doesn't do what we think he should to secure our existence, we *can't* go with it. We can't.' In fact, of course, it is not only Jewish Israelis who need 'security' for Israel. Nahla, for one, is clear about this. Being a Palestinian Arab did not protect her from being wounded in a Hamas bomb attack in Afula.

Something of these differences surfaced when we were due to turn out for a roadside demonstration after the Jerusalem suicide bus bomb in March 1996. Some Jewish members had proposed placards reading 'No to terror. Yes to peace.' Of course, to use the word 'terror' points the finger at Arabs and lets Israeli state violence off the hook. Nahla was pleased to have found that it was not left to a Palestinian Arab woman to argue that point. It was a Jewish woman who took issue and others agreed. The placard was changed to read 'No to violence. Yes to peace.'

Land: the most hurtful issue   Galilee has a special significance in Israeli land policy. This large northern territory adjoining Lebanon and Syria was not intended by the United Nations to be part of the Israeli state. It was acquired by Israel in the fighting of 1948/9, and despite

Often in Bat Shalom the space between differences seems filled with expressive hands.

displacing the great majority of those who had until then been its main inhabitants, Israel nevertheless inherited in Galilee a sizeable remaining Arab population. Thirty years later Jews were fearing, since the Arab birthrate was clearly much higher than that of the Jews, that Arabs might soon constitute a majority in the region. The Koenig Memorandum of 1976, named after its author, then district commissioner for Galilee, recommended a trio of measures to 'Judaize Galilee': make life unbearable for Palestinian Arabs, offer them incentives to leave Israel and settle thousands more Jews (Abdo and Yuval-Davis 1995: 307 and 37). The policy was never fully implemented, but the uproar that ensued has sensitized both Jewish and Palestinian feeling in the region to this day.

Certainly, for Bat Shalom, the land is unsteady under their feet. On many of those kibbutzim you can see among the newer constructions ruined mosques and other old stone buildings. They are uncomfortable reminders to the Jews who skirt them every day, and to the Palestinian Arab women who may glimpse them when they visit a kibbutz for a Bat Shalom meeting, that this land was once home to Arabs.

The women decided while I was there to organize a day-trip to Ikrit and Biram, the ruins of two Arab villages in the north of Galilee, sites of a long-running land rights struggle. We set off in a bus, stopping first at the hill of Ikrit, on which only a church stands today. It is squatted by the Committee of Displaced Residents, children and grand-children of the original population, whose representatives addressed our group. They told us how the Israeli forces in 1948 had tricked them into leaving 'temporarily' and later bombed the village out of existence. With the remaining inhabitants of neighbouring Biram, a village with a similar history, they had won rulings from the Israeli Supreme Court affirming their right to go home. But the Israeli government had never allowed it, the Labour minister of defence, Pinhas Lavon, commenting on the case: 'a revolutionary movement like Zionism cannot consider as sacred all the accomplished facts inherited from the past' (Halevi 1987: 185). But the community went on marrying their young in the church, burying their dead in the graveyard and tolling the church bell for visiting supporters like us.

A palpable wrong. The trouble was, the lands of Ikrit and Biram had long ago been given to a kibbutz and a moshav to farm and build on. We climbed back in the bus and went next to visit the kibbutz, whose representative greeted us courteously, and explained, with refreshments, history as they saw it. The original pioneering kibbutzniks allocated the site by the Israeli state had always sought good relations with the Arabs, he said. They had even supported them, he said, in aspects of their claim. In contrast to the intransigent moshav next door, the kibbutz had been prepared to give up the site where the village had stood. But the villagers wanted their farmland back too: how were they supposed to make a living without it? But, argued the kibbutznik, my generation was born here, we planted these orange trees, it is as much our home as any land could be. Would you do a second wrong to put right the first? It began to sound like a cameo of the history of Israel.

On the way home in the bus, as we drove along the mimosa-lined roads and past shining Kinneret, its waters reflecting the tumbling cumulus of that bright spring afternoon, I listened to the women arguing the wrongs and the wrongs. On each side, a sense of self so tenaciously rooted in land – the very same land. Whatever they said, in this fierce moment, they would hurt each other. 'Look, look at these *sabra* cactuses all along the road! It shows this was all Arab villages. All of it!' 'Of course, it was only those Arabs who had no real roots who fled!' 'Nobody has a historical right to land. It's a dangerous idea.' 'They should remember Germany!'

Maintaining unity: resources and threats

A lot of my questions when I was with Bat Shalom circled around 'What enables you to hold together?', or conversely 'When is group survival in doubt, and why?' The answers focused mainly on three things: organizing as *women*; choice of a productive *agenda*; and finding (or failing to find) a safe and sustainable way of relating, a *democratic process*.

Being a women's group was understood as offering certain practical advantages, even if, for quite a few of the women, it was not an important matter of principle. First, women know from experience just how silenced and marginalized women have been in the mixed-sex Israeli peace movement and in the PLO. To organize with women seems a way to be fully engaged. Second, Jewish women perceive it as being the only way to reach Palestinian Arab women, since they suppose that cultural constraints on the latter might prevent them joining mixed-sex cross-ethnic activities. Not all Arab women would see it in quite those terms. But in any heterosexual community it is true enough that going out to meet women is a more acceptable, and therefore more sustainable, activity for women than going into environments where there are men. Third, there is the security aspect. The 'enemy other', terrorist or soldier, is always first seen as a male. As Suad says, 'Conflict: it's a male agenda.' In kibbutz society in any case a group of Palestinian Arab women coming onto the kibbutz for meetings is seen as less subversive than a group of Arab men would be. A bunch of women arriving in an Arab village prompts fewer questions than a car-load of Jewish men. There is a further pragmatic reason for working with women only. Sometimes demonstrations erupt into violence. Yehudit had noticed how 'every time it happened it threw us backwards. We were much stronger when we didn't respond to violence.' And experience had very often shown that it is easier to keep demonstrations non-violent if men are not involved.

A second set of responses concerning women-only organizing argued from essence: women's biology, and particularly their reproductive role, were seen as giving them a shared love of peace. For example, Amit Cohen, whose youngest son was still serving in the army, said, 'The fact that we are women and we are mothers is a stronger bond between us than any difference ... It's the same for all of us, women and mothers, there's no difference whether the child is Arab or Jew.' Sonia, too, sometimes felt, she said, that women just '*are* more tender than men' and that there is something physical involved in the difference:

> Once I saw a big kite flying in the sky, with words on it about peace. I felt myself shivering, my whole body, as though something happened. I feel I want peace *from my body*. And I think other women maybe feel the same. If men want peace, it's not from their body.

Vera disagreed. She observed that her son seemed, if anything, less prone to violence than she. In any case, quite often women seemed to give simultaneously essentialist and experiential reasons for women's involvement in the peace movement. Nor did they put forward such reasons *against* political arguments. Rather, it seemed to be a kind of everyday, casual language in which to speak of a 'difference' they often felt but less often analysed. Rodaina, for instance, said in one and the same utterance, 'the differences [between men and women] are created *by nature*', and 'they are created *by people*, we are born into *a world that discriminates*' (emphasis added). When invited to think analytically the women chose their words more carefully and stressed that: 'It's *the experience* of raising children that makes us reject violence' or 'It's because we've had *the experience* of being oppressed that we can emphasize with the oppressed.'

A minority of the women altogether sidestep 'women's difference', be it of nature or culture, and stress gender politics as a vehicle for transformative change. Lily is one. She speaks of herself as a socialist as well as a feminist. When I asked her 'why organize in a women-only group?' she said:

I think I have no alternative. I'm a woman. I want real change, revolutionary change. And that can't happen without change for women. We have to change the whole way we see things, the way we talk, behave, work. I believe in equality, that's why I'm a socialist. But I think, whatever men say, they can't really be feminists – only up to the moment it conflicts with their interests. They can't go the whole way with us, they just can't.

While Bat Shalom Megiddo characteristically do not challenge or debate the issue of 'feminism' as such in Lily's terms, I sensed that many other women in the group would have concurred with what she says here, and that quite a large area of agreement on gender issues in fact united them. Lily, certainly, felt confident that:

> We're agreed we want to work in a women's group without men, that we want to be in solidarity with women in their demands and improve women's status. We're agreed that in the kibbutzim as well as in the villages there's covert discrimination against women. Probably we would all agree on abortion and contraception rights and the right to choose a marriage partner freely.

But women have had plenty of experience of the difficulty the word 'feminism' causes back at base and are wise enough to allow actions to speak instead of words.

So it is due to engagement around a *selective agenda* that 'being women' remains a resource, rather than being a source of division in Bat Shalom. Tactful silence and careful speech are central to its practice of alliance. It is an aspect of working process that is subject to a never-ending string of risky choices. Unlike the Women's Support Network in Belfast and also (as we shall see) unlike Medica in Bosnia, Bat Shalom Megiddo prioritizes alliance as a political act in itself. The women meet primarily to build solid foundations for their political bridge, and to manifest their solidarity to a wider audience. Because of this, the quality of the group's work and, in fact, its very survival, depend on careful choice of what is placed on the table for discussion and what is left off. If too little is tabled, if its scope is too cautious and too shallow, the alliance has no meaning, no reality. If too much is loaded onto the agenda, if women are drawn too quickly and carelessly into divisive matters, the group might fail as people get hurt once too often and pull away. The trip to Ikrit and Biram was one of those moments when the lid was abruptly lifted from Pandora's box and Bat Shalom allowed itself to explore dangerous differences.

Bat Shalom has a particular difficulty in respect of defining a workable agenda. Women in Black, aiming to attract women from a wide political spectrum, had adopted the strategy of a very closely defined agenda:

peace-with-justice-and-a-Palestinian-state, and little else. Women and Peace, a particularly well-honed political group, self-selecting from the broader movement as both left and feminist, had been safe to range wider into difficult terrain without destabilizing their alliance. Bat Shalom Megiddo was trying to do two things at once: continue the Women in Black tradition of big demonstrations and ever-widening membership, *and* try for a deeper mutual understanding on a broader range of issues through its meetings, events and workshops.

Different women have different ideas about what was in fact on the agenda of Bat Shalom, and what should be on it. Most of the women told me that party politics was off-agenda. Even though there were no right-wing women in the group, and few even from the Labour Party, they did not want to put at risk what was essentially a Hadash–Mapam coalition by raising the familiar bogeys of Hadash's Stalinist tendencies, Mapam's Zionism. Religion too was skirted around. It might be addressed in its cultural and traditional aspects – there was nothing threatening in comparing food taboos, or the fasts of Ramadan and Yom Kippur. But the issue of observance versus secularity, and the relation between religion and the Israeli state, were too sensitive. And the sensitivities were not only cross-ethnic: Zionism, for instance, would be avoided by Jewish members because of differences among themselves.

So intelligent management of the agenda, knowing what is safe to raise and when, what is necessary to raise and why, was an important resource of Bat Shalom Megiddo. Everyone knew, as Samira Khoury put it, that this was the central task of the project: 'We must find this very thin thread that leads us to common ground.' The fact is, however, that some women felt Bat Shalom was already 'too sharp' for them, while others felt irritated that it was too bland, that difficult things were not being addressed in enough depth.

To feel safe debating everything the more ambitious women would want to place on the agenda called for the kind of participatory *democratic process* that is predictable and agreed, that feels safe because it ensures equality and inclusion. And this was Bat Shalom's main weakness. The women operate under practical constraints of time (they are all busy in their own lives) and space (they live far apart and lack transport). They had so far been unable to obtain funding for an office, a central phone number. Meetings were not being held predictably on fixed dates at known times and in consistent venues. Often arranging a meeting was allowed to hinge on certain women, viewed as key person-alities, being available, so that many weeks might go by without a meeting being arranged. Sometimes the phone-around was incomplete, so that people were vulnerable to feeling left out. Some women felt that the meetings were uncomfortably argumentative and competitive. Group-work skills were lacking so that, when meetings did occur, dominant personalities were not held in check and less confident ones were not empowered.

Even where skilled facilitation was available, inherent problems held the group back. In the particular sub-cultures from which Bat Shalom draws its membership there is no tradition of feminist consciousness-raising or, more generally, of self-reflexive identity work. For its workshop series Bat Shalom employed professional facilitators. One of them experienced it as 'an exceptionally hard group to work with'. Her aim had been to enable women to open up and explore their own feelings, entrust each other with their histories, their vulnerabilities and needs. She felt defeated. 'It was a very very difficult experience for me. I wasn't successful. I tried every method that I know.' She concluded that in Israel today there can be no short-circuiting of single identity work. Jewish women must be prepared to work more self-searchingly with each other around issues of identity and belief, Palestinian Arab women likewise. That, she believed, is the necessary pre-condition for later democratic cooperation.

But Bat Shalom is predicated on the feasibility of working across the communal boundary right here and now. And who could deny the urgency of this? The political situation in 1996 was deteriorating. Soon after I left Megiddo, the Israelis launched 'Operation Grapes of Wrath', bombarding Lebanon in response to Hizbullah's Katyusha rocket attacks on northern Galilee. There was uproar among Palestinian Arabs, inside and outside Israel. A hawkish Likud government was elected. The left-wing political parties espoused by most of Bat Shalom's women, already compromised by their collusion with Labour in the Lebanon operation, were driven into retreat. Right-wing extremism gained confidence. Lily's car, with its socialist window-stickers, was attacked in Afula town.

And through all this Bat Shalom staggered on. Even when a sturdy structure of meetings, demonstrations and workshops could not be relied upon, the filigree-fine safety-net of friendship survived. Soon after the nightmare in Lebanon, Suad brought her mother over to visit Lily at the kibbutz. It was just a social call. Together they went out onto the hillside of Armageddon and gathered a certain herb that Arabs love to cook with, which grows abundantly there. (They were cheerfully breaking the law together, since this herb is protected by the state as an endangered species.) The three women filled some sacks together and chatted of this and that. Not of the war, not of Bat Shalom. But a link was being kept alive for the moment when joint political action again seemed possible.

6
Bosnia-Hercegovina: Women in a disintegrating Yugoslavia

In all wars women suffer in a way specific to women. But to the women working in the refugee projects in the Yugoslav successor states – projects like Medica Zenica – struggling to improve the lot of hundreds of thousands of uprooted families, it sometimes seems as if the Yugoslav wars of 1992–95 were wars waged *against* women, against a feminine principle, against all that women stand for, against, as Staša Zajović puts it, 'the feminine symbolic order' (Women in Black 1994: 2). Eighty-four per cent of the refugees are women and children. Many have been raped and abused *as* women by male fighters. All come with stories about the destruction of everything they had nurtured: offspring, homes, fruit trees, cows and sheep, small businesses. In trying to understand the onslaught that became possible in 1992 women probe the history of Yugoslavia before its disintegration for what it can reveal not just about relations between the ethnic groups, but about relations between women and men.

The characteristic household in the Balkan Region was once the *zadruga*, in which several generations of an extended family would live and eat together. When she married, a woman moved into the home of her husband's parents and accepted their authority. The zadruga system began to break up in the twentieth century as young couples more often set up house on their own (Morokvašić 1986). But a generalized patriarchal structure continued, and during the two decades after the creation of a unified Yugoslav state, the decades between the two world wars, the prevailing legal system embodied a frank subordination of women in which they lacked equality with men in property rights, inheritance and 'family laws' (Božinović 1994).

The Second World War was the start of a new age in gender relations in Yugoslavia. The German invasion of 1941 was countered by a People's Liberation movement, foreshadowed by pro-democracy activism in the 1930s in which many women had been involved. In 1942 these women's groups across the territory coalesced into an Anti-Fascist Front of Women, which had two million members. One hundred thousand women fought in regular Partisan military units. Twenty-five thousand were killed in action and forty thousand wounded (Milić 1993). Yugoslavia differed from some other countries of Eastern and Central Europe that later became part of the Soviet bloc in that its post-war communist regime was a popular choice, the outcome of a genuine local struggle for democracy and independence. One in five women played an active part in that movement. It is not surprising that, as Andjelka Milić says, 'many women experienced the country's liberation as their own spontaneous, unexpected, direct emancipation from the closed world of their traditional patriarchal families' (ibid.: 111).

Women in Tito's Yugoslavia

But women today often say, 'Yugoslavia remained a patriarchal society even under Communism.' After the war the mass organization of women was soon more closely bound in to the party structure, first as the Union of Women's Associations, then as the Conference for the Social Activity of Women (note the shift of meaning in this new title), losing any vestige of autonomy (Mladjenović and Litričin 1993; Božinović 1994). The Communist Party introduced a notional equality between the sexes. Discrimination in employment was banned. Women had the right to one year's maternity leave with full pay. In marriage the couple were equal and they could divorce by mutual consent. Abortion was legal, and in 1974 women won legislation that further protected their 'right to choose' (Morokvašić 1986).

As women elsewhere found, however, the socialist strategy on women responded to men's perception of 'the Woman Question' and in no way challenged male-dominant gender relations (Jančar 1985; Djurić 1995; Morokvašić 1997). As a lot of women have pointed out since Yugoslavia's experiment in socialist brotherhood came to grief, 'emancipation' was always the brothers' policy for the sisters, not something the sisters achieved in their own design. Marxist theory proposes that sex equality will be achieved by means of women's equal participation with men in the paid labour force. Women certainly gain by leaving home and earning an independent income. But nowhere has this resulted in sex equality.

To rely on this strategy was especially misguided in Yugoslavia, since the proportion of women entering paid employment was far smaller than in other communist countries. Many young women did, after the war, get education, find jobs, move to the towns and cities. But even in 1981 two-thirds of women still remained outside Yugoslavia's formal economy. A huge gap opened between urban and rural women (Korać

1991), and between those with higher education (the country had one of the highest rates in the world of university-educated women) and the rest. Seventeen per cent of females remained illiterate at the time of the 1981 census, four times the rate for males (Djurić 1995). Besides, the unemployment created by the successive economic reforms of the 1970s and 1980s affected women more severely than men, driving yet more out of paid work (Morokvašić 1986).

Even those women who had jobs were impeded by lack of nursery provision. They normally relied on older female relatives to care for their dependants and continued to perform the 'second shift' of domestic labour after paid work was done. So Yugoslav women, even when working outside the home, remained firmly rooted in it, defined by domestic roles and responsibilities. As Mirjana Morokvašić puts it, the socialist revolution failed to 'cross the threshold of the family' (Morokvašić 1986: 127). Domestic violence against women was routine and may well have increased the more men's patriarchal authority was challenged by women. Yugoslavia was in many respects a market economy so that women were, as in the West, confirmed in female roles as consumers, their images exploited in commercial advertising. Culturally men and boys were valorized. *Ženska glavo* ('woman's head') is a popular term of abuse.

Most striking of all was women's exclusion from positions of managerial and political authority. It had been supposed that the Titoist system of worker self-management and decentralized administration would give women the possibility of directly participating in local power systems (Božinović 1994). But figures for the ensuing period show that women accounted for fewer than 1 per cent of enterprise managers, only 17 per cent of workers' council members and 6 per cent of workers' council presiding officers (Morokvašić 1986: 125, citing official statistics published in 1973). Although a quota system assured women 30 per cent of the seats in regional and federal parliaments, few women held ministerial posts in the administrations of the 1970s and 1980s.

Andjelka Milić has passionately condemned Yugoslavia's modernization programme, the country's costly investment in education and in technology, as a cheat and a waste. Yugoslavia did diverge from the Stalinist model in many ways. Milić says:

> to our credit, in the early 1960s in Yugoslavia we did measure socialist industrialization by the criterion of a higher standard of living, both for the individual and in the social domain. The alternative common in other Eastern countries, 'tons of steel per capita', would have been intolerable, even for the hardest-headed among us (Milić 1994: 150).

But, she goes on,

> despite renouncing the vulgar formula 'socialism = electrification + industrialization', we never fully embraced the alternative: radical *social* modernization (ibid.).

Instead, political elites used investment for their own self-aggrandizement. And education shrivelled into mere certification for ladder-climbing in the communist system.

> As a result, today the promise of technological modernization has finally perished under the treads of a blazing war machine ... And the promise of modernization through education has its bitter fruit in the self-exile abroad, fleeing the war, of hundreds of thousands of the young women and men it had educated (ibid.: 162).

It has often been remarked that the one area in which the otherwise non-conformist Yugoslavia stuck loyally to the Stalinist model was that of gender relations. Clearly the men in power saw nothing to gain from questioning the 'naturalness' of male leadership and female domesticity. All else under socialism might be seen as amenable to social reconstruction – not gender. And, despite the relative openness of Yugoslavia to a wider world, under this patriarchal socialism within, women were mostly unable to imagine themselves as autonomous political subjects let alone as political actors (Drakulić 1993).

All but a few. Because in the 1970s, not long after the upsurge of 'new wave' feminism in Western Europe and the USA, a similar questioning mood arose among a small minority of women in Yugoslavia (Jančar 1985). Yugoslav women after all were free to travel (money permitting), they were able to read books and journals from all over the world. Djurdja Knežević remembers how, here as elsewhere, the first 'feminist libraries' began to accumulate on the bookshelves of individual women, mainly students and young professionals, coming together for the first time in small groups in a process of collective learning, demystifying gender power relations (Knežević 1995).

Nineteen seventy-six is the year in which Žarana Papić recalls the first mention of contemporary feminism in Yugoslavia – at a Croatian sociological association conference. That same year the first women's studies course was held in Dubrovnik. Many women still remember 1978 for an international conference on women at the Students' Cultural Centre in Belgrade. Activists were invited from all the Yugoslav republics and from countries of both Eastern and Western Europe. The aim was 'to present the phenomenon of feminism, and to hear from face to face encounter what feminism really is' (Papić 1994; see also

Mladjenović and Litričin 1993; Hughes et al. 1995). The event provoked a strong reaction from the official women's organization. 'For women war veterans, feminism was synonymous with disloyalty to Yugoslavia,' recalls the journalist Slavenka Drakulić. The party accused the organizers of 'negating the leading role of the working class and the Communist League' (Drakulić 1993). But in 1979, undeterred, they formed the organization Women and Society in Zagreb and over the following years groups sprang up in Belgrade, Lubljana, Sarajevo and Novi Sad. It looked as though a women's movement was in the making.

The uses of women in the national projects

Feminists, however, were not the only subversives of the 1970s. The regime had also dealt repressively with nationalism, imprisoning a number of writers and activists. Both phenomena can be seen as indicators of the character political ferment was going to take in the decade following Tito's death in 1980. Both feminist and nationalist movements addressed contradictions latent in the Yugoslav system, concealed under communist rhetoric: the failure to transcend on the one hand patriarchal subordination of women and on the other ethnic insecurities and rivalries. But the moment fulfilled June Jordan's prediction that 'when we get the monsters off our backs all of us may want to run in very different directions' (Jordan 1989: 144). For the feminists' aim was to seize the moment to shift gender relations into a genuinely emancipatory mode, while the nationalists' solution to the gender contradiction was, as we shall see, to update patriarchal control of women.

In 1985 the Soviet leader Mikhail Gorbachev was surprising audiences at home and observers abroad with proposals for change in the economy and polity of the USSR. He used a strange new vocabulary of 'transparency' and 'restructuring'. In the next four years *glasnost* and *perestroika* would thaw the rigid regimes and centrally controlled economies of the Soviet Union and of the Eastern European countries under its hegemony. This warming of the political climate incubated growth from below. Civil society, including oppositional movements, flowered in such a way that almost overnight, it seemed, old regimes were pushed aside. The wall separating East from West Berlin, the Iron Curtain in concrete, was demolished in 1989. What came next differed from country to country. The fall of communist parties did not everywhere mean the departure of communist personalities. Some put on new clothes and renamed their parties. Some won elections. But everywhere in the political vacuum a discourse of nationalism was revived.

Many people believed that, given the moderate route it had taken and its political distance from Moscow, Yugoslavia would ride the swell of change with relative ease, steering a course between old-style left and new-style right. But, as we saw in Chapter 1, the austerity measures entailed in the global 'structural adjustment' programme were destabilizing the fragile post-war alliance forged by Tito. Nationalism was a weapon ready to hand for ambitious republican leaders, and as we have seen, nationalism is highly infectious. While Serbian nationalists made expansionist moves, proclaiming 'Serb lands are wherever Serb bones are buried', Croatia and Slovenia began to play the European card, drawing a line between themselves and those uncivilized easterners.

It would have been around this time that Slavenka Drakulić reflected 'in the ten years since Tito's death nationalism has started boiling in this country, like a steam kettle, which is now whistling loudly, becoming our only reality' (Drakulić 1987: 171). Women were being stridently addressed by the new nationalist ideologues. Women's identities were to be reshaped and enlisted for the nationalist projects, their bodies instrumentalized by them.

Whatever the reality, sex equality had been one of the principles of communist Yugoslavia. Now that notion was questioned along with other communist doctrines. The task of a patriotic woman was no longer to build socialism by her labour but to regenerate the nation through motherhood (Bracewell 1996). Returning to ideals of hearth, home and land, Yugoslav nationalisms invoked the zadruga of the past, and woman became symbolic of the reawakening people: Little Mother Serbia. The two-thirds of women who had never left the home for paid employment saw their domestic roles endorsed. Professional women found ideological support for their choices draining away. The few women active in political life also withdrew, or were pushed, from public office: the first multi-party elections in Serbia, confirming Milošević in power, saw women's proportion of the seats fall from 20 per cent to under 2 per cent (ibid.: 26).

Reproduction of the national population became a key theme in nationalist discourse in Serbia, Croatia and Slovenia. In Serbia, nationalists played on the fears of the Serb minority in the Kosovo region, where the birthrate of Muslim Albanians dramatically outpaced their own. The female replacement rate in 1994 was +17.38 among Albanians in Kosovo against -2.93 in the Serbian population. An influential and alarmist document titled *Warning*, published in October 1992 by the Serbian Socialist Party (the former Communist Party), the Serbian Orthodox Church and the Serbian Academy of Arts and Sciences proposed a State Council for population, claiming that Albanians,

Muslims and Roma were 'beyond rational and human reproduction' (Papić 1995: 41).

Albanian fecundity was condemned as deviant and unnatural. But selfish 'emancipated' Yugoslav women were blamed for what was termed the 'white plague': death of the Serb people by failure to reproduce (Bracewell 1996: 27). The 'renaissance' of the constituent peoples of Yugoslavia was interpreted literally, as a question of biological renewal through births. With war, from 1992, it would become a question of replacing dead soldiers with new boy babies. Everywhere 'the same basic thought was echoed ... that it was impossible to wage war with an army of soldiers who were their parents' only sons' (ibid.: 29). We shall see, when we come to consider the anti-war protests of mothers, that there was some truth in this perception.

Of course, the restructuring of gender relations in the nationalist projects involved not only a new woman but a new man: protective, martial, virile, most definitely heterosexual. Some women shared in the retrograde movement. One woman writing in the paper *Duga* celebrated the Yugoslav female for having retained her femininity under communism while 'a significant part of the male population suffered serious injuries in the region of the backbone and the heart'. She appealed to women to help their men stiffen up and be 'that which nature and tradition intend them to be' (ibid.: 27).

After the establishment of the independent states of Slovenia and Croatia in 1991 the conservatism of their newly drafted constitutions was not lost on women (Drakulić 1993). Slovenian women saw themselves relegated to the private sphere, 'just when we almost became citizens!' (Antić 1991: 152). Croatia established a Department of Demographic Restoration and offered women incentives to stay home and rear children (Kesić 1995). Traditional abortion rights were threatened, if not yet restricted. The new constitution for the rump Yugoslavia (effectively Serbia) eliminated Article 191 guaranteeing free choice in the matter of parenthood (Papić 1995).

Women as *symbols*, guardians of home and homeland, women as *mothers*, reproducers of children and culture – we saw in Chapter 1 how these themes are often present in nationalist discourse. Another trope is woman as guarantor of the purity of the bloodline, and this too featured powerfully in the competitive national projects in Yugoslavia. The domestic confinement of women safeguards their purity, and rape by alien men is the ultimate defilement. It was a moral panic in the late 1980s concerning alleged rapes by Albanian men of Serbian women in Kosovo that intensified the Serb nationalist revival there. To the Criminal Code of Serbia was added at that time a new offence of ethnic rape, termed 'inter-national rape with political consequences'. It entailed more severe punishment than rape of women by men of their own nation (Milić 1993; Mežnarić 1994).

By no means everyone in the former Yugoslavia was swept along by nationalism, and women may have been less convinced by the new/old rhetoric than men. Andjelka Milić cites opinion polls showing that women were more sceptical than men about the elections of 1990, giving as their reasons both mistrust of the reality of this apparent democracy and dissatisfaction with the choices offered by the (mainly ethnic and nationalist) political parties. Seventy per cent of women said they did not plan to join a party. Certainly, the manifestos of both the ruling parties and the opposition parties stressed the national issue to the neglect of things that might have been expected to appeal to women voters – social welfare, health, education, childcare. Of those who had a party preference, younger and better-educated women tended to favour the few democratic-liberal parties. Older women, peasant women and housewives strongly adhered to the reformed Communist Party. In the election itself women are believed to have accounted for the greater part of the abstentions (Milić 1993). It is believed that more women than men voted for green parties, and that their support for overtly nationalist parties was considerably less than that of men (Djurić 1995).

Perhaps many women sensed that the new value ascribed to women in nationalist discourse was the kind of value one would ascribe to property, a possession, something that belonged to a husband, a father, a nation-state. Communism had pretended to erase sex differences. In some ways the nationalists were speaking an innovatory language, one that women were ready to hear now: a reassertion of gender specificity. But it was transparently about turning back the clock to an old patri-archal order. No more than communism did these nationalisms envisage an autonomous female subject (Milić 1996). In fact, the autonomous woman was now the Other within society, an unreliable element, dangerous and threatening like the ethnic Other without (Korać 1993).

Women's activism and war

In a minority of women, the blatant repression of women by the nationalist movements awoke a feminist oppositional consciousness (Milić 1993). In the year or two immediately prior to the fragmentation of the Yugoslav state several new women's initiatives occurred. 'Femin-ism', writes Djurdja Knežević (1995: 36), 'reached its peak just before the war'. For example, in 1990 the Belgrade group of Women and Society disbanded, making way for more focused activity responding to the changes shaking the political system. Lepa Mladjenović and other authors have described the projects that ensued in Belgrade in the last two years of its life as the Yugoslav federal capital (Mladjenović and Litričin 1993; Hughes et al. 1995). They filled various needs. One was to expose and counter violence against women. Another was to challenge masculinism in politics.

In March 1990 an 'SOS Hotline' for women and children victims of violence was installed. So long as communist ideology had prevailed, the widespread domestic and street violence of men against women in Yugoslavia had been hidden. One of the gains from the current turmoil was that things once taboo now became sayable. The telephone line and counselling provided by the new service was in continual use as women who had long experienced abuse from male partners at last found the courage to speak about it. As the country moved to war, the women running the SOS Hotline detected an apparent increase in the incidence of domestic violence and, as more men began to keep weapons at home, in its severity.

When elections were called that same year, women from different non-nationalist parties formed an alliance, the Women's Lobby, to put pressure on these male-led organizations from within. They drew up a 'minimal programme of women's demands' on women's work and un-employment, sexist education, reproductive rights, healthcare and legal reform. They called for quotas for women's representation in the parties and in a subsequent parliament and for the establishment of a Ministry of Women. That these political women were not ideologically far removed from their sisters in the Hotline is clear from the inclusion among their demands of a refuge for women and children victims of violence, the recognition of rape in marriage as a crime, and the de-criminalization of prostitution. And the Lobby ridiculed the nationalists' natalist policies that cast women in the role of reproducers of a Greater Serbia: 'One supposes that young Serbian foetuses will immediately be baptized, conditioned to hate and lead the war against the many Enemies of the Serbian nation' (Mladjenović and Litričin 1993: 115).

Some women despaired of shifting even the democratic/liberal parties in a direction congenial to women and formed their own party, Ženska Stranka, or ŽEST (the initials signified 'women, ethics, solidarity and tolerance'). They aimed to offer a new form of politics, transcending what they felt to be an outworn dichotomy between left and right. The manifesto was democratic, feminist and green. They proposed a de-centralized and non-authoritarian government structure, an independent judiciary, a mixed economy, better healthcare, educational reforms, en-vironmental protection and democratic, accessible media. They did not seriously set out to win seats so much as to energize a grassroots women's movement. But they did allow themselves, as a provocation, to put up a man/woman job-share team as candidates for the presidency (Cockburn 1991).

When the result of the elections fulfilled women's worst fears by returning a Serbian parliament in which men held 98 per cent of the seats (it was the lowest percentage of women in any European parliament of the time), they responded by setting up an alternative women's parliament to monitor and intervene in the legislative process (Mladjenović and Litričin 1993; Hughes et al. 1995).

Beside the twin focus on violence and politics, feminists were also active at this time in self-education and mutual support. A Women's Studies Centre, independent of the university, was set up in one Belgrade apartment. In another was located an Autonomous Women's Centre. There was a Girls' Centre. And a lesbian and gay lobby, Arkadia, was founded in the winter of 1990 to enhance the visibility of homosexuals, a brave move in a very adverse climate.

While Belgrade as the federal capital saw most women's activism, there were sister projects in Lubljana and Zagreb – the latter city, for instance, had its Women's Aid Now and Autonomous Women's House, responding to violence against women (Borić and Desnica 1996). As to whether this flurry of activity by now amounted to a movement, different women see it differently. Žarana Papić, for instance, is of the view that it might have been going too far to claim they had a movement, but certainly 'we had feminists' (Papić 1994: 19). Bosnia-Hercegovina seems to have exemplified this dictum. There were certainly individual women living in Sarajevo and other Bosnian cities who were active in the Yugoslav women's movement, but institutions such as women's centres and refuges were still lacking there when the region was overtaken by war.

Whether this was a 'movement' was one question; whether it was 'feminism' was also debated. To some Western feminists many of the Yugoslav women activists seemed quite conventionally feminine, with their lipstick and high heels. But Žarana, for one, defended Yugoslav women, along with others of the former Eastern bloc. At a conference of the European Forum of Left Feminists she explained: 'You cannot imagine how beautiful and attractive consumer culture and glamorous femininity can be – when you do not have it. Only the aggressive presence of consumer culture can bring about an awareness of the abuse of femininity and a critique of the exploitation of women as sex objects.' And she argued, 'at this stage of the transformations in the East, every form of women's activity and struggle is welcome ... The main thing is to broaden the possibilities for women's resistance' (Papić 1992).

The trouble was that not all forms of women's activity could be called resistance and not all forms of women's resistance to the nationalists could be called feminist. For a start, some women agreed with that call for a re-masculinizing of men, a re-feminizing of women. Some were militaristic. In 1990 women influenced by the arguments of the communist 'Movement for Yugoslavia' demonstrated in front of the National Assembly in Belgrade demanding a military coup (Drakulić 1993). The feminist movement was mainly local in character and as such was inherently liable to regionalism and therefore to ethnic differentiation (Antić 1991). And, what is more, not all feminists were opposed to nationalism. At the third national women's conference in March 1990 there was animosity between those women who wanted Yugoslavia to hold together and those from various republics, particularly Slovenia, who wanted to see them break away and refused to countenance any Yugoslav-wide women's organization. The Belgrade women were critical of their own home-grown Serb expansionist nationalism, but hesitated to condemn others' secessionist nationalisms. No agreement could be reached and women went away feeling that the movement had split along a fundamental fault-line (Milić 1996; Duhaček 1993; Mladjenović and Litričin 1993).

When the Slovene leadership did move for Slovenian independence in the summer of 1991 the units of the Yugoslav National Army stationed in that region were dispatched to prevent the breakaway. At that time of course all soldiers, whether Serb, Croat, Muslim or of other origins, were 'Yugoslav' soldiers. Mothers of soldiers, and some fathers too, began spontaneous demonstrations that quickly spread across the country against war and against the military.

On 2 July 1991, the mothers stormed the Serbian Assembly in Belgrade declaring: 'We haven't borne sons to die for Milošević!' (Bracewell 1996: 30). Next day, hundreds of women went to Lubljana to try to bring their sons home. At the end of August 40 busloads of parents, mainly mothers, including some from Bosnia-Hercegovina, converged on the headquarters of the Yugoslav National Army in Belgrade (Hughes et al. 1995). With the failure of ceasefire initiatives women's activism intensified. In a mass demonstration in Sarajevo they interrupted a session of parliament with demands for the discharge of sons, many of whom were being kept in the Yugoslav army beyond the term of their military service. On 29 August an estimated 100,000 people gathered in Zagreb in answer to Croatian women's call to 'surround the generals with a Rampart of Love' (Drakulić 1993).

This was a startling mobilization of angry women and many feminists were at first inspired by it. Lepa Mladjenović describes her reaction to an event in the auditorium of the military barracks in Belgrade:

> It was amazing. Never before in this male space had there been such a scene. At the front of the auditorium, on the podium, were the 'fathers' – the army officers. The women were sitting everywhere, talking and eating. At one point women from the villages in Croatia stopped listening to the men and started to softly sing a tender old Croat song. In contrast to the fathers in uniform with their hard strict military culture, the women's voices were from another world (Hughes et al. 1995: 515).

But disillusion quickly followed. It became clear that different elements in the movement had different demands. Some were protesting against fighting in principle, against 'the disgrace of civil war', and they could rightly be called a 'peace movement'. They were against their sons being obliged to fight brother *Yugoslavs*. But what others objected to was their sons having to fight people of their *own* republics. Thus what some Croat mothers in Croatia wanted was merely to prevent their sons fighting in the Yugoslav National Army alongside Serbs for the purpose of scotching Croatia's move for independence.

Certainly the protest of mothers against the military seemed usefully to undercut the claims of the leaders to be fighting to defend women and children. But the moral authority of the mothers derived precisely from the nationalists' system of values. It was yet one more denial of selfhood to women. The jingoistic and war-mongering media chose to ignore the presence of some men/fathers in the demonstrations and hyped up the symbolism of mothers. The women's protests were ideal material for nationalist propaganda justifying the creation of separate republican armies (Bracewell 1996).

As a consequence the women were easily divided. Mirjana Morokvašić describes how, in the autumn of 1991 in the town of Temerin in Vojvodina, where Hungarians and Serbs had been living together for some centuries, several dozen mothers of all nationalities were gathered in a united protest. This display of cross-national solidarity was destroyed by the arrival of Milošević's ruling party delegates and some Serb refugee women, victims of Croatian nationalism, shouting slogans hostile to Hungarians, whom they characterized as historic (because Catholic) allies of their persecutors the Croats. This effectively split the demonstration and next day only Hungarian mothers remained (Morokvašić 1997).

As Slavenka Drakulić noted, 'the women's uprising was doomed because the generals and politicians – not the women – understood the potential power of their movement' (Drakulić 1993). Ultimately, much as we saw happening in Israel (Chapter 4), the strategy of the mothers proved a false start to the anti-war movement. It was unable to resist ethnic naming and finger-pointing. In the end it even added energy to the centrifugal force hurling the peoples of Yugoslavia away from each other.

Women in anti-war action

Then the unthinkable happened. Yugoslavs began fighting each other with rifles and mortars as well as words. The skirmishes in Slovenia were short-lived, but the ensuing slaughter in Croatia shook the world. Now both 'Serbs' and 'Croats' had their martyrs and their justification. In an atmosphere where even silence could be interpreted as treachery, the outspoken anti-war campaign was isolated and vilified. But the small groups who persisted probably spoke for far greater numbers than dared openly support them.

Although the Anti-war Campaign Croatia (ARK) and the Centre for Anti-war Action in Belgrade were both nominally mixed in gender (as well as ethnicity) the majority of activists were women. Martina Belić in Zagreb pointed out with some bitterness that the percentage of men in these organizations was as low as the proportion of women in government. Men seemed to be the architects of war, women the ones trying to end it (Belić 1995). It is fairer to add that many thousands of male opponents of the war had had to escape abroad to avoid conscription. But it is certainly the case that women opposed men's military conscription more than men opposed their own (Women in Black 1994), and an opinion poll in September 1991 showed that 20 per cent more women than men favoured peace (Milić 1993).

Whatever the reason, women predominated in the anti-war activity and the movement appears to have had something characteristically 'of women' in its way of organizing. Which is cause and which effect is unclear. Vesna Teršelić, coordinator of ARK, remarked that women did seem more interested in 'creating new opportunities and building them from the ground up'. Women were prepared to do the many menial but necessary tasks without making a big fuss about their courage. They also had a working style that encouraged new people to express their opinions (Teršelić 1995: 39).

But Staša Zajović, volunteering at the Belgrade Centre for Anti-war Action, found it operating on the same patriarchal model as every other political organization, with women doing the donkey-work and a man representing it in public. In brings to mind the experience of Vera and other Jewish women in the male-led Israeli peace movement (Chapter 4). Staša and other women broke away to create the network 'Women in Black Against War' because 'I wanted our presence to be visible, so that our work would be seen as a political choice, not just a feminine role' (Zajovič 1994: 49).

Women in Black began their public protest on 9 October 1991. They chose the symbolic centre of Belgrade, Republic Square, and formed a line of women, dressed in black clothes, holding in front of them a long banner identifying themselves: *Žene u Crnom protiv Rata* (Women in Black Against War). It was a Wednesday afternoon. They continued to take this stand every Wednesday, only varying their placards from time to time in response to events. Their statement was essentially that age-old message to the militaristic leaders of nations: 'You're not doing it in my name.' The Women in Black vigils have been classic non-violent direct action, women choosing to put their bodies politically into play, stepping out of line with 'society' by stepping into line with each other. 'We refuse to be the hostages of the regime and a state that makes war. We transform our anger into non-violent actions' (Zajović 1995: 42). The vigils were the only anti-war actions in the whole of Yugoslavia that were visible, regular and permanent. They were also unique in being unequivocally feminist.[1]

In 1992 the news began to break of the extent of rape in these wars. The scale and particularity of the practice was gradually established through inquiries made by international organizations and evidence gathered by those caring for the victims of rape (United Nations 1993 and 1994; Amnesty International 1993; European Commission 1993; Helsinki Watch 1993). In the towns and villages attacked by Serbian soldiers of the former Federal Yugoslav Army and by paramilitary units of Bosnian Serbs and irregulars from Serbia, the local Muslims and Croats were dealt with in a gender-differentiated way. Captured men were taken into detention and subjected to forced labour. Many, it later became clear, were executed *en masse*. For women and children there was a different practice. Those who did not flee, or who were picked up in the fields and woods as they did so, were detained in 'camps' that varied in size. It might be a warehouse, a school, a hotel or house. Here

---

1. The 'Women in Black' form of protest was brought to Yugoslavia at the outbreak of war by Italian feminists who had been in touch with the Israeli movement described on p. 126. In turn, the London group mentioned on p. 1 was inspired by the Yugoslav women's action. Involving regular vigils in public places, Women in Black imagery has resonance with that of the women of the Plaza de Mayo in Argentina and Black Sash in South Africa. Although there is no organizational linkage, Women in Black groups and actions now spring up in many countries when war threatens. A large international WIB demonstration was held at the NGO Forum at the United Nations Conference on Women in Beijing in 1995.

they were questioned, taunted and beaten. They were, by force and with the additional threat of harm to loved ones, made to participate in sexual acts. They were raped alone, in groups, by individual soldiers, or by many men. They were tortured sexually with objects and required to torture each other. Often the rapes of any one woman were repeated and frequent. In many cases they were carried out in front of family members. They went on over weeks or months, and there is evidence that some women in some camps were purposely held until in advanced pregancy before being exchanged for Serb soldiers held prisoner by the BH Army (Hauser 1995; Stiglmayer 1995; Žarkov 1997).

During the 'war within a war' when the HVO (Croat Defence Council) extremists began ethnic cleansing in other areas of Bosnia, they used rape in a similar manner, although more frequently holding women individually or in small groups for the purpose in their own homes or in local houses taken over by the military. The question is often asked: did soldiers of the BH army (mainly but not exclusively composed of Muslims) also rape? Rape characteristically occurred during aggressive moves to 'cleanse' territory, and the BH army was engaged mainly in defence of territory in this war. Unlike the Bosnian Serb and Croat militias, the Bosnian authorities proved themselves ready to use the law to punish indiscipline. But, for all that, evidence later presented at the International Tribunal in The Hague revealed instances of rape and other atrocities by Muslim and Croat combined forces, and by Muslim men alone. The exact number of rapes in the Yugoslav wars will never be known. Reasoned estimates range from 10,000 to 20,000 (United Nations Commission of Experts 1994, cited in Žarkov 1997).

Of course, women have always known, even if historians, war tribunals and war reporters have often overlooked it, that rape is an endemic and not incidental feature of war. Some observers of the war in Bosnia felt that there was an organized, even strategic, intention behind many of the rapes: to demoralize the men through defilement of their most treasured possession, women's honour. This certainly accorded with feminist observations (cited in Chapter 1) on the significance of gender in nationalist ideology (Anthias and Yuval-Davis 1989). Whatever the 'ethnic' dimension to the rapes, what was certainly present was a power structure among the men in which control operated partly through collective misogyny. This too had resonance with feminist theory that rape is an effect not of men's sexual drive but of gender power relations (Lees 1997). Enemy men too were 'reduced' to women, by being raped. One feature of the Bosnian war was the high visibility accorded to the rapes. This was due in part to extensive coverage by the world media. And no doubt Western European audiences were more responsive to media reports because these were 'European women'. But the visibility was also due to the courage of raped women who (in contrast to earlier wars) spoke out quickly, and to the existence by now of a worldwide women's movement ready to take up the issue.

Women in Black Belgrade were hearing many reports of rape through the organizations receiving refugees in Bosnia, Croatia and further afield. They were also getting firsthand accounts from refugees they were meeting as they arrived in Belgrade. The majority were of course Serbian women, some of whom had been raped in actions by the Croat HVO. A minority were Croat and Muslim women expelled from Bosnia, some of them raped by Serb extremists. While the nationalist media exploited the rapes for propaganda against their enemies and in the hope of galvanizing international support, and the international media on the whole carried rape stories only so long as they were a novel sensation, Women in Black, along with women in many other countries, were the ones who maintained public awareness and condemned the barbarity of this gender-specific torture.

Women in Black allowed no one who witnessed their demonstrations to evade the fact that military and domestic violence are connected, that only 'when violence against women ceases, wars will stop'. In this way they found a path that skirted the pitfall into which the 'mothers' had fallen, one that at the same time led them to a vantage point from which they could see and challenge these virulent nationalisms on one of their core principles, male dominance, something the anti-war actions led by men (in Yugoslavia as in Israel) seemed unable or unwilling to address.

Of course the women were subjected to ridicule and aggression, but the regime in Belgrade was not, perhaps surprisingly given all its unpleasant characteristics, totalitarian in its repressiveness and never took steps to illegalize the vigils or the organization, despite the known fact that the women helped men evade the draft and soldiers to desert. The women have been called traitors, which is only to be expected and indeed is to be welcomed: Staša Zajović happily titled one of her articles 'I am disloyal' (Zajović 1994). They have been called 'witches' (Benderly 1997), a term of abuse also applied to five women journalists in Croatia who offended nationalist sentiment by refusing to accept that only Croatian women had been raped in the war by only Serbian men: Croat men too rape, they insisted, and women of any ethnic group may be victims of male aggression (Slapšak 1995).

In language that recalls the Women's Support Network in Belfast, Women in Black put a positive value on difference. They say 'We foster and further differences.' Their practice is also similar to that of the

Northern Ireland women in setting the most divisive difference, ethnicity/nationality, in a context of other, less threatening, differences. They say of themselves, 'We are a heterogeneous group. The age of our members ranges from eighteen to seventy-five. Their backgrounds and life styles differ greatly. Some of them have been active feminists for a long time, while others participate in the feminist discourse for the first time' (Women in Black 1994).

It is not only in Serbia that women peace activists have been at pains to sustain cross-ethnic links. The director of the Centre for Peace, Nonviolence and Human Rights in the Croatian town of Osijek, who identifies herself only as Katarina, describes how they set about breaking out of the spiral of hurt and revenge dividing Serb from Croat in that region:

> First we overcame our fear and then we started working to abolish the divisions of people caused by violence. We refused to be nationalistic in orientation, although it seemed quite logical that priority had to be given to the defence of the nation when the nation was attacked. So we focused on defending basic human, universal values and in doing this we were opening ourselves out to all those who accepted these values. We were experiencing a sort of reconciliation process with people of other nationalities (Bennett et al. 1995: 235).

If such women were acting as mixers, they were also serving as message-carriers. Katarina goes on: 'What we wanted to do was to work on building up civil society and becoming a kind of messenger to the authorities, pointing out the needs of the whole community.' In these modes they became skilled at negotiating common agendas and, again like the women of the Women's Support Network in Belfast and Bat Shalom in Israel, leaving areas of silence where words would shake the alliance. More than one observer has noted that discussions of politics-with-a-big-P have been avoided – for it is this difference that split the pre-war women's movement and indeed, of course, underlies the fighting itself (Korać forthcoming).

The skilled and dedicated work of feminists of the territories of the former Yugoslavia during the wars of course did not lead (any more than it has led women in other wars) to their being included among the actors who negotiated peace on the world stage. The Dayton Agreement of autumn 1995 and all the political moves that preceded and followed it were an all-male matter. But these activists have ironically – and heroically – thanks to the creative use of the *zamir* regional e-mail server (it means 'for peace') begun to create just the unified Yugoslav feminism that warrants the name of 'movement' and that many felt had not quite yet come into being at the moment Yugoslavia fell apart (Korać 1996; Teršelić 1995).

The Internet had also enabled the women of former Yugoslavia to develop productive links with feminist groups all over the world and particularly in Western Europe. Even during the years of warfare there was movement and firsthand contact, with women from elsewhere visiting Belgrade, Zagreb and even Sarajevo despite the siege, and many visits arranged for women from the region to speak in Western European and American cities. Besides, Women in Black, cheerfully defying border controls and security police, were organizing annual international feminist encounters in Serbia from 1994.

There were tensions inherent in the international networking. In 1992 Zagreb women organized a conference on 'Women and War', from which they banned Serb feminists on grounds of nationality. At times Western feminists were intrusive and 'Yugoslav' feminists resented them. But the importance and fertility of the networking was apparent at a second conference in Zagreb in October 1996 on 'Women and the Politics of Peace'. The organizers of the 1992 conference abstained from this one. Framed by an international presence, the many women of the region who attended, meeting each other again with obvious delight, seemed to be the pan-Yugoslav women's movement they would have wished to be five years before. Although to reach each other they now had to pass through newly erected national border fences, have stiff new national passports stamped by officious frontier guards, still there was the feeling that these neighbouring countries were to the women like neighbouring regions of a single country. They felt and spoke as 'us'. Among the women embracing each other in Zagreb were women from the Medica Women's Therapy Centre of Zenica, Bosnia-Hercegovina.

7
Medica Women's Therapy Centre

It was late in 1992 that news began to appear in Western media of widespread detention and raping of women by the soldiers and para-militaries of the Bosnian Serb forces. Monika Hauser, an Italian woman living and working in Köln, Germany, was one of many people in Western Europe who began to understand that these rapes were on an appalling scale, seemingly part of the Serb nationalists' project of destroying the Muslim community in the region and eradicating Muslim culture.

Perhaps because she was specializing in gynaecology, acutely aware of what rape means in physical and emotional trauma, this doctor began making contact with humanitarian organizations to see what she might usefully do in support of the Bosnian women. She was dismayed to find a lack of response wherever she turned. Someone who did respond was Gabi Mischkowski, the coordinator of a German women's anti-war network called Sheherazade. She put Monika Hauser in touch with women in Croatia working among refugees fleeing across the border from Bosnia-Hercegovina. From them she understood that the women with the least support and the greatest need would be those refugees from Serb ethnic cleansing still clustering in the government-held areas of Bosnia itself. In December 1992, travelling overland along roads deep in snow and slush, rutted by military vehicles and convoys, she managed to reach the industrial centre of Zenica in central Bosnia.

Zenica – is this a town or a city? The cluster of high-rise flats and office buildings in the centre, the chimney-stacks of its great steelworks, suggest a city. The River Bosna surging under its bridges, swollen with snowmelt, gives the place a certain stature. But the urban housing quickly runs out into apple orchards on the foothills of the mountains all around. It is a city where the cocks crow at dawn and in the evening there is an aroma of woodsmoke. But in 1992 firewood and fowl were already becoming scarce commodities in central Bosnia.

Zenica's main industrial employer had been the steel factory, now almost at a standstill. Most of its male workers had 'gone to the hills'. They had taken up arms on one side or the other. Zenica had become a city of women, children and old men. Monika began making enquiries around town, met other concerned women and put to them her idea for a therapy centre for women, run by women, that would combine medical with psycho-social care. In the local hospital and other health services she met gynaecologists like herself, and physicians, nurses and psychologists. Overwhelmed by the need they were witnessing in the refugee camps, they readily supported Monika's proposal.

Together the small group of women set about obtaining a building, talking with the municipality and making sure they would have the support, or at least not the opposition, of the religious authorities in the city. While the local women started to convert an unused kindergarten to their needs, Monika went back to Germany to raise money. She struck lucky, with a grant of DM 250,000 donated by listeners to a women's television programme that had featured the rape story. With this she bought all the equipment needed for a gynaecology clinic, hired vehicles and drivers and set out on the long and hazardous road back to Bosnia. She arrived in Zenica in January 1993 and found a team and a building ready and waiting. Medica Women's Therapy Centre opened its doors three months later.

Responding to trauma

The women who founded Medica believed that women who have been abused by men need treatment and care from women in a woman-only environment. They understood that, first and foremost, women survivors of rape must be believed and respected. Medical treatment should involve a recognition of the woman as an individual, a caring and not merely professional contact between doctor and client, and go hand in hand with psychotherapeutic and social care. The service must be free. The provision must be of the highest quality possible in these hard circumstances, because the women deserved nothing less. These principles made Medica unique in the Yugoslav region.

Medica quickly developed its work in three buildings, with a total staff of 70, all Bosnian. Medica-1 was a utilitarian two-storey structure surrounded by much taller housing blocks, not far from the centre of town. Here were the gynaecology unit, a psycho-therapeutic centre and accommodation for twenty or thirty women and children. In the gynaecology unit on the ground floor were doctors (like Amira Frljak), anaesthesiologists (such as Meliha Branković), and head nurse Paša Kovać and her team of six. Some worked full-time in Medica, others shared their time between Medica and the local hospital. They treated both in-patients and out-patients (the latter being mainly but not

Zenica, Central Bosnia, city of the living, the uprooted and the dead.

exclusively refugees). They offered family planning, reproductive healthcare, supervision of pregnancy and abortions. Often they found themselves treating injuries and disease, as well as pregnancies, arising from rape.

Medica had a good relationship with the local health authorities, and was able to operate with a degree of freedom in the matter of abortion. Bosnia-Hercegovina had barely had time to form a national government when it was plunged into war. Consequently the old Yugoslav legislation still held, under which abortion was permitted freely until the tenth week of pregnancy, and up to the twentieth week after referral to a medical panel. The Muslim authorities were supportive. The Catholic Church of course was opposed, but it had no influence during the war.

One member of the psychotherapy team, Nurka Babović, a Montenegran by origin and a sociologist by training, was in continuous contact with the local refugee population, visiting the various centres and seeking out those who had found lodgings in private homes. This was one of the hardest jobs in Medica, because it meant constant exposure to the desperation of the refugee population, making judgements about relative need and being gatekeeper to the sanctuary that Medica quickly became.

It was important to ensure that women coming to Medica were not publicly identified as 'raped'. In Yugoslavia before the war, as in many countries, particularly in the more traditional rural communities, a raped woman would be shunned, unmarriageable, effectively blamed for what had been done to her. Medica obtained a helpful *fatwa* by the Imam of Zenica urging respect for raped women. All the same, it advertised itself on local radio and through other means in coded terms as a 'gynaecology clinic', a centre for women 'traumatized' in the war. In fact Monika and the other founders of Medica recognized that rape was not the only, and in many cases not even the worst, trauma women were experiencing. A significant proportion of the project's clients were from the start women and children who had not been raped, but who had experienced terrorization and loss in other forms.

The majority of the six-strong psychotherapy team had not practised as therapists before the war. The demands of Medica were very different from those of the educational and occupational psychology they had typically practised in peacetime. They had to set quickly about acquiring new knowledge and new skills. They read everything they could find on trauma and began to identify the symptoms of women after rape and other forms of torture and terror. They learned the stages of healing and how it can be helped. They treated women and children, individually and in groups (Medica 1997). Together with the gynaecology unit they cooperated in staffing a mobile clinic, 'Martha', which went out three days a week into nearby villages, where long queues of women would be waiting.

Medica-1's household staff consistently provided, despite increasingly severe shortages, warmth, comfort and good solid food. These were also a kind of therapy to people who had arrived in Zenica hungry and cold, after being driven from their homes and hunted across mountains and through forests before reaching the relative safety of Zenica. So Nusreta Ćatović, who had formerly catered for three thousand in the steelworks canteen, was jokingly called Medica's 'psycho-cook', on account of the homely and nutritious meals she made out of the most unpromising ingredients. Downstairs Vahida Mustafić, helped by Amela and Sanela, ran a nursery and play-school for the children, who of course were no less traumatized than their mothers. It had been recognized from the start that women would need to have time for themselves and help with feeding, clothing and caring for their children.

As the project grew, administration became a complex matter, requiring its own team – Nuna Zviždić, Hana Vuković and others. A logistics-person dealt with orders and supplies, ferrying food, equipment and medicines via Croatia, and coordinating with UNHCR and NGO convoys. The project had four-wheel-drive vehicles equipped with radio. An information department, Infoteka, was staffed by young women who quickly learned how to handle computers and maintain contact with the outside world by fax, phone and e-mail whenever these links were not interrupted by the fighting. Talking over strong sweet coffee at any time of day around Infoteka's long table with Duška Andrić, Selma Hadži-halilović and Belma X was the way the information was exchanged between the project and the town and flowed to and from the many humanitarian organizations operating in the region, and to visitors from abroad.

Medica's two other centres were residential units. When patients began to show signs of improvement they might move from Medica-1 to Medica-2, a separate house across the town where they would continue to have care and therapy. This homely place was under the care of Zilha Hadžihajdić, the mother-figure of Medica, who had been a schoolteacher of German language and literature before the war and had a special fondness for her teenage residents. When well enough, the younger women would go from here to town each day to attend those schools and colleges that were still open. The older women would spend their days here sewing, weaving, knitting or hairdressing. This was therapeutic activity but, since everyone had lost their usual livelihood in the war, the workshops involved training too, through which they might

restore themselves to some kind of independent existence. Several of the trainers were themselves refugees, and quite a few of Medica's patients as they recovered took up employment in the project.

A separate house some miles away in a country location was called Medica-3. Although it was served by the same psychotherapists, it operated somewhat independently, with mainly rural refugees and activity focused around horticulture, keeping livestock and a small dairy.

No sooner had Medica opened its doors than war broke out on a second front. This Croatian exercise in ethnic cleansing, in which the victims were Muslims and remaining Serbs, effectively blockaded Zenica and shrank the enclave of central Bosnia still in government hands. By summer 1993 only a fraction of the needed aid was reaching the area. Electricity and water supplies were erratic and petrol almost unobtainable. Keeping the convoys rolling from the coast became more and more hazardous. The Medica women had to use all their resourcefulness and their contacts to keep themselves and their refugees from starving, let alone maintain the flow of pharmaceutical and medical supplies. On the road, like all the humanitarian aid-workers, they wore safety helmets and flak-jackets. They learned how to get what they wanted from bureaucrats, soldiers, mercenaries and *mujahedeen*, how to talk their way through checkpoints, how to smuggle, to be devious, to confront, to persuade.

If conditions in Medica were hard, in the town they were unspeakable. The luckier of the refugees were living in overcrowded flats and houses. The least fortunate were in appalling camps. One of the young women in Medica told me she had come from among seven hundred people sheltering in a cinema, with no windows, mostly with no lighting, without soap, without medicines, with the most meagre daily hand-out of food. Another had experienced seven months with four hundred others in a gymnasium hall with broken windows and scanty bedding. But perhaps worse than the physical conditions were uncertainty about the fate of loved ones and the lack of prospect of any return to a life of normality, familiarity and meaning.

Even two years into its operation and after the Croatian 'war within a war' had ended, around half the women passing through Medica had been subject to rape. The psychotherapy team analysed the data concerning these women for 1995. Forty-eight per cent had been raped in group situations. One in three had been multiply raped. Almost half had been raped in front of members of their family or acquaintances. Their average age was 27. The youngest was 12, the oldest 52. Half of the women were married. Forty per cent had never experienced sexual intercourse before. Thirty per cent of this Medica sample had become pregnant as a result of the rapes and most of the pregnancies had resulted in live births. Of the women giving birth in Medica, the great majority kept their child. The proportion was as high as it was partly because of the support and counselling they received there. Only 2 per cent of the raped women did not need treatment for adverse gynaeco- logical symptoms. Most found it difficult at first to talk about what had happened to them. Many were severely withdrawn and nearly half attempted suicide or gave signs of being suicidal. Fifty per cent were suffering anxiety and depression. Feelings of shame, fear, repulsion and aggression were a common reaction (Medica 1995).

From the women's testimony a picture emerged of the extent of the war's atrocities, of the many villages and towns where these thousands of rapes had taken place, of the buildings used to detain women, the identity of their torturers, the names of the many women 'taken out' who were never returned and must be presumed dead.

The meaning of Medica to the team

Medica became a place of refuge not only to the refugees it sheltered but to its staff. To a greater or lesser extent everyone was traumatized by the war, and they too gained by the warmth the place radiated, from the friendships and from having meaningful work to do. Some of them were now doing for work what had been a hobby before, like Zdenka X, a town planner and architect now teaching weaving in Medica-2. Emsa Hodžić, working alongside Zdenka, training the refugees in hairdressing, had lost her own little salon to the flames of Serb aggression in her home town of Jajce. When she came to Zenica as a refugee she had only the clothes she was wearing. She said, 'We went to the Red Cross. We had nothing, no clothes, no tissues. I got a nightie and cut it short at the hem. The offcut we made into hankies to dry our tears.' For Emsa, Medica had become a substitute home and family. 'I can't wait to come in on Mondays,' she said.

Some were pleased to have found war-relevant uses for their skills. Doing psychotherapy seemed more fulfilling than the research into worker absenteeism and alcoholism that some of them had been doing in the steelworks' social department. Marijana Senjak said, 'What was very important for me was that here we were free to imagine, to find out things we didn't know, think how we might do it, make it our own creation.' Medica seemed to be one of those spaces in which finding the resources to survive war can be experienced by women as empowering. 'I think this work involves all of me for the first time, I feel more human,' said Mirha. 'War is one of the worst things you can experience

Medica: individual and group therapy for women raped and traumatized in the war, and for their children.

in your life. But there's this other side – the war is drawing the best from me.'

But day to day the work was exhausting, totally draining. The therapists were the recipients of scarcely bearable news from the front-line, borne by women whose suffering threatened to overwhelm everyone who witnessed it. Edita Ostojić sometimes felt 'This violence we're all seeing may be eating us away inside like a cancer.' The doctors too were shaken by what they encountered. 'I sometimes feel there's no one in the whole world who's seen the wounds I've seen,' said Meliha Branković. 'I mean all of us here. This kind of war hasn't been written about anywhere.' The refugees' great need and desperation made them very demanding patients. 'Every woman who comes here leaves a trace in us,' said Zilha. There is always one leaving who takes a bit of you with her, and another arriving to whom you have to give yourself afresh.

But there was an ethic of care for each other as well as for the patients. Nobody had to pretend they were perfect, cover up mistakes or inadequacies. They learned to open to their own feelings. In this they were helped by 'supervision' and psychodrama sessions from visiting therapists and trainers from Germany and elsewhere with experience in post-traumatic stress disorder (PTSD). 'Nobody had asked me in my work before how I was feeling,' said Nurka. The socialist system had allowed no room for that. The first time someone had given her such space for unburdening, she hadn't stopped crying for days.

From the start Medica was conceived as a women–only project. One or two exceptions were made for safety's sake: the warehouse-keepers and armed guards, and later one or two drivers, were men. Otherwise Medica was all female. The definition of Medica as a project run by women for women was that of Monika and other feminist women sup-porters in Germany, including Gabi Mischkowski of Sheherazade (who had set up an office for Medica in Köln during the year Monika was in Zenica). But the core group of Bosnian professional women agreed that women would be more likely to understand the feelings of women who had been raped, the particular experiences of women in war, and that in turn the women coming to Medica for treatment and care would be more likely to trust women doctors and therapists. Mostly the other members of the staff in Zenica that I spoke with agreed. They believed there was a 'more human' approach, greater patience and less competitiveness than there would have been if men had been involved. They were happy to prove that 'women can do everything'. They were particularly proud to see Kirsten Wienberg and Mirjana Idrizović driving the big vehicles, Nuna controlling the finances, the women in Infoteka teaching them-selves all they needed to know about computer technology.

Feminism and democracy

Whether Medica can be called a feminist project is an open question. Its first report certainly described the project as 'autonomous, feminist, politically independent, decentralized and in conjunction with women from all the republics of the former Yugoslavia'. This statement was drafted by Monika Hauser, and it located Medica firmly within the context of an international feminist movement. As we have seen, however, the Yugoslav women's movement, focused in Belgrade, Zagreb and Lubljana, had had slight expression in Sarajevo and had passed the rest of Bosnia-Hercegovina by. Although since then the catastrophe of the war had given rise to numerous women's charities and humanitarian organizations in the new nation-state, many were religious, most were 'patriotic' and some were outright nationalist. Medica, at the outset, was on the cusp between this women's voluntary sector and the feminist movement.

It was Monika of course who, without imposing anything, simply tended to speak in her own feminist language from the start. Later, as Gabi Mischkowski, Kirsten Wienberg and other German women came to work with Medica, they too were heard to speak this language. There had been no opposition to the assumption that Medica would be a feminist project, perhaps because of the extremely gendered nature of the issue it was addressing. But the experience of communism had left Yugoslavs sceptical of socially engineered Utopias. Three years into the project, some of the women I spoke with expressed a little distance from feminism as they read it in Monika, Gabi and other Western visitors.

Zilha, for instance, was dubious about this quest for women's autonomy, 'a woman living for herself', which she felt was alien to the Bosnian ideal of family and friendship loyalties. Rada X, Medica's interpreter and translator, said that at first she'd felt impatient with these Western women who seemed to have no responsibilities. Without husband, home and children, of course they had time for feminism! She, Zdenka and several other women said they could not recall ever having felt disadvantaged under communism. Strong women like this had felt some distaste for 'women's issues'. Rada had thought the official fuss made about International Women's Day each year just 'kitschy', a matter of flowers and flattery. Some women felt frustrated in Medica by a sensitivity about feelings that could amount to a lack of straight talking. And in so far as feminism was seen as distancing women from men, that seemed too cruel a thing, an unthinkable thing, while the men you loved, your husband or your son, were away fighting for their lives and for yours. So here again, as in Belfast, I found women saying 'I'm feminist in my own way', 'We're *Bosnian* feminists'.

An important measure and test of Medica's feminism was its governance. Management was always bound to be a challenge. It called for both hard-headed efficiency and sensitive caring. Decisions had to be made fast, but also democratically. The women involved came from very different backgrounds. They were, as we shall see, of different ethnic groups. But in addition they had different levels of education, and, important in the Bosnian context, were from both urban and rural environments.

While Monika was in Zenica during 1993, she tended to be looked to as leader of Medica. But she was anxious from the start, first that decision-making should be consensual and second that the project should as soon as possible operate without her. When she went back to Germany one of the psychotherapists, Marijana Senjak, became nominal leader and spokesperson, but she did not relish the role. In terms of structure, between 1993 and 1995 the project was run as a loose assemblage of functional teams. The psycho-team, the medical team, the kitchen-and-nursery team, and so on, ran their own affairs, chose their own co-ordinator, and sent her to a regular coordinators' meeting. But this team-leaders' meeting soon felt too big and the time it stole from the practical work was resented. Yugoslavs had unpleasant memories of time-consuming 'socialist self-management' and forms of democracy that had in practice been disempowering. The truth was, nobody in Medica really wanted to be a manager.

The German women had come with ideas of feminism and democracy, Rada said, 'but our project was founded during the war. It was an extreme situation, you couldn't give much thought to democracy, things you'd normally think about. With shelling on the street, it was a matter of survival ... Democracy seemed funny for us, crazy, a luxury. We wanted something practical and quick. Democracy was exhausting, it took so much energy.'

In 1995–96 Gabi Mischkowski spent many months in Zenica trying to serve as midwife to a viable management structure, foreseeing a time when Medica must be independent of Köln, capable of raising its own funding from international sources and controlling its own budget and its own destiny. By late 1996 a formula for a democratic collective leadership, a more streamlined management committee, had been painfully thrashed out, and Gabi and the Köln office felt able to turn their attention to the plight of Bosnian women refugees in Germany. But a tension remained in Zenica around these issues.

So the feelings of these women about feminist democracy had been shaped between the relentless hammer of the daily need to act and make decisions, and the resistant anvil of war conditions and refugees' desperate need. It is not surprising then that each of them (rather like the women of the Women's Support Network in Belfast) had worked out a personal relationship with it, given it her own twist.

Perhaps the most striking thing about Medica, though, was how little serious conflict there was among them over this divergence. It was permissible to differ on feminism. Perhaps it was because the German women were loved and valued, as indeed were the many ex-Yugoslav feminists everyone knew were giving Medica moral support from Zagreb and Belgrade. It was also certainly because many women had a new openness in their sense of themselves and others as women, due to their work and their war. Duška wondered, 'Was it that the war turned us into feminists, or did it just show us we'd been feminists all along?' Meliha, anaesthesiologist and practising Muslim, had been entirely non-political before the war, had had 'no feelings for women'. 'You realize', she said now, 'it's not enough to be a doctor. You have to be engaged in a political sense too. Through the project I've met a lot of women who are in the women's movement and I've found my place in it.'

Selma, 20 years old, was already a veteran of two years' army experience. She clearly liked men, knew a lot of soldiers and had fun in their company. These men often ridiculed feminism. But Selma was undeterred, because, she said, 'In Medica I heard them say "the personal is political" and that has created me.'

Maybe men laugh in the first couple of minutes if you decide to present yourself as a feminist. Probably the first image they have is 'Oh my God, she's a witch, she's against men, she wants the world to become a women's world and so on.' But I don't think we're like this. We're just for equal rights, that everybody should have what belongs to them. So after a couple of minutes he'll understand, 'This is a strong woman and she knows what she wants. I shouldn't blame her – I should appreciate that.' But people here in Bosnia are the same as everywhere else. All around the world now you have propaganda against feminism, saying women should go home and have children because there's social crisis. Here, England, it's all the same.

The fact is that, despite or because of its almost-feminist profile, Medica had achieved respect and self-respect. Most of the women had been employees of hospitals and factories with rigidly conventional structures. They were proud of the freedom and choice in Medica, its client-centred regime. Gynaecologist Amira said, 'The patients perceive Medica differently from other medical institutions. You can tell by their reactions how much they appreciate the way they're treated.' In the wider world of national and international authorities and NGOs Medica was acknowledged as serious and professional. And those women who had the opportunity to travel abroad during the war and speak on feminist platforms felt continually affirmed in their politics and their approach.

Ethnicity in Medica

Before the Serbian aggression began, Zenica had a population of about 120,000 of whom around 22,000 were Serb by declared nationality and a similar number were Croatian. The war saw the departure of all but about 3,000 each of the Serb and Croat population, and the arrival of about 70,000 refugees, many Muslim. Ethnic mixity was thus drastically reduced within a matter of months. That is the effect achieved by ethnic cleansing, even in a city well behind the frontline.

Medica Women's Therapy Centre reflected the remaining, drastically diminished, ethnic richness of the city. Only one or two per cent of the refugees were non-Muslim. (One was Dara, an elderly Bosnian Serb woman who had fled Serb aggression along with her Muslim neighbours saying '*These* are my people.') Of the staff, only around 10 per cent were not Muslim by background. There were three women whose parentage was Bosnian Serb, three whose parentage was Bosnian Croat and one Slovenian. I interviewed all of these. But everyone emphasized that these distinctions felt new and distasteful to them. They simplified 'belonging' beyond anything they recognized. For example, Zdenka, the teacher of weaving, was of Slovenian Catholic background. She had been living with her partner for seven years when they decided to formalize their union in marriage. On jointly filling out the marriage form she had been surprised, though in no way dismayed, to see that he was 'Croatian' – a fact she had had no reason to know till then. Such knowledge comes much sooner today and bears danger with it.

'Religion' was perhaps more meaningful. Slovenians and Croatians are historically both Catholic peoples and this similarity between Zdenka and her partner perhaps reduced the significance of 'national' difference. But that itself must be in question, since both of them professed atheism. As we have seen, Bosnian Muslim identity has heretofore never been unambiguous as to whether it signifies 'nationality' or 'religion'. The Yugoslav census of 1971 gave it official status as 'nationality', but Muslim identity has never been coterminous with Bosnia-Hercegovina. Nurka, for example, is of Muslim background but is not originally Bosnian. She comes from the significant Muslim community of neighbouring Montenegro.

Then again, is 'Muslim' a matter of religious conviction or of 'tradition'? Certainly only two of the 18 'Muslim' women I interviewed went out of the way to describe themselves as observant Muslims. Anyway, as Paša, Medica's head nurse, said, 'Belief in God is very demanding, it asks a lot of your free time. That's something I don't have.' Like many others, she had settled for morality in place of piety. Because the Yugoslav state had discouraged religion and disadvantaged those who practised it, the present generation of women in Medica mainly had parents who had been non-religious, members of the officially atheist Communist Party. But they often mentioned grandmothers who had been religious, whose beliefs and practices they had been intrigued by and had respected. Probably most women in Medica in principle welcomed the re-enfranchisement of religions in the region. But for most of these women personally, being 'Muslim' was 'only' a matter of family and community culture. They were anxious that religion 'know its place', not a matter for the state or party politics but one of individual spirituality.

To state that Medica had seven 'non-Muslims' is to understate its mixity in other ways too. First, there were several additional women who were brought up as, came to think of themselves as, or were ascribed the identity of, Bosnian Muslim who actually had one parent who was not of that culture. They had been officially 'undetermined'. Second, several of Medica's 'Muslims' were married or had been married to men of different or of mixed parentage. Finally, of course, there had been in Yugoslav days the option of declaring oneself 'Yugoslav' rather than one of the constituent nationalities. At least half the 26 women I interviewed had chosen this option and only since Bosnian 'independence' had they been required to think again, to re-adopt (or newly accept) a latent ethnicity.

In the confused identity-environment of BH since the disintegration of Yugoslavia, names have taken on a special significance. The new official identity card issued to the citizens does not specify 'nation' or 'religion' – only your name, your father's name and your married name are shown. Both personal and family names in the Yugoslav region are read as indicators of religious background and/or nationality. The trouble is, people frequently have the 'wrong' name. First, gender may introduce an ambiguity into ethnicity here: some women, like Rada, proudly challenge patriarchy by keeping their 'own' – albeit their father's – surname on marriage. And parents sometimes break tradition in naming their children. Hana's 'modern' parents, she says, fancied a name for their daughter that in Bosnia happens to have a 'Christian' ring to it. They did not imagine what that might mean to a young

Medica still harbours something of Bosnia's old mixity:
Muslim, Serb, Croat. All Slavs, all Bosnians.

Muslim 30 years later. But you can also feel inauthentic if, like Ferida, a Medica nurse, your personal name says you are Muslim, while you were in fact born in Croatia to a Croatian mother (though a Muslim father) and have now married a Bosnian Serb. She says, 'I don't want to be judged by my name, but by my personality, by my soul.' It is distasteful to her that in today's circumstances, in ethnic disguise, she steals an illegitimate advantage over, let us say, Belma, who says, 'I know now someone could rape me for my name.'

Holding together

These women are where they are partly by chance, partly by choice. They were mainly born and bred in the Yugoslav republic of Bosnia-Hercegovina and so are, *de facto*, whatever their 'religion' or 'nationality', effectively 'Bosnians'. Even the non-Muslims among them say that when they went out of Bosnia to other Yugoslav republics as students they were made to realize a certain Bosnian-ness in themselves by others' comments on their accent, the little jokes invoking a Bosnian stereotype. (Popular stories portray Bosnians as endearing fools who nevertheless get the better of those who underestimate them.) Most happened to have been living, here in Zenica, in an area of Bosnia that had not been 'ethnically cleansed' (yet). They had not been forcibly moved (yet). But also they were against nationalism and the ethnicizing process. The 'Serbs' and 'Croats' among them had chosen not to interpret the current course of events as necessitating a move. They had chosen to remain in what they hoped could survive as a democratic, open and mixed society.

The paroxysm of nationalist fear and murderous loathing that was induced in many people in the Bosnian Serb and Bosnian Croat communities did not occur among Bosnian Muslims. And there were in any case many stories of 'good neighbours' on all sides befriending each other despite the convulsion of hatred. Nevertheless the events of the war had inevitably, even in central Bosnia, coloured Muslim opinion of the 'others'. Duška, for instance, recognizably a Bosnian Serb, had found human excrement deposited, an unambiguous message, on the doorstep of her home in the town.

How was this enmity avoided in Medica? The cohesion was made possible by a number of shared principles, more or less explicit within the discourse of the project. One was the belief that the experience of women gave them a commonality that did not always, but could sometimes, override ethnic differences. In particular they felt themselves to share three things: domestic experience, and (because of the nature of Medica) nurturing skills and vulnerability to rape. In this sense Medica's democratic feminism, discussed above, however each woman might adapt it to her leaning, gave them some immunity to the epidemic of ethnicism. This can be seen in their determination to re-establish contact with Bosnian Serb women after the hostilities ended. In May 1996 a group from Medica (facilitated and accompanied by feminists from Zagreb and Belgrade) went north into the 'Bosnian Serb Entity' (the Republika Srpska) for an exploratory meeting with Duga, a women's group in Banja Luka. Duga was known to be non-nationalist, even though not feminist, and Medica believed they might be suitable partners in re-establishing common ground, despite the total non-cooperation of the authorities of the Entity with the remainder of the Bosnian state, the Muslim–Croat Federation. As we saw in the previous chapter, Croatian women had similarly built bridges back to women of the Serb minority in the Croatian Krajina and Osijek as soon as the fighting stopped.

A second source of cohesion in the project was a shared analysis of who and what was to blame for the disaster into which Yugoslavia had fallen. I met with no departure from the view that ordinary people's vulnerability to nationalist extremism (sometimes they termed it fascism) had been exploited by ambitious individuals and groups to further their own power. They included academics, politicians and religious leaders with access to organizations and the media. The leaders of the Yugoslav National Army were blamed for betraying the constitution and its federal ideal. And it was believed that nationalism had been whipped up by the return from Western countries of extremist right-wing émigrés, vestigial Četnik and Ustaša groups with money and arms, profiting by the fall of communism. Self-interested world powers were criticized for having reacted irresponsibly in the vacuum left by the internal collapse of communism in the Soviet Union and Eastern Europe. They had been concerned only to have the world learn the lesson of the failure of the socialist experiment and to install a capitalist market in the region. It was widely felt that the USA and the countries of the European Union could have prevented or stopped the war, and that they should not have reinforced ethnic separatism with their tidy partition plans. They also believed that the Muslim community and political organizations had been naive in failing to protect democracy (and their own communal interests) sooner.

The shared belief that the fears of 'ordinary Bosnian Serbs' and 'ordinary Bosnian Croats' were manipulated was crucial to Medica as an alliance of women of mixed ethnicities. But one very troubling area of uncertainty was widely shared too: how was it that so many people had been open to manipulation? 'How did they make all those Serbs think the same way?' Emsa asked herself. 'They left our town one by one before the fighting began, without even telling me they were going – men, women and children. They went out on the hills and shelled us.' Everyone had this experience of trusted neighbours and friends who had turned against them. Despite the incomprehension, it felt important to everyone not to ascribe ethnic labels, to evaluate each person as an individual, not to 'put everyone in one basket' (a phrase I heard many times). So this was another important factor in Medica's cohesion. They said to each other, 'There's no such thing as collective guilt.'

There is a difference between the ethnic mixity of the Women's Support Network in Belfast, Bat Shalom in Israel and this mixity at Medica. In Ireland and Israel the women had positively sought each other out in a political move after decades of separation. The mixity in Medica was residual. The separation of Bosnia's ethnic groups was recent. Until three years previously they had been living closely intermingled. In rural areas few villages were comprised of only a single ethnic group. Almost all had distinct communities of Muslims living side by side with groups of Catholic (Croat) homes or Orthodox (Serb) families. They maintained separate cultures, acknowledged difference and often discouraged their young from intermarrying. But they had been social with each other, exchanging coffee visits, sharing in family celebrations and cooperating in local affairs. In her ethnographic study of a mixed Muslim/Croat central Bosnian village Tone Bringa writes:

> Socializing between villagers, Muslim and Catholic, provided an opportunity for identifying with one's ethnoreligious Community and expressing this belonging to nonmembers. At the same time, however, it gave members of the two communities an opportunity to focus on shared experiences and other aspects of their identities that were common to both (being women, neighbours, villagers, Bosnians) ... It is precisely this tension between perceived similarities and difference which created the dynamic of social life (Bringa 1995: 66).

The cities and towns had been different in two respects. A secular Yugoslav culture had replaced religious tradition. Women were less bound by patriarchal traditions and had jobs, even careers, and a degree of social and sexual freedom. And there was not the territorial sorting that persisted in the villages. People related to each other more as individuals, according little significance to each other's ethnic identification. Names might be distinctive, but the difference the names signified had become negligible in the urbanizing and modernizing half-century since the Second World War.

Edita said of the effective mixity into which her generation had grown up, 'It was Bosnia's greatest wealth.' And the current ethnic diversity in

Medica was not strategic, it was just a little of this wealth living on. In its first two years there was a taken-for-grantedness about it: 'Of course, that's how we always were.' But in late 1995 at the time of my first visit, there was beginning to be a new consciousness, partly awoken by the interest of foreign visitors like me, that combined pride in the continued presence of non-Muslims in Medica with a self-questioning about how to celebrate difference without over-emphasizing it.

That year for the first time they took a collective decision to hold a Christmas party. (Medica as a project had always celebrated Bajram, the closing festival of Ramadan.) The Muslim women at first thought of a special meal on Christmas Eve. Then someone said, 'No. That's when Christians like to celebrate at home with their families. Better choose another day.' Nudžejma Y, herself a practising Muslim, said, 'Of course we would invite the refugees too. We weren't sure if they could accept the idea of celebrating a Christian holiday. Most of them at that time had just been expelled from Srebrenica. But they did come, and we celebrated together and it was very very positive.' Each 'Christian' there, Bosnian Serb, Bosnian Croat, Bosnian Slovenian, German and English (for I was there too) was given a present by the group as a whole. Musing on the way the event had been thought through, Selma said, 'I think it was a sign Medica grew up, that we really understood what we've been fighting for.'

Before that moment, the concern in Medica had been less a question of celebrating difference than one of how to avoid hurting each other. The refugees flooding into the town were 99 per cent Muslim. The aggressors at that time were the Bosnian Serbs. Refugees coming to Medica would have been aware of the three women of Serb background, and others with names that suggested they were married to Serbs, working in the project. Medica's Bosnian Serb driver, Mirjana, for instance, would have been waiting for women at the reception centres when they arrived in flight from the Serb atrocities. Duška and Rada were always visible in and around Infoteka. But it was not until the disaster of the second front opened up by the Croatian extremists that women in Medica began to worry about mutual hurt between refugees and staff.

This was particularly because two of the psychotherapists were of Bosnian Croat background. When patients began to arrive in the project who had been raped by men of the Croat forces, the psycho-team, particularly Edita and Marijana themselves, wondered how the women might react to having a Croat woman as therapist. 'I was always asking myself,' said Edita, 'will this client look on me as one of the ones who hurt her? Will she put me in the same basket as them?' Medica's policy

Refugee children perform the Charleston at a Medica party.

was to nominate a therapist, but make her ethnic identity clear and give the patient a chance to refuse. On the rare occasion she did, the hurt to Edita or Marijana also became a concern of the psycho-team, and was made explicit and worked through.

The potential crisis for relationships between Muslim and Croat in Medica and the way they moved through it together is exemplified in the arrival of Nudžejma Y, who was recruited to Medica's psycho-therapy team as a Muslim theologian and counsellor. One of the most ferocious actions of the Croat HVO was to besiege and destroy Stari Vitez, the old Muslim centre of the major town of Vitez. Nudžejma and her family lived in the area consumed by fire in the sacking of Vitez. In Spain, at the Mijas workshop, she told us how she had come to Medica:

> We lived in a mixed village with Croats. We never had any conflict between us. They must have known the HVO's intentions, yet they gave us no warning of any kind. At that moment my trust in Croats was pulled from underneath me. I simply put all Croats in one basket. We were put in prison.
>
> Eventually, we were released into a Muslim area and made our way to to Zenica. And even then, when I arrived in Zenica, whenever I heard a Croat name, I felt hate. Then when I came to work in Medica I met colleagues in the psycho-team and later the other Medica staff. And I saw that Croats, Serbs and Muslims worked in the team together. At that time the conflict with the HVO was intensifying all the time. Although the Croats and Serbs had a chance to flee out of the Muslim area, they didn't. They were friendly to Muslims and wanted to help these refugee women. They expressed their discomfort to me about the acts perpetrated by their 'nations'.
>
> Then something broke in me. And at that moment I told them: I love you, as a Croat, and *because you stayed here to suffer with us and to help*. And I started to rebuild my trust in the other nations. And I know how relieved they felt at that moment. I'm proud to belong to a team where we can enjoy our nationality but have respect for others. I specially love the national ingredients in our psycho-team, including Croats in mixed marriages with Serbs and Muslims. They helped me overcome my trauma.

Edita, another of the psychotherapy team, and a Croat by origin, shared equally in this tension and this love. She had suffered great pain over the outrages being perpetrated by paramilitaries in the name of 'her' people, and knew that her colleague Kadrija's parents had spent eleven months under siege in Stari Vitez. She carried the potential for guilt and shame within her. She also felt doubt and confusion, because of two conflicting feelings: anger that the Bosnian government army did not or could not inflict retribution on these Croat forces, and fear for the suffering of many innocent Croats if they were to do so.

Some months after Kadrija joined the team they were together at a seminar in Bonn. It was a time and place where the two women could really talk for the first time, when Edita could show her grief for Kadrija's suffering and hear her say: 'I don't hold you guilty.' Edita says now, looking back to those hard times when every day they were hearing 'unforgettable and unforgiven things' that that conversation with Kadrija 'was a gift from the heavens. It was beyond compare with any gift I ever had from anyone. I felt she saw me as the person I am, that I feel I am.'

As we have seen was the case in Belfast and in Megiddo, these kinds of situations call for crucial choices about silence and speech. There are times you cannot talk, times you can talk, and times you must talk. The moments when talk becomes possible or necessary differ for different things. The entire work of Medica's psycho-team was helping traumatized women to find the moment and the words to speak about what happened to them, and so bring nearer the moment of healing. But, working under stress as they all were, the learned wisdom did not always transfer into project relationships.

When Rada told me about her situation as a Bosnian Serb in Medica, it was clear that 'speech or silence' was central. Like everyone else, when Medica began, she had submerged any identity problem she may have felt and focused her energies exclusively on work. Most of them felt, I think, as Nuna put it, that if they indulged in too much self-analysis they 'might drown in it'. Rada's work involved German/Bosnian interpretation at meetings between Medica personnel and visitors to the project. On several occasions she found herself interpreting hurtful things, things her professional role prevented her challenging. While Medica staff would always be careful, for example, to distinguish the aggressors of Prijedor, Foča or Višegrad as 'the Bosnian Serb forces' or 'Četniks', visitors to the project might thoughtlessly lump all 'Serbs' together as criminals.

When they did this, Rada just swallowed the hurt and did not show what she felt, even to her friends. She said to herself, 'I don't want to bore them with that. We all have our hurts in this war. I think I can handle it myself.' It was only during a psycho-drama session organized for Medica staff by a visiting German colleague, Gabi Müller, that Rada was able to allow herself to show just how much it hurt to be one of an ethnic group who had become the world's monsters. The others were mortified and shocked when she broke her silence. Zilha was there. She said, 'We were amazed. We had just respected Rada as an expert in her field. She had nothing but praise from us, praise was what she deserved. We didn't know where all those frustrations came from. Then we understood that she had been trying to repress the Serb in herself,

to be free from identification with the people who'd done terrible things
– but she didn't want to reject her nation.'

Later, at Mijas, in conversations with Protestant women from Northern Ireland and Jewish women from Israel, also dealing with the pain
of being identified by others with a group positioned as aggressors/
oppressors, Rada was able to say more about this. But still in day-to-day
working in Medica she maintains, unobserved, a private and personal
balance in the matter of silence and speech. Because the problem of
being a Bosnian Serb today goes far wider than Medica, Zenica or even
Bosnia. And her loyalty to Medica, anyway, has primacy: 'Medica is my
oasis, after all.'

Ethnic and gender relations: adaptive renewal

Even if the Dayton peace accord holds in Bosnia-Hercegovina, it
will be a long time before Medica's work with refugees is no longer
needed. Thousands are now being returned by host countries but
without the prospect of re-establishing life in their original homes.
The demand for Medica's gynaecological clinic is as great as ever. The
psychotherapy team are finding that as old traumas heal, new ones
arise: accepting that those who have gone missing will now never come
back, accepting that those who come home have become different
people.

The Medica team foresee needs (possibly conflicting) on the one
hand to institutionalize the project as an accepted part of the health
provision of central Bosnia, on the other to be a vocal, campaigning
organization. Abortion rights will need to be defended against nationalist and religious reaction. Even the Bosnian gynaecological profession is
not wholly committed to women's right to choose (unpublished report
on e-mail, November 8/9 1996). The experience of the war has made
it possible to speak openly of rape, but the maximum penalty still
remains only four years' imprisonment and the project will probably
find itself campaigning for the legal system to take rape more seriously.
In all the former Yugoslav countries women working on SOS 'hotlines'
and in refuges believe they are seeing increased domestic and street
violence against women with the return of men from the fighting
(Mladjenović and Matijašević 1996; Borić and Desnica 1996). By 1996
the Medica women were preparing to shift focus from war rape to
domestic violence, increasing popular awareness and providing support
for battered women. There were plans to set up and run their own SOS
phone line.

Because of the new poverty, prostitution has been growing fast in

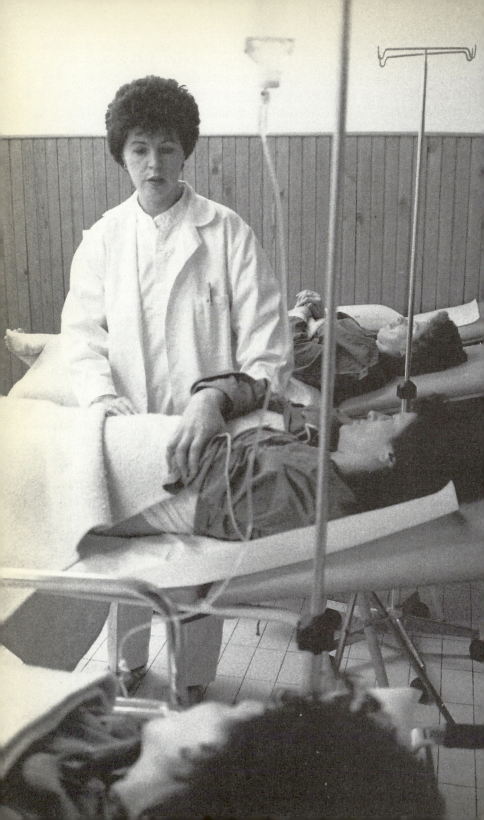

Zenica. Those who buy sex from prostitutes include the many foreigners who have flooded into the city during and since the war. Medica has appealed to the military, international agencies and NGOs to discipline their male employees about the use of under-aged prostitutes, some of them as young as 14. One day they may find themselves organizing healthcare and counselling for prostitutes. So, provided funding continues to be found, Medica seems likely to live on.

It is interesting to wonder about the future of ethnic and gender relations in the project. Will it continue to be ethnically mixed? It has been said often enough: this was a war waged against the principle of mixity itself. The aggression involved the destruction of cultures. Intellectuals and other educated and professional people were the first to be singled out for assassination. Religious buildings, libraries and historically significant buildings were purposely destroyed. Certain street names were changed so that 'We can forget those others ever lived here.' Many people felt it was a war waged by barbarians from the hills on urban civilization, on the cities and towns where people had gone to leave tradition behind, where they had mingled and where, not incidentally, women had been most free. War is a powerful device for convincing the survivors that: 'We can't live together ever again.' And it had worked on many of the refugees in Medica. The trust of the young women living in Medica-2 in anyone other than Bosnian Muslims had been quite destroyed. Those I spoke with were clear in their minds: the only safe world now would be a Muslim world.

Medica staff, on the other hand, had not lost their optimism. The demise of Yugoslavia had been a deep disappointment. They had clung to the possibility of a multi-ethnic Bosnia as a kind of redemption of the Yugoslav ideal. I think a simple valorizing of ethnic coexistence had been a golden thread to lead them through the moral morass of the war. Vahida used the metaphor of a forest in which diverse species of tree coexist to make the rich mixed environment she wanted to live in. Nusreta, speaking as a Muslim, said, 'I wouldn't want us to be *alone* here.' In any case, would that even be possible? Where there's scarcely a 'clean' family, an ethnically 'clean' territory is a chimera. The Muslim women in Medica felt a new and special loyalty to the Bosnian Serb and Bosnian Croat women who had survived the war with them and who, like them, had given all they had to Medica. What they longed for now was reconciliation and democracy. And they still believed, *had to* believe, that it was possible.

The rest of Bosnia does not look like living up to the heterogeneous ideal that Medica tries to exemplify. While the Republika Srpska and

Post war, Medica's gynaecology unit responds to increased domestic assault and prostitution.

many Croat nationalists refuse full cooperation in a new Bosnia, while war criminals are not delivered for trial and Muslims and Croats are not welcomed back to their homes in the Serb-controlled territory, it is impossible to begin any process of 'truth and reconciliation' between ethnic groups on the lines South Africa is attempting. Without a renewal of trust an open society will be impossible to sustain. Bosnian Serbs, who remain as a 'national minority' in the Muslim–Croat Federation area of Bosnia-Hercegovina, wonder about their future. Hana and her Serb husband are a case in point. They are depressed by little signs of an Islamicizing of Bosnian society. Will their child be discriminated against in school? Will you need to be Muslim to get a good job, just as you needed to be a communist in Yugoslavia? (At least you'd had a choice over that!) With these thoughts in mind they have applied for immigration visas to Australia. Mirjana, the driver, also in a mixed marriage, is set to emigrate too. Rada cannot help but sympathize. She says, 'I do sometimes dream of finding one small part of the earth to live in where I never have to hear the words Serb or Croat or Muslim again.' But if the same, oh-so-understandable, impulse drives thousands of others to opt out of the remaking of a mixed Bosnia, the country will follow the path of Northern Ireland and Israel to maximal segregation. Years hence an organization such as Medica may have to think of 'positive action', like the Fair Employment measures of Northern Ireland, to sustain its own mixity. It is a thought that has not yet been articulated.

Although it is not spoken about in quite the same terms, it is clear that a post-war settlement is also needed between women and men. The many mixed marriages and the incidence of rape make this war an extraordinary manifestation of the intimate, violent interlacing of gender with ethnic relations. This so-called ethnic war was totally gendered. Men and women played different parts, were used symbolically for different meanings, tortured with different weapons, dealt different deaths. Bosnian women had been the ones who reproduced cultural difference but also took care of those little courtesies that kept Muslim, Serb and Croat families in touch with each other. It was precisely those threads of connection spun by women that the ethnic aggression was directed towards tearing asunder. Aggression that was, *de facto*, by men.

The discussions in Medica about post-war heterosexual relations were not so explicit as those about the re-creation of hetero-ethnic relations. There were clearly strong forces favouring a recovery of the old habitual relationship between women and men. Those women whose loved men had survived the fighting were simply grateful to have them back. There was a hunger for normality, for the renewal of family life.

For some women on Medica staff, normality would mean the project becoming less exclusively female. They saw no reason why men should not be included on the staff – supportive, 'feminist' men, of course. And there was a widespread feeling that men too would need psycho-therapy to overcome on the one hand the traumas and on the other the brutalization they had undergone.

But there were also forces pressing the other way, favouring a degree of 'provisionality' in relations between women and men. Rape had been one of the strategies of the aggressor groups to make the nations believe 'We can't live together.' But it had also had the effect of driving women away from men. Research by Medica's psycho-team shows that a signifi-cant number of raped women they treated felt unable to consider relationships with men (Medica 1995). Even among women who had not suffered direct abuse from men there was an observable alienation from the masculine culture that seemed to be particularly implicated in the barbarism. There was a new critique of 'patriarchy'. The formal position of the project, as reflected in the Medica's *Bulletin*, was that 'war rapes are an inherent part of each and every war. The reason for them has nothing to do with ethnicity but is *based in relationships constructed by patriarchy*' (my italics). What Serb and Croat strategists 'in their ethno-mania' were using strategically was male power (Medica 1996). And women I talked with in the project often did cite male dominance in Yugoslavia, boys brought up 'like little emperors', women subordinated in every sphere. Add a militarized war culture and put a gun in a man's hand ... In this respect the end of the war was likely to bring more of the same. Already local men seemed to be coming back wild, gun-toting, different from the boys they were when they were conscripted. Women worried about what their own menfolk had seen. And what, perhaps, they had done.

Most of the women I talked with felt a deep reluctance, despite easy references to 'patriarchy', to believe that violence against women could actually be an effect of, sanctioned by, social structures. To explain how so many men raped under orders they fell back on individual pathology, blamed drink, drugs, insanity, perversion and 'evil'. Only 'abnormal' men raped. But this question was opening up more and more as the women in Medica began to shift their attention to post-war domestic violence. During the war people had been able to say of violence against women, 'It was the war, those men were the enemy.' That your attacker can be one of the men you call your own, that meant a painful re-thinking. If 'normal' men also batter and rape, new and troubling questions had to be asked about 'normal' gender relations and gender cultures. The Bosnian women were finding their way to the same issues

It's one thing to call a ceasefire, another to decommission militarized masculinity.

of gender power and violence that the Irish and Israeli women were dealing with.

So some women, like Mirjana, believed that there must now be 'a change in the position of men themselves, and their relations with one another'. And they must change in their expectations of women. Meliha stressed that the marriages that were being taken up again with the end of the war were not, and had never been, 'equal, modern relationships'. Yugoslav marriage had been gender mixity without gender democracy. So, for that matter, had the Yugoslav workplace and Yugoslav society. A future Bosnia different from a past Yugoslavia would need men willing to question the nature and meaning of their masculinity. One such man, Trivo Indjić, writing in a Women in Black journal, said a man, now, 'must dare get out of his own skin', and 'accept feminists' offer of finding a new mode of organization and expression' (Women in Black 1994: 134). Until that happens, many women wanted Medica to remain a women-only project.

8

Identity and Democracy

Each of these three projects, then, has its own distinctive work. The Women's Support Network in Belfast was formed to give women from the city's poorer districts a unified voice to express their common interests in the wider political world. In Israel, Bat Shalom brings Jewish and Palestinian Arab women together to take a public stand for peace and justice. Medica came into being in a time of brutal aggressions in Bosnia to provide social, psychological and medical support to raped and traumatized women and their children. But they are alike in having chosen cooperation between women of polarized ethno-national groups, contradicting the norm in their countries, where those identifications have been mobilized for war. They are *alliances*. What does that mean exactly? There are friendships among them, but these are not just groups of women who like each other.

Mariam Mar'i, an Israeli Palestinian Arab, in a conversation she recorded with Naomi Chazan, an Israeli Jew, stressed this matter of not-just-friendship. 'On the personal level,' she said, 'of course, you can like an Arab and an Arab can like you. That is a different story. But what I'm trying to say here is that the issue is *not social but rather political*' (my italics, Chazan and Mar'i 1994: 31). In a similar vein Simona Sharoni, in her discussion of Israeli Jewish/Palestinian groups working together across the Green Line, stresses the difference between mere 'dialogue groups' and true collaborative projects whose success hinges on facing up to difference and constantly renegotiating the terms of solidarity (Sharoni 1995: 141, 147).

This is the crux of an alliance: *a creative structuring of a relational space between collectivities marked by problematic differences*. The significant differences, in the case of the three projects, spring from politicized ethno-national identities. As alliances they are committed to cooperative action, and that requires of them a shared belief that apparently deadlocked situations can transform (can be transformed) over time, as needs are differently felt. Impelling them towards that belief is a deep desire to visualize an end to violence.

Identity process and democracy

An important asset of these three projects, helping them to survive as alliances, is a particular understanding of the individual in relation to collective identities. It is part implicit, part explicit, partly brought by individuals to the projects, partly learned in them, and it has a lot in common with recent academic thinking on the subject. To say it reflects theory would be to put the cart before the horse, because they have not read books about it. Their concepts have evolved through hard experience in a world in which ethno-national identities are implicated in more than the usual suffering and danger. If anything, it is theorists who have learned from the way people respond to circumstances like these.

Not many years ago, the prevailing belief concerning selfhood was, as Stuart Hall describes it, that in each of us there is a 'stable core of the self, unfolding from beginning to end through all the vicissitudes of history without change; the bit of the self which remains always-already "the same", identical to itself across time' (Hall 1996: 3). Today we are more inclined to think of an individual's sense of self 'as a *production*, which is never complete, always in process' (my italics, Hall 1990: 222). So we expect collective identities, such as gender and national identities, no matter in how essentialist a form they are dressed by politically interested parties, actually to be lived by individuals as *changeable* and unpredictable. And the way they take shape and change is *relational*. In other words, there is no thinkable specification of selfhood that does not have reference to other people, known or imagined. We feel ourselves to resemble these; those seem different from us. And because a social formation has so many structured differentiations, potential categories of inclusion and exclusion, belonging and alienation, the self is seen potentially very *complex*, shaped through many attachments.

Perhaps because we live in an age of commercial advertising, of powerful visual imagery on TV screens and sophisticated political propaganda, we are acutely aware today (both academically and pragmatically aware) of the persuasive, hectoring, identity discourses that authorize and offer us subject positions, push and pull the self. A great many people and institutions clearly have a vested interest in whom we feel ourselves to be, how we position ourselves in relation to other individuals and groups.

For a start, few of us today escape the moulding and differentiating influence of capitalist production and marketing. Think of the way the leading capitalist countries, through conditions imposed by the International Monetary Fund on former communist countries such as

Yugoslavia, seek to reshape their inhabitants into entrepreneurs and consumers. As Donna Haraway says, 'Stabilization of identity is a world industry. You can think of the history of capitalism as the stabilization of some identities and not others' (Bhavnani and Haraway 1994: 32).

Those who govern us use identity processes to do so. Dominant groups maintain hegemony for the most part by discursive means rather than by direct force, mobilizing consent by inclining us towards particular identifications. Louis Althusser stressed the ideological power of state apparatuses to summon us to our subject positions (Althusser 1971). Administrations need us calculable and biddable, so they consign us to formal categories such as 'head of household' or 'dependent', 'homosexual', 'disabled' or 'refugee', and use these as a basis for assigning rights and responsibilities. The categories emerge through official discourse as collective identities, inviting certain behaviours (Moore 1994).

But without doubt it is those social groups that drive competitive ethnicist and nationalist movements that are the master-spinners of identity tales designed to make some of us feel part of their imagined community, and others quite clear we are not so favoured. They fix, eternalize and essentialize the identities that are the vehicles of their control: our primordial nation, man and woman as nature intended. The contrary view of identity, as something complex, ambiguous and shifting, is anathema to projects of power: a Serb is a Serb, by descent, by blood! Yet, ironically, to win hearts for the Serb project the nationalists must contradict their own logic, behaving as though people do in fact have a choice: '*Be* Serb! *Feel* Serb!' the new lyrics of fascist turbo-rock seem to appeal from a million transistor radios in Belgrade. And of course, we do have a choice. But how much, and over what?

The factors that limit an individual's agency derive both from the social formation in which she lives and from her individual circumstances. The social formation and the moment certainly shape the range of identities in play. Where an ethnic group has not conceived of a national project, its members will not feel a national identification. If a feminist movement has not yet occurred and been named, a woman can hardly 'identify as' a feminist – she is likely to feel simply a discontented woman, or a misfit. Individual circumstances too prepare possible identities. Whether a person is born into wealth or poverty, her education and her work, whether she has children or not, how mobile she is, will suggest some identifications and rule out others. History has a bearing too. The individual who, as a child and in the course of her life, has lacked love and affirmation may have more difficulty in developing a strong subject self, individuated, un-'determined', and in forming reasoned, steady and multiple attachments.

But within the scope afforded by circumstance, the 'I' is a creative actor in making the self. Three concepts provide a way into thinking about our part in producing ourselves. First, Wendy Hollway suggests the term *investment* to describe an individual's commitment, a buying-in, to those among available subject positions that appeal to us as providing pleasure, satisfaction or reward, or playing to our fantasies (Hollway 1984; see also Moore 1994: 65). Second is the concept of *articulation*, the designing of a joint, connection or link between one element of identity and another (Laclau and Mouffe 1985; Hall 1996). A similar notion is *inflection*. We may be constrained by circumstances and contexts, including the current 'availability' of identities, but a certain agency lies in articulating one element of identity to another, inflecting each towards particular interpretations, bending and changing their significance. Sometimes we 'real-ize' an element or inflection of identity through meaning consciously made of an involuntary change of circumstance. Rodaina Jarisy (Israeli Palestinian Arab) went abroad and was conscious of 'feeling more Israeli when I was out of Israel'. And Tagreed Yahia-Younis (who helped me as interpreter in Israel) was, she said, conscious of feeling more Israeli when sharing with Jews the fear of being hit by Iraqi missiles.

But agency, choice, operates in another way too, and it is this above all that the three projects exemplify. The arrangements we choose to make for our interactions with each other, the structures and processes we create for our organizations, shape the way we deal with identities. A creative handling of difference is central to democratic process, and democracy disposes towards non-essentializing conceptualizations of identity.

We normally use the word democracy in connection with larger and more official institutions – councils, parliaments. But the women themselves, at the Mijas workshop, raised as an important focus of discussion between them the question 'How do we make democracy out of difference?' Their projects may be small and loosely framed organizations, 'out there' in civil society, a long way from the structures of power. But they are (and the Women's Support Network is most conscious of this) obliged to 'do' democracy if their alliances are to survive, and to model democracy if they are to have a wider influence for coexistence, development and peace.

In thinking through their situation I have been helped by the ideas of William E. Connolly, a US political scientist. In his book *Identity/ Difference* Connolly begins from the assumption that identities are an indispensable feature of social formations, that 'every stable way of life invokes claims to collective identity that enter in various ways into the interior identifications and resistances of those who share it'. Unfortunately, 'no god created humanity so that contending claims to identity will coalesce into some harmonious whole or be dissolved into some stable, recognizable, and transcendent principle'. How, he asks, are we to respond to this depressing reality (Connolly 1991: 158)?

A key issue is the mode of differentiation. As William Connolly puts it: 'An identity is established in relation to a series of differences that have become socially recognized. These differences are essential to its being. If they did not coexist as differences, it would not exist in its distinctness and solidity' (Connolly 1991: 64). For every 'us' there is a 'them'. The question is, in what shape will we imagine our definitional others in the process of imagining our own community? Alternatives do exist. Identities can be complementary, in such a way that (as Connolly puts it) 'the voice of difference is heard as that with which one should remain engaged'. Or alternatively a self can invoke a wholly alien other, with a voice that is heard as 'sickness, inferiority or evil' (ibid.: 64). And in that mode it can bring the other to angry life, as one nationalism stirs another.

Again the mode of self-differentiation is partly prepared by history. If you lack a secure self, are caught up in inner conflict, you are likely to disown the hated or feared parts of yourself and project them onto the unknown 'other'. This is well recognized in the individual, and an analogous process goes on at the level of the collectivity. But politically it is important to stress that the framing of the moment is influential as well, and again it applies at both levels. If the space is safe, the process transparent and the self (let us say a grouping) feels affirmed, then it may feel able to 'own' rather than project its fears. It is more likely to hear and engage with, rather than fantasize and demonize, the other.

Connolly suggests a rethinking of democratic theory and practice, in which we set out to find:

> a practice of democracy – or a strain of politics within democracy broadly defined – that responds to the problematic relation between identity and difference ... Let me call [he says] this political imaginary 'agonistic democracy', a practice that affirms the indispensability of identity to life, disturbs the dogmatization of identity, and folds care for the protean diversity of human life into the strife and interdependence of identity/difference (Connolly 1991: x).

And so we come back to decisions about political practice, whether it is the little-p politics of the projects or the big-P Politics of Northern Ireland, Israel/Palestine and Bosnia. It is only political practice that can create spaces, spaces affording both sufficient distance and sufficient

closeness for differences to constitute themselves safely there as contending identities. 'Agonistic' democracy, in Connolly's formulation,
breaks with the comfortable and dangerous illusion of 'community' and
the politics of communitarianism, that assumes consensus is (must be)
possible. Instead it settles for the difficult reality of unavoidable, unending, careful, respectful struggle.

National and gender identity and the sense of self: Rada's story

Many (sometimes it seems most) identity processes are coercive. We
are labelled, named, known by identities that confine us, regulate us and
reduce our complexity. The subtleties in our sense of self are difficult
to convey in the terms available to us. We often feel misunderstood and
misrepresented. And these processes are the more painful because they
exploit our irreducible need to belong, our happiness in belonging.
When war breaks out between national collectivities, extraordinary pressures descend on people that force them to rethink who they are in
relation to collective identities.

The experience of Rada, who will be remembered from the account
of Medica in Chapter 7, brings to life two things: the identity plight
that war can throw us into, and the challenge that dealing with identity
can represent to an alliance. And here in this narrative, Rada and I
become co-authors as our two discourses flow together and mingle. She
reflects on her experience, while I reflect on what she says, using terms
from the readings I refer to above, concepts that have taken on a new
life for me listening to her and other women.

Rada was born in 1955 in a little town in central Bosnia, not far from
Zenica, and grew up in Tito's communist state. On leaving school she
studied for a degree in German language and literature in the Philosophy Faculty at the University of Sarajevo. For a while she was a
schoolteacher, but in the period just before joining Medica she had been
working as an interpreter and translator in the international department
of the Zenica steelworks. Of her ethnic identity Rada says, 'The background of my parents was Orthodox. And the usual name for that is
Serb.' But for her, this was not a very developed facet of her identity.
She had little invested in it. 'I can sincerely say that nationality was
totally unimportant to me, my relatives, friends, my circle.' At the
census, given a choice between identifying herself as Serb or Yugoslav,
it seemed natural to her to choose the latter. As we have seen, the
resonance of 'Yugoslav' was less with 'nationality' than with a kind of
'citizenship'. But for Rada it did involve a settled sense of belonging –

not to a nation but to one of the world's 'countries'. She realized this especially when the disintegration of the federal state deprived her of it. Then, deluged with violent nationalist discourses from all around, 'I felt naked,' she said.

Then the fighting began, and Rada found that people were ascribing her a national identity that had nothing to do with the person she thought herself to be. 'All at once, I became a "Serb". It was clear from my name that I wasn't a Muslim. So I didn't have to declare myself a Serb, people declared *me*.' This seemed to her not just an abuse of her self-sense, but an abuse of history. 'We were all just Slavic people. The Orthodox and Catholic Christians living in Bosnia-Hercegovina only began to be called "Serb" and "Croat" in the nineteenth century, in response to political changes in the neighbouring territories bearing those names. And now it's supposed I should have some connection with the Serbs who live in Serbia! I don't feel I have any more in common with them than I do with my Muslim and Catholic neighbours in Bosnia.'

The Serb project of ethnic cleansing was legitimated by invoking 'our land' where 'Serb bones are buried'. (The new Bosnian government national anthem that was soon to be heard on the radio and learned by schoolchildren in Zenica also celebrated 'our beautiful land'.) But Rada said, 'I'm cosmopolitan and I don't have a developed feeling for my "homeland", for "roots". It's difficult for me at the age of forty to think of building up such an identity. Somehow it's underdeveloped. I like to know what my country is, but that doesn't mean it's the only place I'd want to live.' Rada shares with her husband Goran both a 'Serb background' and a non-national politics. Rada says of Goran, 'He feels himself to be a person from "nowhere".'

And of course the name Serb now connoted evil. How could 'Serbs' not be hated, in a Zenica threatened by the shells and mortars of Serb nationalist extremists? 'From the government media, all the time you get the message that Serbs are guilty.' And Rada could only agree. In common with many people in Bosnia, she felt that many forces outside Yugoslavia were implicated in the preparation of war in Yugoslavia. But she had not a moment's hesitation in blaming Serb and Bosnian Serb politicians and the Serb-dominated Yugoslav National Army and Serb paramilitaries for the actual aggression. And however she might twist and turn in her thoughts, she 'was' (in the sense of what is ascribed to name and inheritance) a Serb. 'I took on this feeling of guilt.' She recognized the feeling in some of her many German friends, on account of the Second World War and the Holocaust. Like them, she was now pushing the limits of choice for the subject self. Some kinds of identity, she was finding, cannot be evaded at will. There may be no 'collective guilt', but the very bearing of a national name mysteriously entails some responsibility – difficult to define, difficult to act on, and burdensome. What did you have to do to prove your innocence?

Her two school-age children made her acutely conscious of this dilemma. One day her daughter, aged seven, asked, 'Mum, what are we?' Rada says, 'She had never had to ask that before. It was difficult. But I feel she has the right to an answer. I told her, in Bosnia there are these three nations and we are Serbs. She made a face, "Why do we have to be *that*?" She felt ashamed. And at that moment I felt shame in front of this child of mine.' But she tussled with the gap between meanings, tried to recover some self-respect 'as a Serb', to inflect the identity in a way she could feel comfortable with, or at least to render it tolerably neutral. She explained, 'It's not that I hate or reject the term Serb. I'm not trying to escape from it. I would like it if I were more mixed, but I'm not. So no, I'm not ashamed of being Serb. I'm not proud of it either. It's just a fact. I might as well have been born a Bushman or a Zairean, whatever.'

One inhibition against disavowing her Serbness (were that even possible) was respect for her parents. But she sometimes wondered whether a religious identification could serve instead, a less politically positioning sort of belonging. But her family had not been a religious family. The word Orthodox was hardly ever mentioned. She said, 'I'm not baptized, I don't pray, and I don't go to church. I'm not against it, but for myself don't have anything to do with religion.'

All around her in Zenica, neighbours and friends who were unresponsive to the interpellation of the new nationalisms were nevertheless tending to fill the gap left by a vanished Yugoslavia with revived religious identities. Catholics were rediscovering Christian culture, celebrating Christmas and Easter. Muslims were showing renewed enthusiasm for the fast of Ramadan and festivals such as Bajram. 'They take their children to the mosque. Why don't I take mine to the Orthodox church? I feel guilty about this empty space I'm bringing up my children in,' she said. 'In the old days, in Yugoslavia, we used to celebrate unifying socialist holidays: New Year was the biggest. And May Day. Now I miss the cultural celebrations, and I try to make a cake, light a candle. But somehow it's only improvisation. But I do find it's nice. Candles, singing some nice songs. It's nice to take care of these things. At Easter we colour eggs. My mother used to do it.'

At the Mijas workshop Rada found she wasn't the only one who worried about the lack of cultural colour in socialist politics and secular life. Yehudit, an Israeli kibbutznik, sometimes felt the same. She seems to herself, as she puts it, to be lacking the 'nation' bone in her body, and feels angry at being forced towards nationalism in Israel today. And religion. But she admits, 'The secular, there's always a kind of difficulty in feeling it well. Religion is more sure.' The challenge for her was to make a culture that draws convincingly on political resources in place of religious or nationalist ones. She said, 'I don't need God. Democracy is something spiritual for me. The culture of democracy is the space I could educate my children in. My mother never sang to me the songs her mother sang, or told those stories. Our childcare workers in the kibbutz told stories to all us children. They weren't folk tales, but socialist stories. In our agricultural society we've created holidays that connect us with the land. So in our kibbutz we emphasize spring, freedom.' And Rada said, laughing, perhaps a bit envious, 'Like the pagans of ancient Rome!' Joy Poots understood the problem too. She and her partner are left-wing, anti-nationalist and non-religious. But their children inevitably share the Christian culture of school and the 'Irishness' of the country. How to construct a satisfying culture for such a family? Their answer had been a kind of pragmatic multivocalism. She said, 'We sing, first, *Bandiera Rossa*, and next *Jesus Loves Me*, and then *The Fields of Athenry*.' It would be funny, they agreed, were it less serious.

So the collective identity 'Yugoslav', agreeable to so many like Rada as a confederal, a statist, non-national identity, vanished with history. The collective identity that was being compellingly thrust on her today was 'Serb', with two subtle variants, 'Bosnian Serb' and 'Orthodox Christian'. Ideally, now, perhaps Rada could reject both and invest in Bosnian-ness, listen with self-recognition to those who speak of the survival of a democratic, open, multicultural Bosnia-Hercegovina.

But this discourse was being drowned out by a daily more clamorous Muslim nationalism, kicked into life through being cast as Other by an aggressive Serb (and Croat) Self. In fact, a calculated piece of identity engineering was under way. The adjective to describe 'a person of Bosnia' in the days when Bosnia-Hercegovina was a republic within the Yugoslav state used to be *Bosanac* (feminine: *Bosanka*). That was agreeable enough to Rada. But war had subverted this concept too. Increasingly on the media the adjective *Bošnjak* (feminine: *Bošnjakinja*) was being used. At first people were confused by this antique-sounding word – what did this revival imply? Gradually the politics behind it became clear. It was a conscious ploy, proposed by the writer Alija Isaković in the Bosnian parliament in 1993 and favoured by Alija Izet-begović, to create a new version of Bosnian belonging. The effect is to annex the root word for 'Bosnia' to the meaning 'Muslim'. *Bosanac* might include Bosnians of all varieties, not only Muslim but Orthodox/

Serb, Catholic/Croat, Roma, Jew. Bošnjak, by virtue of repeated usage in this sense, could mean Muslims only (for a fuller discussion see Bringa 1995: 34–5). Rada said, 'The entity now is called the "Federation of Bošnjaks, Croats and Other Nations", so now I'm the Other, a minority. That's a new feeling of myself.'

I was with Rada on the anniversary of the day her parents died. They had been killed two years before, by a Serb shell (the irony is bitter) pitched on the largely Muslim central Bosnian town they had lived in all their lives. She took me to the Orthodox church in Zenica where a service was in progress, because she wanted, atheist though she was, to remember them through the ritual of lighting candles. We stood and listened, watched the faces around us, enjoyed the gold vestments and icons reflecting the soft light. And then we stood awhile outside in the crisp December sunshine and she told me about her remaining relatives, all living on the Bosnian Serb side of the Dayton border, in the Republika Srpska. She said, 'When my parents were killed, for the first time in my life I longed for my family, for my "roots". I felt so alone here. For everyone around me the main issue had become family, where they were, how to get to visit each other, support each other. I scarcely mentioned "mine", because they were "over there", those who remained.'

Not long after the hostilities ended, an opportunity occurred for Rada to visit the Bosnian Serb Entity. As we heard in the last chapter, Medica women established contact with Duga, a women's project in Banja Luka. A visit was arranged, and a group of women set off from Zenica in the Medica vehicle. They were all tense and excited as they crossed the 'border' into Serb territory. The city of Banja Luka surprised them by its normality, still spacious and gracious, with its wide leafy avenues. The streets were busy; the people 'looked just like in peacetime'. But there were no mosques left standing. Ethnic cleansing had swept away the Muslim population in its entirety, but for a handful of the very old.

While in Banja Luka, Rada went eagerly to meet her father's sister, her mother's brother, her Bosnian Serb cousins. But it was difficult. 'In the beginning words failed us. We could only repeat tacky phrases like "How are you doing?", "How's life?", "What's new?".' But gradually the conversation deepened. And that's when Rada's pleasure in rediscovering her only surviving relatives began to drain away. They were all soon using the words 'we' and 'our place', 'you' and 'your place'. To her disappointment, all of these Bosnian Serbs justified the Serb part in the war. The fault lay with the Muslims, with Alija Izetbegović, the SDA. They refused to acknowledge Serb atrocities. (But, she couldn't help but wonder uneasily, how often do 'we' acknowledge Muslim atrocities? They may have been fewer, been more defensive, but a death is a death.)

The relatives found it difficult to believe that Rada was not treated badly as a Serb among Muslims. They urged her to consider coming to live in the Serb Republic. They said, 'What about your children? Think about where they are growing up, whether that's good for them.' She felt that they denied the reality and the validity of her life as she experienced it. But both sides made efforts to bridge the gulf. They even dared little 'ethnic' jokes between them. When Rada accepted coffee, calling it, with a smile, by the Bosnian Muslim term *kahva*, the aunts and uncles smiled too and said, 'You certainly are truly Islamicized now.' And the words, like the coffee, left an aftertaste. And as they went back to Zenica, Rada felt, 'I belong nowhere. I hang in mid-air.'

So national identity gave nothing but hurt and confusion to Rada. But there was another aspect to her sense of self that was less problematic. In fact it was a new source of strength and pleasure. She was investing in being a woman and, increasingly, feeling herself to be a feminist. Where reliance on relatives had dwindled, the importance of friends had grown – especially the friendships among the women in Medica. In a reflective moment she said, 'I really am fascinated by the unpredictability of this country. It's an enigma. Relationships I thought of as eternal have disappeared, behind new walls we've built. And people who meant nothing to me before the war are now my friends.'

The work they were doing together, specifically as women, at Medica had taken on great importance for her. And she was newly conscious of what, as a mother, she could do to counteract patriarchal values and the growth of nationalistic culture and their grip on children. 'If mothers have a cosmopolitan democratic spirit they can educate their children in that, independently of their husband. Or if they are religious, they can teach that other religions have equal value, that it's a richness that there are many religions, but in a spirit of equality. So women aren't just powerless living in patriarchy. If we have the confidence and the courage.' She was articulating motherhood to feminism and inflecting it away from nationalism.

She wasn't saying that women are nothing but good. She saw women all too often contributing to nationalist extremism. And she wasn't saying that men were to blame, as a sex, for the maelstrom of violence Bosnia had fallen into. She recognized an aggressive side to her own nature too. But masculine culture and the patriarchal inheritance she did believe were deeply implicated in the war, the too-valued manly traits of pride, bravado, superiority. And she believed men were not without agency, and therefore responsibility, in matters of self and identity. 'Men are conscious beings, with consciences. They have the power to define themselves, to be or not to be manipulated.'

Working with women as women seemed to open up a path through the thickets of ethnic and national identity. Perhaps she could produce herself anew for new times, with a downplayed sense of nationality articulated creatively to the identity of a feminist woman, a linguist, perhaps a writer. She began to see a subjectivity that would do for today, one that contained (and here I paraphrase Jonathan Rutherford 1990: 24) traces of its past and what it could become, an identity that was contingent, a provisional full stop in the play of differences and the narrative of her own life. After the visit to Banja Luka, Rada at first felt no desire to see her relatives again. Later, she felt, 'I can accept them. No matter that we disagree. They suffered from the war too.' And politically the visit to Republika Srpska opened up to her that necessary vision of repositioning and transformation. She said, 'I do want us to work with Duga. I even see an epochal meaning in it. It is part of my longing for the birth of an international women's movement, to resist nationalist, patriarchal insanity. Step by step.'

Spaces of violence and democracy

There is a point at which discourse ends and killing begins. And Rada's identity crisis has to be read in the context of a cataclysm in which extremists bearing her 'name' were exterminating perhaps two hundred thousand Muslims and an unknown number of Croats because of their presence in places they had decided to make their own. It was identity murder. The group identifying themselves as Serb patriots had severed the links of relationship with those they discursively constructed as 'Muslims' and 'Croats' and smashed the mirror in which they saw their hated alter-egos. In the vortex of destruction came a number of other annihilations and erasures: attachments were ruptured, homes destroyed, economies wrecked, cultures uprooted.

And, as we have seen, a particular kind of aggression was visited on women, and that too had a great deal to do with identity. Thousands, perhaps tens of thousands, of women were raped. The rapes had both a meaning specific to the ethnic and patriarchal relationships of this war and a meaning common to rape everywhere and at all times. Ruth Seifert, a military sociologist in the Federal German Army's Institute for Social Science, suggests several dimensions to the meaning of the rapes. They were part of the generally understood rules of war, in which the women of the routed forces are historically seen as available to men of the winning side. They conveyed a message of humiliation from the winning to the losing men. They were a mechanism of control among men within the aggressive forces, exploiting negative aspects of masculine cultures. They aimed at destroying the enemy nations' culture by undermining family relationships. In this sense rape of women was all of a piece with the dynamiting of mosques and libraries. And finally, the rapes were expressions of a perennial contempt for women that gets uninhibited expression in a time of chaos (Seifert 1995).

Several times in Medica I heard rape described as 'the assassination of the subject self' (Medica 1995: 1). They mean, I think, that what is murdered is the woman's sense of herself as she lived it before the rape. 'As if I had lost myself,' one such woman said (Medica 1996: 15). Certainly, identity does not die as an issue for the raped woman. In fact it becomes more acute than she has ever known it. The self that survives is thrown into a crisis in which she is left with a minimal sense of continuity with the person she was, struggling to resist the appalling array of new identities competing to claim her – victim, traitor, outcast. Any self-sense she can muster begins from worthlessness: raped woman. A young woman of 19 receiving therapy in Medica said, 'Now, when somebody says the word rape, it's as if they are calling my name' (Medica 1996).

And that is why those who have organized *political* support for the women raped in Bosnia, alongside those who organized therapeutic and medical support, have contributed significantly to the resources for their healing. They have made available to the raped woman a new, alternative and self-respecting identity. Cynthia Enloe, whose has long studied the gender implications of war, sees it as something new that in the Bosnian situation women's organizations then and there carried the issue into what quickly became an international political network of feminists, 'using news of the Bosnian women's victimization not to institutionalize women as victims, not to incite men to more carnage, but to explain anew how war makers rely on peculiar ideas about masculinity' (Enloe 1995: 220). Lepa Mladjenović and Vera Litričin, active in this network from Belgrade, write: 'There is a lot of identity work to be done. Women-identified women have a strong basis of identity to begin that work … Raped, murdered women will never be considered brave, except by us.' But they did not doubt it would be uphill, counter-discursive work. 'We know that if we are to say aloud who we are and what we want there will be no historically accepted political patterns for our experience or our language' (Mladjenović and Litričin 1993: 119).

Rape is, oddly enough, a good place to start thinking about demo-cratic space, the creative space between differences. Because rape, like other forms of torture, is outrageous bodily closeness, violent touching,

224 / THE SPACE BETWEEN US

a travesty of intimacy. And the word 'rape' is used metaphorically to convey that feeling of abuse, as when someone or some group penetrates, invades and damages the space (the land, perhaps, or culture, or thoughts) in which another or others dwell. Closeness and contiguity are the ultimate in pleasure and the ultimate in horror, depending on the quality of the relationship in which they occur.

A good deal of effort therefore goes into structuring a comfortable democratic distance between us, as individuals in a marriage, as collectivities in a multicultural city, as nations sharing a world. The space has to afford an optimal distance between differences, small enough for mutual knowledge, for dispelling myths, but big enough for comfort. It needs to be criss-crossed with the webs of a structure and a process capable of sustaining stable relationships and conveying clear meanings from one side of it to the other. It has to be strong enough to prevent implosion, a collapse of differences into rape, silencing or annihilation. But it also has to be flexible enough to permit differences to change their form and significance, and for increased intimacy as and when the quality of relationships allow of it. Love, even. The word recurred in my conversations in Bosnia. And Paša said, of Bosnia before the wars, 'We had mixed marriages. Our children were raised together, they went to school together. *We loved each other.* I don't know what happened.' Ferida, a Muslim, said, 'The patients at Medica know I'm married to a Serb but they never said anything against me and *I have a feeling they really love me.* I feel proud of that.'

It is in this dynamic field of love and hate that the Women's Support Network, Medica and Bat Shalom are trying to sustain their alliances. And in constructing democratic polities, the best tools they have, the tools they share, are identity processes. Reflecting back, I can distinguish six, all of which we have seen them use well and less well.

First, at their best, the projects *affirm difference*. They resist the temptation of erasing it, of collapsing mixity into mere heterogeneity or, worse, a pretended homogeneity. Sometimes of course they make the error (as in Chapter 7 we saw Rada complain) of not acknowledging politicized difference openly enough. Sometimes (as in Bat Shalom) the differences are so clear-cut that they structure the group uncomfortably into two halves. But it is an important principle in all three projects that difficult differences 'don't have to be left outside the door in order for us to work together'. Marie Mulholland put this nicely:

> My republican views are very strong and my fierce desire is to see a united Ireland. But I've never felt the battles had to be diluted in any way to work in the Network with women, say, from the [Unionist/Protestant] Shankill

Road. For me it's about – well, the nearest analogy I can give to this is about sexual identity. I'm the only lesbian in the Network. My sexual orientation is well known, I'm very open about it. Equally, I'm open about my politics. And I've found that, you know, where there's no mystery, it's easier for people to work with you. Because the contact is one of honesty from the outset.

But we should not be tempted by the women's goodwill to forget just how explosively politicized are the ethno-national differences they are dealing with. To refer back to Pieterse's categorization of ethnicities, mentioned in Chapter 1, the ethnicities in these countries are not optional nor dormant. On the contrary they involve on the one hand dominant, on the other highly competitive, combative, ethnicities.

Second, an important corollary, the projects are on the whole good at *non-closure on identity*. They do not essentialize identities and therefore do not predict what might flow from them. They are unusually willing to wait and see, to believe there may be many ways of living, for example, a Protestant identity. You may be a Protestant, yes, but one in whom that identity is inflected towards secularism, socialism and internationalism. You may live your Protestant-ness articulated tightly with 'woman', so that it is a little detached from the masculine interpretation, and thereby given a different meaning. You may invest more in your woman-ness than in your Protestant-ness, and, what is more, choose to inflect it towards feminism. These things will shape a meaning for Protestant very different from the stereotyped 'Prod' that some 'Catholics' like to hate. So, interrogating themselves, watching each other, they seem to believe, with June Jordan, that 'The final risk or final safety lies within each one of us attuned to the messy and intricate and unending challenge of self-determination' (Jordan 1989: 114).

So the women take great care in the way they deal with identities in individual interaction and relationship. Sometimes mistakes are made. And even mistakes have their uses, because if a person is hurt now and then it alerts her to the hurt others may feel. So, most of the time, they avoid ascribing thoughts or motivations or qualities to others on the basis of their ethnic or national label. One woman will wait to hear the other's telling of history, her view of the event, idea of herself, reading of the situation, preference for action – rather than making suppositions because she 'is' Catholic/Croat/Jew. Likewise she will avoid ascribing collective guilt: you are not to be held accountable for everything done in your name. As the Medica women like to say, 'You don't put everyone in one basket', but expect Protestant/Serb/Muslim/Palestinian Arab to come in many colours. 'You judge people by what they do, not what they are.'

In relation to this, the projects have found useful ways of *reducing polarization by emphasizing other differences.* Of course, the single most important feature of their alliances is that by organizing around political interests shared with women, yet framing difference from men in non-essential terms, they reduce the significance of ethnic difference and the plausibility of nationalist discourses. But they also blur sharp ethno-political dividing lines by two other devices. On the one hand they emphasize other kinds of differentiation within the project. Medica, for instance, stresses that not everybody falls into one or the other: there are many project-workers and refugees who are of mixed parentage or in mixed marriages. They also seek out evidence of greater diversity in the surrounding community, as when the Irish women enlisted the Chinese minority in Belfast to remind the Catholic and Protestant youngsters that their communities were not the only ones in the town. On the other hand, they look beyond the divided community, putting communal boundaries into softer focus by stepping outside and looking back at them from an international vantage point. In this sense, all the projects gained strength from their involvement in a global feminist movement and its networks.

The fourth tool the projects bring to bear in alliance-building is an *acknowledgement of injustices* done in the name of differentiated identities. In none of the three countries is ethnic difference the difference of equals. These regions are not just sites of war between peoples who for some inexplicable reason hate each other. They are societies founded on terrible wrongs.

Creating an alliance is therefore not just a matter of mutual opening. It involves a willingness to face ethical issues, to dig deep into layers of advantage, exploitation and oppression. It is a painful process. As Yehudit Zaidenberg says, herself a Jew, 'It's hard to explain to Jews, to get them to accept, that after all our suffering we now cause suffering to others. Our suffering should have made us sensitive to that of others, but it hasn't.' Only when that self-sensitizing work is taken on board by project members who, like Yehudit, are identifiable as a member of an oppressor group does the next, and equally difficult step become possible. Then, those of the societally subordinated group may find they can acknowledge and understand the oppressor group's deep-seated fears, the memories of suffering that have been allowed (and often unscrupulously exploited) to justify acts of repression and aggression. They may also be able to acknowledge the threat the aggressor/oppressor perceives from external populations that may seem to them to majoritize their 'enemies' – all the 'Catholics' of the Republic, the Vatican, the USA; all the Arabs of 'the Arab World'.

There are plenty of factors that inhibit the tabling of ethical issues of power and justice. In Bat Shalom the fact that Jewish women usually outnumber Palestinian Arab women in the organizing group may make it difficult for the group as a whole consistently to achieve what Sharoni calls 'the unequivocal acknowledgement of power disadvantage between the two communities and a willingness on the part of Israeli Jewish women to account for their power and privilege' (Sharoni 1995: 149). In the Belfast Women's Support Network the problem is complicated by the fact that women whose background associates them with the Catholic community (numerically, politically and economically disadvantaged in Northern Ireland society) have the edge in political initiative in both community and feminist activism, so creating a potential inversion of Protestant power in such projects. In Medica women who bear the ethnic identity of the aggressor groups (Bosnian Serb and Bosnian Croat) are present only as a small minority. The Muslim majority tend simply to take the fact of these women having stayed on in Zenica, when they could have fled, as saying what they need to hear: 'They're not doing it in my name.' There is a natural reluctance to start conversations that can seem to make a painful situation worse. Nevertheless, the projects operate well as alliances only when they do recognize and make explicit this ethical asymmetry. They cannot move any distance towards peace without facing issues of right and wrong.

A fifth and further way the women put to use what they have learned about identity pain and identity work is in *defining the agenda* of the projects, those matters on which it is safe to engage with each other, those that should be avoided if the group is to hold together and, most importantly, those that become possible as the group gains in ability to deal creatively with difference, or cease to be possible as violence closes in.

The sixth and final tool is *group process*. A democratic polity has to ensure that all its voices are heard, that all are given equal weight and that decision-making is fully shared. At the level of the individual in a face-to-face group, the destructive 'othering' processes to which collectivities (such as ethno-national groups) are prone can be contradicted, and an alternative modelled. In a situation where everyone speaks, in a safe context where defensive masks can be set aside, each person can afford to be more 'herself'. Less projection occurs, and the group coheres.

The Women's Support Network and Medica have both been conscious of group process and have devoted a good deal of discussion, and practical trial and error, to democratic ways of managing their work. In this sense, having a shared, daily, absorbing, practical task gives them an advantage over Bat Shalom, with no office or centre to manage, no staff

to employ or accounts to keep. Bat Shalom hold meetings only sporadic-
ally, their membership is more variable and there is less continuity of
action. As a result they have not been forced to develop such conscious
group processes, and sometimes that lack is felt. Friendship, the last
resort of an alliance, is something on which Bat Shalom more often
have to fall back than the Network or Medica.

So, yes, the women of the three projects long ago learned that
identity is negotiable and that agonistic democracy is the only durable
alternative to war. Looking back now it seems to me that their special
talent is for: helping each other give up dangerous dreams, helping each
other leave room for things that do not at first fit comfortably, and
helping each other make unnerving journeys.

It was Rodaina Jarisy who said to me one day in Nazareth, 'We have
to give up certain dreams', and Yehudit out on the kibbutz said something similar, 'We're not in Bat Shalom for dreams but for what we can
have now.' The dreams they meant were wish-dreams that inhabit
people's minds not only in Israel but in Ireland and Bosnia too, a
longing to live among your own kind, in your own land, where difference
keeps its distance and so conflict is unknown. They are dreams of
home. But what they imply is a great deal of screening out of uncomfortable realities, things that do not fit.

Nationalist renderings of the nation are highly selective histories
that delete everything that does not contribute to the story of a unitary
people ('always-already "the same", identical to itself across time', as
Stuart Hall said of identity, see p. 212). Their 'people' have a common
origin, are like each other and different from others, march together
along a given road, travelling towards a shared destiny. All the di-
vergencies and convergences of real historic social time, the departures
of some and arrivals of others, the mixing and splitting, the dyings-out
and the illegitimate births, are ignored.

Something similar happens in contemporary conceptions of 'community'. Community speaks of something we feel we want, a sense of
belonging, where identity is not problematic, a political home where our
sense of self matches the identity that others ascribe to us without any
feeling of misfit or pain. But whatever community you choose to look
at you find inside it deep differences, currents of dissension, some on
the surface, some causing turbulence from the hidden depths. For
instance, most ethnic 'communities' inhering around a traditional culture
and religion involve men controlling and representing women – whose
voices, if heard, might seriously destabilize the very idea of community.

Patriarchal stories of the family involve similar erasures. When a
'family tree' is drawn up it usually shows (it is designed to show) the

descent from one common male ancestor, through the male line, to a living inheritor of his genes, usually also a male. Entirely rubbed out of the story are the swelling hosts of ancestors and descendants of every wife, cousin and sister-in-law that also contribute and inherit genes and culture in the social world of which these two are a part. The line from great-great-great-grandfather to today's son-and-heir that is marked so boldly on the 'family tree' would be lost to view if all the other actually existing lines and connections were sketched in. In this sense the family, with its notion of purity of bloodline, is a fiction, an artefact of patriarchal discourse.

Nora Räthzel (see p. 40) said of German people's dreams of a cosy, unproblematic Heimat, a home with no intrusive foreigners and no strife: they involve *radical deletions*. You can maintain dreams of home and homeland, family, community and nation only by removing from within the frame of the picture everything that in real life complicates it. Those who dream Marie's dream of a united Ireland might love to delete from the island the Protestants who spoil its Irishness. Those who dream Vera's dream of Jerusalem as a home of the heart might love to resurrect the temple and discard the mosques, the churches and the tourist routes history has overlaid on it. But Marie and Vera themselves know that it is just the complexity that promises movement, learning and development. It is by transcending the contradiction, the dialectic tells us, not by wishing it away that progress unfolds. The dreams cannot deliver a future because they are trapped in a purified imagined past.

In trying to create sustainable democratic polities, then, the three women's projects are involved in helping each other individually to distinguish between dangerous fantasies and reasonable hopes. For the Self to give up its dream without the Other doing so too is impossible, or impossible without defeat and debasement. What the women do, in a sense, is respect each other's fears but see these dreams of simple futures for what they are, impediments to a life now. They are also, as collectivities, resisting the seductions of a collapse into false homogeny, taking care not to imagine a total agenda, complete consensus or common language. We have seen them instead negotiating their partial agendas, living with mixity and learning to translate each other's languages.

Women in Belgrade wrote in a letter to their sisters in Sarajevo about their shared resistance to 'the lethal belief in the *proper* name, *proper* land and blood' (my italics, Mladjenović and Matijašević 1996: 131). And that is a neat reminder: as women making over our worlds our first task is *impropriety*. So the three projects are resisting the temptation to erase things and people who (like a lesbian aunt left out of the family tree) do not conform with the dream. They are withstanding the allure of tidy closures and conclusions.

They help each other to keep travelling too, stepping out into public space and across international borders, but most importantly keeping a forward momentum. Because it is only possible for partners in an alliance to hold on in there, to survive the compromise and anger, if they believe that new times will come (can be brought about) in which the outline of future justice is discernible. They have to be able to think that the view from tomorrow's subject positions, howsoever slight their distance from today's you and me, will afford a fresh perspective from which the conflict has shapeshifted and no longer seems impossible to resolve.

Bibliography

Abdo, Nahla (1994) 'Nationalism and feminism: Palestinian women and the *Intifada* – no going back?' in Moghadam, Valentine M. (1994b).

Abdo, Nahla and Yuval-Davis, Nira (1995) 'Palestine, Israel and the Zionist settler project' in Stasiulis, Daiva and Yuval-Davis, Nira (eds) *Unsettling Settler Societies: Articulations of Gender, Race, Ethnicity and Class.* London: Sage Publications.

Abu Rakba, Saniya (1993) 'Arab women in the Israeli labor market' in Swirski, Barbara and Safir, Marilyn P. (1993).

Althusser, Louis (1971) 'Ideology and ideological state apparatuses' in Althusser, Louis, *Lenin and Philosophy and other Essays.* London: New Left Books.

Amnesty International (1993) 'Bosnia-Herzegovina: rapes and sexual abuse by the armed forces'. January. London: Amnesty International.

Anderson, Benedict (1983) *Imagined Communities.* London and New York: Verso.

Anthias, Floya and Yuval-Davis, Nira (1989) 'Introduction' in Yuval-Davis, Nira and Anthias, Floya (1989).

Antić, Milica G. (1991) 'Democracy between tyranny and liberty: women in post-"socialist" Slovenia', *Feminist Review*, No. 39: 149–54. Winter.

Applegate, Celia (1992) 'The question of Heimat in the Weimar Republic', *The Question of 'Home'*, issue of *New Formations*, No. 17, Summer: vii–xi.

Article 19 (1994) *Forging War: The Media in Serbia, Croatia and Bosnia-Hercegovina.* London: International Centre Against Censorship.

Ashkenasi, Abraham (1992) *Palestinian Identities and Preferences: Israel's and Jerusalem's Arabs.* New York: Praeger.

Aughey, Arthur and Morrow, Duncan (1996) *Northern Ireland Politics.* London: Longman.

Augustin, Ebba (1993) 'Developments in the Palestine women's movement during the Intifada' in Augustin, Ebba (ed.) *Palestinian Women: Identity and Experience.* London: Zed Books.

Belić, Martina (1995) 'The biggest victims of the war', *War Report*, No. 36: 32–4. September. London: Institute for War and Peace Reporting.

Bell, Geoffrey (1978) *The Protestants of Ulster.* London: Pluto Press.

Ben-David, Ya'acov (1975) *Work and Education on the Kibbutz: Reality and Aspirations.* Rehovot: Center for Research of Urban and Rural Settlements (in Hebrew).

Benderly, Jill (1997) 'Rape, feminism and nationalism in the war in Yugoslav successor states' in West, Lois A. (1997).

Bennett, Olivia, Bexley, Jo and Warnock, Kitty (1995) *Arms to Fight, Arms to Protect: Women Speak Out About Conflict.* London: Panos.

Bhavnani, Kum-Kum and Haraway, Donna (1994) 'Shifting the subject: a conversation between Kum-Kum Bhavnani and Donna Haraway on 12 April

1993, Santa Cruz, California' in Bhavnani, Kum-Kum and Phoenix, Ann (1994).

Bhavnani, Kum-Kum and Phoenix, Ann (eds) (1994) *Shifting Identities, Shifting Racisms: A Feminism and Psychology Reader*. London: Sage Publications.

Billig, Michael (1995) *Banal Nationalism*. London and Thousand Oaks, New Delhi: Sage Publications.

Bloom, Anne R. (1993) 'Women in the defense forces' in Swirski, Barbara and Safir, Marilyn P. (1993).

Borić, Rada and Desnica, Mica Mladineo (1996) 'Croatia: three years after' in Corrin, Chris (1996).

Bowes, Alison M. (1986) 'Israeli kibbutz women: conflict in Utopia' in Ridd, Rosemary and Callaway, Helen (1986).

Božinović, Neda (1994) 'Key points in the history of the women's movement in former Yugoslavia' in Centre for Women's Studies, Research and Communication (1994).

Bracewell, Wendy (1996) 'Women, motherhood and contemporary Serbian nationalism', *Women's Studies International Forum*, Vol. 19, Nos 1/2: 25–33.

Bringa, Tone (1995) *Being Muslim the Bosnian Way: Identity and Community in a Central Bosnian Village*. Princeton, NJ: Princeton University Press.

Burton, John (1987) *World Society*. Lanham, MD: University Press of America. Reprint of 1972 edition.

Burton, John (1990) 'Unfinished business in conflict resolution' in Burton, John and Dukes, Frank (eds) *Conflict: Readings in Management and Resolution*. London: Macmillan.

Centre for Women's Studies, Research and Communication (ed.) (1994) *What Can We Do for Ourselves?* Report of the East European Feminist Conference, Belgrade, June.

Chazan, Naomi and Mar'i, Mariam (1944) 'What has the occupation done to Palestinian and Israeli women?' in Mayer, Tamar (1994c).

Cockburn, Cynthia (1991) 'A women's political party for Yugoslavia: introduction to the Serbian Feminist Manifesto', *Feminist Review*, No. 39: 155–60. Winter.

Cockburn, Cynthia (1996a) 'Different together: women in Belfast', *Soundings*, No. 2. Spring.

Cockburn, Cynthia (1996b) 'Refusing ethnic closure: a women's therapy centre in Bosnia-Hercegovina', *Soundings*, No. 3. Summer.

Cockburn, Cynthia (1997) 'Wrong and wrong again: women for peace in Israel', *Soundings*, No. 5. Spring.

Cohen, Philip (1988) 'The perversions of inheritance: studies in the making of multi-racist Britain' in Cohen, Philip and Bains, Harwant S. (eds) *Multi-Racist Britain*. London: Macmillan.

Connolly, William E. (1991) *Identity/Difference: Democratic Negotiations of Political Paradox*. Ithaca and London: Cornell University Press.

Corrin, Chris (ed.) (1996) *Women in a Violent World*. Edinburgh: Edinburgh University Press.

Curle, Adam (1971) *Making Peace*. London: Tavistock Publications.

Dajani, Souad (1994) 'Between national and social liberation: the Palestinian women's movements in the Israeli occupied West Bank and Gaza Strip' in Mayer, Tamar (1994c).

Davis, Uri (1987) *Israel: An Apartheid State*. London: Zed Books.

Deutsch, Yvonne (1994) 'Israeli women against the Occupation: political growth and the persistence of ideology' in Mayer, Tamar (1994c).

Djurić, Tatjana (1995) 'From national economies to nationalist hysteria – consequences for women' in Lutz, Helma, Phoenix, Ann and Yuval-Davis, Nira (eds) (1995) *Crossfires: Nationalism, Racism and Gender in Europe*. London: Pluto Press.

Drakulić, Slavenka (1987) *How We Survived Communism and Even Laughed*. London: Vintage.

Drakulić, Slavenka (1993) 'Women and the new democracy in the former Yugoslavia' in Funk, Nanette and Mueller, Magda (1993).

Duhaček, Daša (1993) 'Women's time in former Yugoslavia' in Funk, Nanette and Mueller, Magda (1993).

Dunn, Seamus and Morgan, Valerie (1994) *Protestant Alienation in Northern Ireland*. Belfast: University of Ulster, Centre for the Study of Conflict.

Edgerton, Lynda (1986) 'Public protest, domestic acquiescence: women in Northern Ireland' in Ridd, Rosemary and Callaway, Helen (1986).

Enloe, Cynthia (1989) *Bananas, Beaches and Bases: Making Sense of International Politics*. London: Pandora.

Enloe, Cynthia (1995) 'Afterword', in Stiglmayer, Alexandra (ed.) (1995) *Mass Rape: The War Against Women in Bosnia-Herzegovina*. Lincoln and London: University of Nebraska Press.

Espanioly, Nabila (1993) 'Palestinian women in Israel respond to the *intifada*' in Swirski, Barbara and Safir, Marilyn P. (1993).

Espanioly, Nabila (1994) 'Palestinian women in Israel: identity in light of the Occupation' in Mayer, Tamar (1994c).

European Commission (1993) *Final Report of the Investigative Mission into the Treatment of Muslim Women in the Former Yugoslavia*. Brussels. February.

Evason, Eileen (1991) *Against the Grain: The Contemporary Women's Movement in Northern Ireland*. Dublin: Attic Press.

Flapan, Simha (1987) *The Birth of Israel: Myths and Realities*. New York: Pantheon Books.

Funk, Nanette and Mueller, Magda (eds) (1993) *Gender Politics and Post-Communism*. London: Routledge.

Galtung, Johan (1975–1980) *Essays in Peace Research*. Five volumes. Copenhagen: Christian Ejlers.

Gellner, Ernest (1983) *Nations and Nationalism*. Oxford, UK and Cambridge, MA: Blackwell.

Gluck, Sherna Berger (1997) 'Shifting sands: the feminist–nationalist connection in the Palestinian movement' in West, Lois A. (1997).

Grossman, David (1994) *Sleeping on a Wire*. London: Jonathan Cape, Picador.

Gurr, Ted Robert (1995) 'Transforming ethno-political conflicts: exit, autonomy or access?' in Rupesinghe, Kumar (1995b).

Halevi, Ilan (1987) *A History of the Jews: Ancient and Modern*. London: Zed Books.

Hall, Stuart (1990) 'Cultural identity and diaspora' in Rutherford, Jonathan (1990a).

Hall, Stuart (1996) 'Introduction: who needs identity?' in Hall, Stuart and du Gay, Paul (eds) *Questions of Cultural Identity*. London and Berkeley, CA: Sage Publications.

Hassan, Manar (1993) 'Growing up female and Palestinian in Israel' in Swirski, Barbara and Safir, Marilyn P. (1993).

Hauser, Monika (1995) 'War against women and their resistance', paper given at the International Congress for the Documentation of Genocide in Bosnia-Hercegovina. Bonn, 31 August–4 September.

Helsinki Watch (1993) *War Crimes in Bosnia-Herzegovina*. New York.

Hobsbawm, Eric (1990) *Nations and Nationalism since 1780: Programme, Myth, Reality*. Cambridge: Canto.

Hollway, Wendy (1984) 'Gender difference and the production of subjectivity' in Henriques, Julia et al. (eds) *Changing the Subject: Psychology, Social Regulation and Subjectivity*. London: Methuen.

Hughes, Donna M., Mladjenović, Lepa and Mršević, Zorica (1995) 'Feminist resistance in Serbia', *European Journal of Women's Studies*, Vol. 2: 509–32.

Hurwitz, Deena (1992) 'Introduction' in Hurwitz, Deena (1992a).

Hurwitz, Deena (ed.) (1992a) *Walking the Red Line: Israelis in Search of Justice for Palestine*. Philadelphia: New Society.

Institute for War and Peace Reporting (1994–97), various issues of *War Report*. London.

Izraeli, Dafna N. (1993) 'Women and work: from collective to career' in Swirski, Barbara and Safir, Marilyn P. (1993).

Jackson, Peter and Penrose, Jan (eds) (1993) *Constructions of Race, Place and Nation*. London: UCL Press.

Jančar, Barbara (1985) 'The new feminism in Yugoslavia' in Ramet, P. (ed.) *Yugoslavia in the 1980s*. London: Westview Press.

Jayawardena, Kumari (1986) *Feminism and Nationalism in the Third World*. London and New Jersey: Zed Books.

Jiryis, Sabri (1976) *The Arabs in Israel*. New York: Monthly Review Press.

Jordan, June (1989) *Moving Towards Home: Political Essays*. London: Virago Press.

Kandiyoti, Deniz (1993) 'Identity and its discontents: women and the nation' in Williams, Patrick and Chrisman, Laura (eds) *Colonial Discourse and Post-Colonial Theory: A Reader*. London: Harvester Wheatsheaf.

Kaplan, Gisela (1997) 'Feminism and nationalism: the European case' in West, Lois A. (1997) *Feminist Nationalism*. New York and London: Routledge.

Keogh, Dermot and Haltzel, Michael H. (eds) (1993) *Northern Ireland and the Politics of Reconciliation*. Washington and Cambridge: Woodrow Wilson Center Press and Cambridge University Press.

Kesić, Vesna (1995) 'From respect to rape', *War Report*, No. 36: 36–8. September. London: Institute for War and Peace Reporting.

Knežević, Djurdja (1995) 'Rulers and rhetoric change – but reality?', *War Report*, No. 36: 35–6. September. London: Institute for War and Peace Reporting.

Koonz, Claudia (1987) *Mothers in the Fatherland: Women, the Family and Nazi Politics*. London: Methuen.

Korać, Maja (1991) 'Prisoners of Their Sex.' Belgrade: Institute of Sociology, Faculty of Philosophy, University of Belgrade. Master's thesis. (In Serbo-Croat.)

Korać, Maja (1993) 'Serbian nationalism: nationalism of my own people', *Feminist Review*, No. 45: 108–12.

Korać, Maja (1996) 'Understanding ethnic-national identity and its meaning: questions from women's experience', *Women's Studies International Forum*, Vol. 19, Nos 1/2: 133–43.

Korać, Maja (forthcoming) *War, Violence and Women's Organizing: The Case of Post-Yugoslav States*. Uppsala: Life and Peace Institute.

Kretzmer, D. (ed.) (1990) *The Legal Status of the Arabs in Israel*. Boulder, CO: Westview Press.

Laclau, Ernesto and Mouffe, Chantal (1985) *Hegemony and Socialist Strategy*. London and New York: Verso.

Lees, Susan (1997) *Carnal Knowledge: Rape on Trial*. Harmondsworth: Penguin.

Lustick, Ian (1980) *Arabs in the Jewish State: Israel's Control of a National Minority*. Austin: University of Texas Press.

McCready, S. H. (1993) 'Community Development in Protestant Communities: A Study of a District Council in Northern Ireland'. Research report. Belfast: University of Ulster, Department of Applied Social Studies and Centre for the Study of Conflict.

MacCurtain, Margaret (1978) 'Women, the vote and revolution' in MacCurtain, Margaret and O Corrain, Donncha (1978a).

MacCurtain, Margaret and O Corrain, Donncha (eds) (1978a) *Women in Irish Society: The Historical Dimension*. Dublin: Arlen House.

McKittrick, David (1994) *Endgame: The Search for Peace in Northern Ireland*. Belfast: Blackstaff Press.

Malcolm, Noel (1994) *Bosnia: A Short History*. London: Macmillan, Papermac.

Mar'i, Mariam M. and Mar'i, Sami Kh. (1993) 'The role of women as change agents in Arab society in Israel' in Swirski, Barbara and Safir, Marilyn P. (1993).

Massey, Doreen (1994) *Space, Place and Gender*. Cambridge: Polity Press.

Massey, Doreen (1995) 'Imagining the world' in Allen, John and Massey, Doreen (eds) *Geographical Worlds*. The Open University. Oxford: Oxford University Press.

Mayer, Tamar (1994a) 'Heightened Palestinian nationalism: military occupation, repression, difference and gender' in Mayer, Tamar (1994c).

Mayer, Tamar (1994b) 'Women and the Israeli Occupation: the context' in Mayer, Tamar (1994c).

Mayer, Tamar (ed.) (1994c) *Women and the Israeli Occupation: The Politics of Change*. London: Routledge.

Medica Women's Therapy Centre (1995) 'Research: dominant gynaecological and psychological consequences of rape'. Report by Mirha Pojsić, unpublished.

Medica Women's Therapy Centre (1996) *Surviving the Violence.* Bulletin No. 1/ 96. English version. Zenica.

Medica Women's Therapy Centre (1997) *Rape – a Specific Trauma, a Specific Type of Violence.* Internal report. Zenica.

Menuchin, Ishai (1992) 'Occupation, protest, and selective refusal' in Hurwitz, Deena (1992a).

Mežnarić, Silva (1994) 'Gender as an ethno-marker: rape, war and identity politics in the former Yugoslavia' in Moghadam, Valentine M. (1994c).

Miles, Robert (1989). *Racism.* London and New York: Routledge.

Milić, Andjelka (1993) 'Women and nationalism in former Yugoslavia' in Funk, Nanette and Mueller, Magda (1993).

Milić, Andjelka (1994) 'Women, technology and societal failure in former Yugoslavia' in Cockburn, Cynthia and Fürst-Dilić, Ruza (eds) *Bringing Technology Home: Changing Technology in a Changing Europe.* Buckingham: Open University Press.

Milić, Andjelka (1996) 'Nationalism and sexism: Eastern Europe in transition' in Caplan, Richard and Feffer, John (eds) *Europe's New Nationalisms.* Oxford: Oxford University Press.

Mladjenović, Lepa and Litričin, Vera (1993) 'Belgrade feminists 1992: separation, guilt and identity crisis', *Feminist Review*, No. 45: 113–19.

Mladjenović, Lepa and Matijašević, Divna (1996) 'SOS Belgrade July 1993–1995: dirty streets' in Corrin, Chris (1996).

Moghadam, Valentine M. (1994a) 'Introduction and overview' in Moghadam, Valentine M. (1994c).

Moghadam, Valentine M. (ed.) (1994b) *Gender and National Identity: Women and Politics in Muslim Societies*, London and New Jersey: Zed Books.

Moghadam, Valentine M. (ed.) (1994c) *Identity, Politics and Women: Cultural Reassertions and Feminisms in International Perspective.* Oxford: Westview Press.

Moore, Henrietta (1994) *A Passion for Difference.* Cambridge: Polity Press.

Morokvašić, Mirjana (1986) 'Being a woman in Yugoslavia: past, present and institutional equality' in Godout, Monique (ed) *Women of the Mediterranean.* London: Zed.

Morokvašić, Mirjana (1997) 'The logics of exclusion: nationalism, sexism and the Yugoslav war' in Charles, Nickie and Hintjens, Helen (eds) *Gender, Ethnicity and Political Ideologies.* London: Routledge.

O Connor, Fionnuala (1993) *In Search of a State: Catholics in Northern Ireland.* Belfast: Blackstaff Press.

O'Leary, Brendan and McGarry, John (1993) *The Politics of Antagonism: Understanding Northern Ireland.* London: Athlone Press.

Orr, Akiva (1994) *Israel: Politics, Myths and Identity.* London: Pluto Press.

Oz, Amos (1994) *Israel, Palestine and Peace.* London: Vintage.

Palgi, Michal (1993) 'Motherhood in the kibbutz' in Swirski, Barbara and Safir, Marilyn P. (1993).

Papić, Žarana (1992) 'The possibility of socialist feminism in Eastern Europe' in Ward, Anna, Gregory, Jeanne and Yuval-Davis, Nira (eds) *Women and*

Citizenship in Europe: Borders, Rights and Duties. London: European Forum of Left Feminists and Trentham Books.

Papić, Žarana (1994) 'Women's movement in former Yugoslavia: 1970s and 1980s' in Centre for Women's Studies, Research and Communication (1994).

Papić, Žarana (1995) 'How to become a "real" Serbian woman?', *War Report*, No. 36: 40–1. September. London: Institute for War and Peace Reporting.

Peterson, V. Spike (1996) 'The gender of rhetoric, reason and realism' in Beer, Francis A. and Hariman, Robert (eds) *Refiguring Realism: International Relations and Rhetorical Practices*. East Lansing, MI: Michigan State University Press.

Peterson, V. Spike and Runyan, Anne Sisson (1993) *Global Gender Issues*. Boulder, CO: Westview Press.

Pieterse, Jan Nederveen (1997) 'Deconstructing/reconstructing ethnicity', *Nations and Nationalism*, Vol. 3, No. 3: 365–95.

Pope, Julia J. (1993) 'Conflict of interests: case study of Na'amat' in Swirski, Barbara and Safir, Marilyn P. (1993).

Raday, Frances (1993) 'The concept of gender equality in a Jewish state' in Swirski, Barbara and Safir, Marilyn P. (1993).

Räthzel, Nora (1994) 'Harmonious "Heimat" and Disturbing "Auslander"' in Bhavnani, Kum-Kum and Phoenix, Ann (1994).

Ridd, Rosemary and Callaway, Helen (eds) (1986) *Caught up in Conflict: Women's Responses to Political Strife*. London: Macmillan.

Rooney, Eilish and Woods, Margaret (1995) *Women, Community and Politics in Northern Ireland: A Belfast Study*. Belfast: University of Ulster.

Roulston, Carmel (1996) 'Equal opportunities for women' in Aughey, Arthur and Morrow, Duncan (1996).

Roulston, Carmel (1997) 'Women on the margin: the women's movements in Northern Ireland' in West, Lois (1997).

Rowthorne, Bob and Wayne, Naomi (1988) *Northern Ireland: The Political Economy of Conflict*. Cambridge: Polity Press.

Rupesinghe, Kumar (1995a) 'Conflict transformation' in Rupesinghe, Kumar (1995b).

Rupesinghe, Kumar (ed.) (1995b) *Conflict Transformation*. London: Macmillan.

Rutherford, Jonathan (1990) 'A place called home: identity and the cultural politics of difference' in Rutherford, Jonathan (1990a).

Rutherford, Jonathan (1990a) *Identity: Community, Culture, Difference*. London: Lawrence and Wishart.

Ryan, Louise (1997) 'A question of loyalty: war, nation and feminism in early twentieth-century Ireland', *Women's Studies International Forum*, Vol. 20, No. 1: 21–32.

Ryan, Mark (1994) *War and Peace in Ireland: Britain and the IRA in the New World Order*. London: Pluto Press.

Safir, Marilyn P. (1993a) 'Religion, tradition and public policy give family first priority' in Swirski, Barbara and Safir, Marilyn P. (1993).

Safir, Marilyn P. (1993b) 'Was the kibbutz an experiment in social and sex equality?' in Swirski, Barbara and Safir, Marilyn P. (1993).

Safran, Hannah (1995) 'From denial to equal representation', *Palestine–Israel Journal of Politics, Economics and Culture.* Vol. II, No. 3: 22–5.

Said, Edward (1995) *The Politics of Dispossession: The Struggle for Palestinian Self-Determination 1969–1994.* London: Vintage.

Seifert, Ruth (1995) 'War and rape: a preliminary analysis' in Stiglmayer, Alexandra (1995).

Sharoni, Simona (1992) 'Every woman is an occupied territory: the politics of militarism and sexism and the Israeli–Palestinian conflict', *Journal of Gender Studies*, Vol. 1, No. 4: 447–62.

Sharoni, Simona (1994) 'Homefront as battlefield: gender, military occupation and violence against women' in Mayer, Tamar (1994c).

Sharoni, Simona (1995) *Gender and the Israeli–Palestinian Conflict: The Politics of Women's Resistance.* New York: Syracuse University Press.

Shiran, Vicki (1993) 'Feminist identity vs. Oriental identity' in Swirski, Barbara and Safir, Marilyn P. (eds).

Silber, Laura and Little, Allan (1995) *The Death of Yugoslavia.* London: Penguin Books, BBC Books.

Silver, Vivian (1993) 'Male and female created he them' in Swirski, Barbara and Safir, Marilyn P. (1993).

Slapšak, Svetlana (1995) 'Silence kills, let's speak for peace', *War Report*, No. 36: 30–1. September. London: Institute for War and Peace Reporting.

Smith, Anthony D. (1995) *Nations and Nationalism in a Global Era.* Cambridge: Polity Press.

Smith, Anthony D. (1996) 'Memory and modernity: reflections on Ernest Gellner's theory of nationalism', *Nations and Nationalisms*, Vol. 2, Part 3, November: 371–88.

Smyth, Ailbhe (1995), 'Paying our disrespects to the (bloody) states we're in: women, violence, culture and state', *Journal of Women's History*, Vol. 6, No. 4 and Vol. 7, No. 1, Winter/Spring: 190–215.

Sontag, Susan (1979) *On Photography.* Harmondsworth: Penguin.

Stiglmayer, Alexandra (ed.) (1995) *Mass Rape: The War Against Women in Bosnia-Herzegovina.* Lincoln, NE: University of Nebraska Press.

Strum, Philippa (1992) *The Women are Marching: The Second Sex and the Palestinian Revolution.* New York: Lawrence Hill Books.

Swirski, Barbara (1993) 'Israeli feminism new and old' in Swirski, Barbara and Sasfir, Marilyn P. (1993).

Swirski, Barbara and Safir, Marilyn P. (eds) (1993) *Calling the Equality Bluff: Women in Israel.* New York: Teachers College Press.

Teršelić, Vesna (1995) 'Women dominant in antiwar campaign', *War Report*, No. 36: 39–40. September. London: Institute for War and Peace Reporting.

United Nations (1993) Third Situation Report, UN Commission to Investigate the Human Rights Situation in the Former Yugoslavia (Mazowiecki Report). Geneva. February.

United Nations (1994) Commission of Experts (Pursuant to the Security Council Regulation 780, 1992). *Final Report.* Annex II and Annex IX. United Nations Security Council S/1994/674.

Usher, Graham (1995) *Palestine in Crisis: The Struggle for Peace and Political Independence after Oslo.* London: Pluto Press.

Warnock, K. (1990) *Land before Honour: Palestinian Women in the Occupied Territories.* New York: Monthly Review Press.

Warschawski, Michel 'Mikado' (1992) 'The long march towards Israeli–Palestinian cooperation' in Hurwitz, Deena (1992a).

West, Lois A. (1992) 'Feminist nationalist social movements: beyond universalism and towards a gendered cultural relativism', *Women's Studies International*, Vol. 15, Nos 5/6: 563–79.

West, Lois A. (ed.) (1997) *Feminist Nationalism.* London: Routledge.

West, Lois A. (1997a) 'Introduction: feminism constructs nationalism', in West, Lois A. (1997).

Women in Black (1994) *Women for Peace.* Belgrade: Women in Black.

Women's Support Network (1992) *Grant Aided ... or Taken for Granted? A Study of Women's Voluntary Organizations in Northern Ireland* (researched by Ruth Taillon). Belfast.

Women's Support Network (1996) *Development Plan.* Belfast.

Woodward, Susan L. (1995) *Balkan Tragedy: Chaos and Dissolution After the Cold War.* Washington: Brookings Institution.

Woolf, Virginia (1966) *Three Guineas.* New York: Harcourt Brace Jovanovich. Originally published 1938.

Young, Elise G. (1992) *Keepers of the History: Women and the Israeli–Palestinian Conflict.* New York: Teachers College Press, Athene Series.

Yuval-Davis, Nira (1985) 'Front and rear: the sexual division of labour in the Israeli Army', *Feminist Studies*, No. 3.

Yuval-Davis, Nira (1987) 'The Jewish Collectivity' in Khamsin Collective (ed.) *Women in the Middle East.* London: Zed Books.

Yuval-Davis, Nira (1994) 'Women, Ethnicity and Empowerment' in Bhavnani, Kum-Kum and Phoenix, Ann (1994).

Yuval-Davis, Nira (1997) *Gender and Nation.* London and Thousand Oaks, New Delhi: Sage Publications.

Yuval-Davis, Nira and Anthias, Floya (eds) (1989) *Woman-Nation-State.* London: Macmillan.

Zajović, Staša (1994) 'I am disloyal' in Centre for Women's Studies, Research and Communication (1994).

Zajović, Staša (1995) 'The guardians of "national values" and biological reproduction', *War Report*, No. 36: 42–3. September. London: Institute for War and Peace Reporting.

Žarkov, Dubravka (1997) 'War rapes in Bosnia: on masculinity, femininity and the power of the rape victim identity', *Tijdschrift voor Criminologie*, Vol. 39, No. 2: 140–51.

Index

242 / THE SPACE BETWEEN US

189–92, 197; in Northern Ireland, 60–3, 74; in Women's Support Network, 80, 88, 92–8; in Yugoslavia, 163–73
Ferida Y, 196, 224
Frljak, Amira, 175, 191
funding of women's projects, 76, 77, 96, 131, 190

Galilee: Judaization project, 150; territorial significance of, 147
gender, 11; and nationalism, 39, 42–3; and media, 12; and war, 12–14; in relation to ethnicity, 203–11
General Union of Palestinian Women, 118
Gibson, Gillian, 82, 86, 92
Gorbachev, Mikhail, 160
group process, 44, 96–8, 154–5, 227; see also democracy
Gulf War, 127, 129

Hadžihajdić, Zilha, 181, 188, 189, 202
Hadžihalilović, Selma, 181, 191
Hadash (Israel), 143, 154
Hall, Stuart, 212, 228
Hamas (Palestine), 27, 113, 127
hamula (clan structure), 112
Haraway, Donna, 213
Hasan, Amal Muhammad, 128
Hassan, Manar, 112
Hauser, Monika, 174, 188, 189, 190
Heimat, movement, 40, 229
Herceg-Bosna, 32, 34
Hildesheim, Pesi, 133, 146
Histadrut (Israel), 101, 137
Hodžić, Emsa, 185, 197
Hollway, Wendy, 214
Holmes, Rosanna, 94
Holocaust, 25, 217
home see homeland
homeland, 8, 23, 30, 39, 40, 44, 116, 145, 217, 228–9; see also Heimat movement, land
Hume, John, 21

identity, 8–11, 14–16, 155; and agency, 213–14; and democracy, 211–30; and sence of self, 212–22; as process, 10, 212–16; collective,

14, 34–5, 212–16; crisis of, 72, 222; definition of, 14, 15, 212; essentialized, 13, 215, 225; non-closure on, 225
Idrizović, Mirjana, 188, 199, 206, 210
Ikrit village, Galilee, land rights struggle in, 150
impropriety, 230
Indjić, Trivo, 210
International Monetary Fund (IMF), 31, 212
International Relations (IR), 7, 8
International Women's Day, 131, 189
Internet, use by women, 173
intifada, 26, 111, 118, 123; women's movement within, 119
Iraq, invasion of Kuwait, 27, 127
Ireland: history of, 16–21; partition of, 19; Republic of, 19, 21; see also Northern Ireland
Irish Republican Army (IRA), 20, 21, 22, 41, 56, 58, 61, 68, 72, 82, 83, 86
Irish Suffrage Movement, 40
Isaković, Alija, 219
Islam, 22, 23, 42, 180, 205; in Bosnia, 28; in Palestine, 27, 113, 118, 127; Islamic movements, 27, 113, 118, 127, 206; observance of, 193
Israel, 12, 99–128; as Jewish state, 25, 109, 116, 147; history of, 22–7; invasion of Lebanon, 122, 155; militarization in, 139, 147; Six Day War, 26, 110, 121, 145; Yom Kippur War, 121, 122
Israel Women's Peace Net (Reshet), 126
Izetbegović, Alija, 32, 220

Jarisy, Rodaina, 136, 137, 152, 214, 228
Jayawardena, Kumari, 42
Jerusalem, 25, 27, 146–6
Jerusalem Link (Israel), 130
Jews: history of, 22, 23; Ashkenazi, 23, 120, 132, 138; Misrahi, 23, 120, 132, 138; Sephardic, 23; see also Zionism
Jezreel Valley, 39
Jordan, June, 160, 225